W9-CFE-922

PRAISE FOR *MAKE A SCENE*

Make a Scene breaks the scene down to its vital elements in such a clear, thorough—and thoroughly helpful—way. Jordan Rosenfeld has created an invaluable resource for any fiction writer who wants to imbue each page with sparkle and power.

> —Gayle Brandeis, author of *Fruitflesh: Seeds of Inspiration for Women Who Write*, *The Book of Dead Birds*, and *Self Storage*

Make a Scene distills years of study into one clear, concise book. Even for advanced writers, the examples and explanations are sure to inspire.

> —Jody Gehrman, author of *Notes From the Backseat* and *Tart & Summer in the Land of Skin*

Make a Scene will answer all the questions you might ask—and some you won't think of asking—on the scene. In clear and concise language, using innumerable examples from James Joyce's "The Dead" through Joseph Conrad's *The Secret Sharer* and on to Harry Potter, with explanations of terms from "the reveal" to the epiphany, Jordan Rosenfeld explores all the secrets of the scene. For the beginning writer, as well as one who thinks he/she knows it all.

> —Sheila Kohler, award-winning author of *Cracks*, *Crossways*, and *Bluebird: Or the Invention of Happiness*

This book, which arrived when I was deep in the writing of my second novel, provided both the encouragement and wise counsel to get me to THE END—one scene at a time. Packed with practical advice and superb examples, this guide will help any writer, whether novice or veteran, infuse their scenes and their stories with authenticity, tension, and power.

> —Patry Francis, author of *The Liar's Diary*

In *Make a Scene*, Jordan E. Rosenfeld magnifies with intelligence and insight the underpinnings of powerful story making. Demonstrating in a step-by-step manner why a scene works, Rosenfeld shows how fiction writers can apply this knowledge to their own work. The astonishing depth and breadth of this guidebook, which utilizes a wide range of narrative styles to underscore a point, make it a vital tool for writers serious about their craft.

> —Jessica Keener, fiction editor of *AGNI Magazine*

MAKE A
SCENE

Crafting a Powerful Story
One Scene at a Time

JORDAN E. ROSENFELD

WRITER'S DIGEST BOOKS

Cincinnati, Ohio
www.writersdigest.com

12 11 10 09 08   5 4 3 2 1

Distributed in Canada by Fraser Direct, 100 Armstrong Avenue, Georgetown, Ontario, Canada L7G 5S4; Distributed in the U.K. and Europe by David & Charles, Brunel House, Newton Abbot, Devon, TQ12 4PU, England, E-mail: postmaster@davidandcharles.co.uk; Distributed in Australia by Capricorn Link, P.O. Box 704, Windsor, NSW 2756 Australia.

Library of Congress Cataloging-in-Publication Data

Rosenfeld, Jordan E.
  Make a scene : crafting a powerful story one scene at a time / by Jordan E. Rosenfeld.
      p. cm.
  Includes index.
    ISBN-13: 978-1-58297-479-8 (pbk. : alk. paper) -- ISBN-13: 978-1-58297-532-0 (hardcover : alk. paper)
  1. Fiction--Authorship. 2. Narration (Rhetoric) I. Title.
  PN3383.N35R69 2008
  808.3--dc22   2007029982

Edited by Kelly Nickell
Cover designed by Claudean Wheeler
Interior designed by Eric West and Claudean Wheeler
Illustrations by Kirsty Pargeter/iStockPhoto
Production coordinated by Mark Griffin

F+W PUBLICATIONS, INC.

DEDICATION

This book is dedicated to the multitude of teachers and mentors I've had the fortune to work under who are, amazingly, too many to name. Most importantly to the memory of Stephanie Moore, who first introduced me to the scene and who left the world far too soon in 2006.

ACKNOWLEDGMENTS

This book was inspired by my editing clients, whom I thank for their vulnerability and tenacity, but it could never have come to fruition without the support of Rebecca Lawton (Write Free). Thanks to the Wellspring Renewal Center for hosting me as I gave birth to the outline (and to Marlene Cullen for being the most gracious roommate). To the rest of Wild Mindz—Susan Bono, Ellen Bichler, Christine Falcone, Lizzie Hannon, Claudia Larson, and Barbara Spicer—who help me remember why I write, and to the women of El's Kitchen—Ellen Meister, Myfanwy Collins, Kathy Fish, and Maryanne Stahl—who always sympathize when I need it. Also to Maurie Traylor, client turned friend, who read early drafts; and to my cheerleading squad during revisions, Stephanie Anagnoson, Emily Brady, Tracy Burkholder, Laura Griffith, and my dear "sister," Patricia Schiavone. Also to Sheryl Glubok, for convincing me this book title was better. And a huge debt of gratitude goes to my editor, Kelly Nickell—without her vision and critical prodding, this book absolutely would not exist.

And of course, I want to thank all of my family, who always remembered to ask "So how's the book coming?" And especially my mom, for being my lifelong, unflappable, one-woman PR team.

Lastly, but most importantly, to my beloved, Erik, who makes ALL things possible.

ABOUT THE AUTHOR

Jordan E. Rosenfeld is a contributing editor to *Writer's Digest* magazine, and a freelance writer and author. Her articles, essays, and reviews have appeared in numerous publications, including AlterNet.org, the *St. Petersburg Times*, the *San Francisco Chronicle*, and *The Writer*, and her book reviews are regularly featured on NPR affiliate KQED radio's The California Report. She's co-founder of Write Free, a method to help people attract a creative life, which has spawned the book *Write Free: Attracting the Creative Life* (with Rebecca Lawton) and a monthly newsletter. Find out more about Jordan at: www.jordanrosenfeld.net and about Write Free at: www.writefree.us.

TABLE OF CONTENTS

PART IV OTHER SCENE CONSIDERATIONS

PREFACE

Three years after I graduated from college, my lifelong aspiration to be a working writer foundered. I'd become sidetracked by massage therapy, a career I undertook to support myself but which wound up absorbing most of my actual writing time.

One quiet afternoon at the Marin County health club and spa, where I worked as spa director, my co-workers and I assembled on the exercise floor in mild anticipation, summoned by an all-staff memo. What did our boss, Michael, have in store for us this time?

He bounded out, dressed in skimpy Spandex bike shorts: "Today, we're having a morale-boosting exercise," he cried, exuberant as always.

Fourteen of us, crammed into sports leggings and identical staff T-shirts, shifted and murmured on the exercise floor. What would it be—another power meeting or mini-marathon? A large-toothed motivational speaker to teach us to feel the burn? None of my fears materialized, but the tall, Scandinavian blonde who emerged from the locker room at a purposeful clip did not quell my concern. There was a mischievous twinkle in her blue eyes that made me a touch nervous.

"This is Stephanie Moore," said Michael, waving in the beautiful woman's direction with equal parts awe and respect.

With her straight posture and serious demeanor, she looked like she was there to teach us how to walk elegantly with books on our heads, or to count every last calorie. The look in her eye said clearly that she had plans for us.

"You guys look great!" she gushed in a throaty, nightclub-singer voice after appraising us. What was this—an auction? Take-home-a-trainer for a day?

"Are you ready? You better be ready!" she continued.

Unlike Michael's dogged cheerfulness, which had a tendency to grate on the staff's nerves, Stephanie's exuberance commanded our attention, as did her astonishing good looks, and a powerful authority in her long, lean body that suggested she could turn drill sergeant at any second and demand we drop and give her sixty.

"I hope you're ready to dance!" she cried, and before we could argue that, while we were fitness buffs, dancing was another story, she'd turned on raucous Latin music and started swinging her hips in rhythm to it.

"You're going to learn to salsa," she cried, raising a slender arm, "in an hour. Pair up!"

I had recently recovered from bad bronchitis and was weak and slow-moving. This did not escape Stephanie. She grabbed me by the arm. "You'll be my partner," she said. "I'll lead," she added, as if I had any doubt.

"One, two, one-two-three," she said, demonstrating the beat to the music with her knees.

Despite my klutzy nature, under her surprisingly steady hand my body showed a kinetic intelligence I didn't know it had. Within minutes even the beefiest and most graceless among us were hip-swinging away, unembarrassed, to the vivifying salsa beat.

"Oh, you've got it now!" she shouted. And for a few moments, I did feel as though I had it, if that meant control over my body in a whole new way.

Afterward, in the locker room, still giddy and panting with effort, I stopped her. "You're a great teacher," I said. "My creative outlet is writing, but I can see how dancing could be a great one, too."

"Thanks." She flung her blonde hair out of her face and lasered in on me with those royal blues. "I also teach writing, and as it happens, I can write like I dance." I was all prepared to drop and bow to her multitalented nature when she offered, "I can teach you to do the same."

Inspired by her skills as a dance teacher, I knew fate had handed me an avenue back to my writing, and I gladly took it.

Stephanie was the first person to teach me about the scene—the tool I just used to illustrate the essential idea of this book. To write well, you must take the readers in hand and teach them how to move to your beat, or follow a mystery, or care about two lovers whose relationship is coming apart at the seams. Your reader must be able to enter your story as if it were the auditorium of a theater, or an empty dance floor with strange music playing. It is my hope that this book will teach you how to, well, *make a scene* with as much confidence as I had when I once danced like a salsa queen.

INTRODUCTION

I feel a bit sorry for the scene: It's a misunderstood element of writing be-cause, unlike other elements, it is not a *singular* thing, but a *sum* of all the parts of great fiction. Many writers understand one element of the scene, but not how all the elements work together, inform each other, and create a nar-rative that is compelling and capable of maintaining a reader's attention.

I feel confident saying that if you can understand what a scene is, how all its elements collaborate to create a vivid and compelling snapshot, and how those moments add up to a story, you'll write your drafts differently and become a more self-assured writer with a page-turner on your hands.

In order to make scene construction clear, start with the basic func-tion and structure of a scene, because even if you can identify a scene in someone else's work, you may not be sure what constitutes a scene in your own writing (and I have worked with plenty of writers who weren't). Where does a scene stop and start? Can too much or not enough of one element ruin the whole stew? I want you to know why you should bother to write scenes and how a single scene is built before you go on to learn how to build a house out of them.

The bulk of this book looks at the different kinds of scenes that compose a narrative, from suspense scenes to contemplative scenes. These different types of scenes are like the notes in a symphony: Individually they may be intense or mild, contemplative or dramatic, but when they are used in combination, they form a fantastic narrative that feels rich and complex.

By the book's end, you should be able not only to build a vivid scene, but to link each of your scenes to create a compelling narrative that will engage the reader and make you proud.

Plus, throughout this book I've included sidebars in which published authors share their insights on all aspects and techniques of scene writing. These exclusive thoughts prove that even best-selling authors can be inspired and moved by a well-written scene.

To help you avoid tactics that could bore the reader, I leave you with this caveat: *The audience is watching.* Never forget this. Even though the audience isn't actually present at the moment of your writing, you should write (and especially revise) as if the reader is sitting behind your desk, awaiting your finished pages. What this means is that, if your eye is ultimately on publication, it is your job to entertain and inform the reader through clear writing and powerful scenes; if you are using fancy prose or showy strategies to amuse yourself or prove something, you aren't keeping your audience in mind.

Though it's not wise to write *first* drafts with the super-ego breathing its foul, critical breath down your neck, your readers should be the most precious people imaginable after your characters. You see, most readers are not writers; they don't know how hard it is to write. They have very little patience or empathy for your struggles. They just want a good story, and they will put down one that doesn't hold their interest. It's up to you to ensure that they don't lose interest in *your* story.

PART I

ARCHITECTURE OF A SCENE

You climb a long ladder until you can see over the roof, or over the clouds. You are writing a book. You watch your shod feet step on each round rung, one at a time; you do not hurry and do not rest. Your feet feel the steep ladder's balance ... you climb steadily, doing your job in the dark.

—*ANNIE DILLARD*

1
FUNCTIONS OF A SCENE

You've felt the pulse-pounding drama of a good story, you've turned pages at a furious clip, caught up in a book so real you felt as though it was happening to you. What makes that story, book, or essay come to life? Strong, powerful scenes.

Writing is a wildly creative act, and therefore often seems to defy rules and formulas. Just when a rule seems agreed upon, some writer comes along to break it. While there *is* a formula to scene-writing, it's not straightforward. It's not like a paint-by-numbers kit, where you fill in the listed colors and voilà, you have a perfect painting of dogs playing poker, in all the right proportions. The scene-writing formula is more like the messy spontaneity of cooking: You start with the ingredients the recipe calls for, but you work them in creatively, and variations on the main ingredients yield different, even surprising, results.

The only certain result you want is to snare the reader's attention with your very first sentence. Since writing competes with the fast-paced, seductive intensity of television and movies, your challenge is to write engaging scenes.

THE SCENE DEFINED

So what is a scene, exactly? Scenes are capsules in which compelling characters undertake significant actions in a vivid and memorable way that allows

---

the events to feel as though they are happening in real time. When strung together, individual scenes add up to build plots and storylines.

The recipe for a scene includes the following basic ingredients:

- Characters who are complex and layered, and who undergo change throughout your narrative
- A point of view through which the scenes are seen
- Memorable and significant action that feels as if it is unfolding in real time
- Meaningful, revealing dialogue when appropriate
- New plot information that advances your story and deepens characters
- Conflict and drama that tests your characters and ultimately reveals their personalities
- A rich physical setting that calls on all the senses and enables the reader to see and enter into the world you've created
- A spare amount of narrative summary or exposition

Arguably, the one thing in that list that makes a scene a scene is action—events happening and people acting out behaviors in a simulation of real time—but well-balanced scenes include a little bit of everything. Mixing those ingredients together in varying amounts will yield drama, emotion, passion, power, and energy; in short, a page-turner. Some scenes need more physical action, while others may require a lot of dialogue. Some scenes will take place with barely a word spoken, or with very small actions. Other scenes may require vivid interaction with the setting. As you make your way through this book, you will get a better grasp of the power of the scene and how to use it to achieve your desired effects.

In part two we'll discuss all of the above ingredients, as well as these more complex scene considerations:

- Dramatic tension, which creates the potential for conflict in scenes
- Scene subtext, which deepens and enriches your scenes
- Scene intentions, which ensure characters' actions are purposeful

- Pacing and scene length, which influence the mood and tone of individual scenes

These latter ingredients deepen your scenes and help you take them beyond the perfunctory. Dramatic tension will make the reader worry about and care for your characters and keep her riveted to the page. Subtext can build imagery and emotion into the deeper layers of scenes so that your writing feels rich and complex. Scene intentions help to guide your characters and take them through changes in as dramatic a way as possible. By pacing your scenes well and choosing the proper length for each scene, you can control the kinds of emotional effects your scenes have, leaving the reader with the feeling of having taken a satisfying journey.

ANATOMY OF A SCENE

To help clarify how all of the elements just discussed function within a scene, here is a complex snippet of a scene from Joseph Conrad's richly layered short story "The Secret Sharer," which I have labeled to show its parts.

> Before entering the cabin I stood still, listening in the lobby at the foot of the stairs. [*First-person point of view.*] A faint snore came through the closed door of the chief mate's room. The second mate's door was on the hook, but the darkness in there was absolutely soundless. [*Physical setting that invokes one of the senses: hearing.*] He, too, was young and could sleep like a stone. Remained the steward, but he was not likely to wake up before he was called. I got a sleeping suit out of my room and, coming back on deck, saw the naked man from the sea sitting on the main hatch, glimmering white in the darkness, his elbows on his knees and his head in his hands. [*Action that provides a sense of real time.*] In a moment he had concealed his damp body in a sleeping suit of the same gray-stripe pattern as the one I was wearing and followed me like my double on the poop. Together we moved right aft, barefooted, silent.
>
> "What is it?" I asked in a deadened voice, taking the lighted lamp out of the binnacle and raising it to his face.
>
> "An ugly business." [*Dialogue.*]

He had rather regular features; a good mouth; light eyes under somewhat heavy, dark eyebrows; a smooth square forehead; no growth on his cheeks; a small brown mustache, and a well-shaped round chin. His expression was concentrated, meditative, under the inspecting light of the lamp I held up to his face; such as a man thinking hard in solitude might wear. [*Detailed physical character description.*] My sleeping suit was just right for his size. A well-knit young fellow of twenty-five at most. He caught his lower lip with the edge of white, even teeth.

"Yes," I said, replacing the lamp in the binnacle. The warm heavy tropical night closed upon his head again.

"There's a ship over there," he murmured.

"Yes, I know. *The Sephora.* Did you know of us?"

"Hadn't the slightest idea. I am the mate of her—" He paused and corrected himself. "I should say I was."

"Aha! Something wrong?'

"Yes. Very wrong indeed. I've killed a man." [*Dramatic tension and plot information.*]

"What do you mean? Just now?"

"No, on the passage. Weeks ago. Thirty-nine south. When I say a man—"

"Fit of temper," I suggested, confidently.

The shadowy, dark head, like mine, seemed to nod imperceptibly above the ghostly gray of my sleeping suit. It was, in the night, as though I had been faced by my own reflection in the depths of a somber and immense mirror. [*Using physical setting to create the desired eerie mood.*]

Think of the elements illustrated in the marked sections above as crucial ingredients that you want to employ in your own writing. Conrad's story is an example of how unique each scene will be, even when you're using the same essential ingredients. You might choose a different method of creating dramatic tension—like writing in the third-person point of view, opting for more or less dialogue (or none), or using very different actions to create a sense of real time—but you can see that Conrad did, in fact, use all the foundational ingredients of a scene, and held your attention. This is exactly what your scenes need to do for your readers.

THE OLE "SHOW, DON'T TELL" DILEMMA

What exactly does it mean to show and not tell? Should your characters be doing wild strip-teases or crying "Look, nothing up my sleeve," before pulling out a rabbit? Only if you want, but in this case *show* is a caveat that means "don't over-explain; trust your reader."

Telling, also referred to in this book as narrating or narrative summary, is a form of *explaining*. And while every narrative has some necessary summary, it must be used judiciously. Imagine yourself as the storyteller to a group of enthralled children gathered around and hanging on your every word. Say that right at the climax where Snow White bites into the poisoned apple (a juicy bit of action), you go off on a tangent like this: "Snow White thought about taking a bite of the apple, but she had been having trust issues since her stepmother had hired the woodcutter to kill her. Remembering her stepmother's betrayal sent her into a whirlwind of doubt. ..." Bored yet? You can bet those kids would be bouncing in their chairs asking, "But what happened to Snow White after she bit into the poisoned apple?!" Grown-up readers respond the same way to telling.

Think about it another way: Most people read with their physical eyes and a handy little part of the brain known as the visual cortex. The brain is, in fact, considered more important in the function of sight than the eyes, and in the act of reading, this is even more true. The brain helps the reader with the most important organ of reading, the inner eye, meaning the eye of the imagination (not some mystical link to spiritual realms). This eye is responsible for constructing in the mind the visual images that are rendered only in text on a page. You want the reader to see what you describe as vividly as you see your dreams at night; therefore, you must give the reader as much opportunity to do so as possible. You must be detailed and specific, and provide enough sensory clues to make the task of seeing easy.

Narrative summary, on the other hand, offers words only to the reader's inner ear, as if someone were standing off to the side whispering right to him. While the eye allows the reader to become emotionally involved, and activates the heart and the viscera, the inner ear seems to be linked more closely to the function of sound. Too much stimulation on the inner ear can temporarily lull your reader, or even put him to sleep. This is one of the reasons that narrative passages should be kept to a minimum.

Scenes use the ingredients mentioned earlier to construct a powerful, vivifying experience that mimics life for the reader. At its best, powerful scene-writing allows a reader to feel as if he has entered the narrative and is participating in it, rather than sitting passively by and receiving a lecture. You know you're in a scene when your own heart is pumping and you're white-knuckling the pages waiting to see what happens next. When you fall into the story and forget the world around you, the author has done a good job of immersing you in a scene.

Narrative summaries, when used in place of scene work or when used in excess, cause the reader to feel that the writing is boring, condescending, or lecturing—which will not win more readers. That said, narrative summaries, when used correctly, do have a place and a function in scenes, and we'll take a closer look at those functions throughout this book.

SCENE LENGTH

Before we wrap this chapter up, let's talk about another issue that's sure to rise up in your mind: scene length. One of the benefits of writing in scene form is that the ending of a scene provides a place for the reader to comfortably take a pause. You may wonder when to use a short scene versus a long scene. Once again, the decision rests with you, but we'll take a quick look at the benefits of using either kind.

Long Scenes

Generally speaking, if a scene runs to more than fifteen pages, it's on the long side. A scene can be picked up, read, and put back down (though not too easily!), leaving the reader with more information than he had before. Even the most avid reader wants to pause eventually, and scene and chapter breaks offer them chances to do so.

Long scenes don't need to be avoided, but they should be peppered in sparingly. Too many long scenes in a row will cause your narrative to drag.

Use long scenes in the novel when you want to:

- Intentionally slow down the pace after lots of action or intense dialogue to allow the protagonist and the reader to digest what has happened, and to build new tension and suspense
- Include a lot of big action in a given scene (fights, chases, explosions)— so the scene doesn't hinge on action alone
- Add a dialogue scene that, in order to feel realistic, needs to run long

Short Scenes

A scene that takes place in ten or fewer pages can comfortably be considered short. Some scenes are as short as a couple of pages. Short scenes often make readers hungry for more. But remember that too many short scenes in a row can make the flow of the plot feel choppy, and disrupt the continuity that John Gardner said creates a dream for the reader.

A short scene has to achieve the same goals as a longer scene, and in less time. It must still contain main characters engaging in actions based upon scene intentions. New information must be revealed that drives the plot forward. The setting must be clear. In the short scene, you have even less room for narrative summary.

You're best using short scenes when you need to:

- Differentiate one character from another (a secretive, shy, or withdrawn character, for instance, might only get short scenes, while an outspoken character may get longer scenes)
- Pick up the pace right after a long scene
- Leave the reader hungry for more or breathless with suspense
- Include multiple scenes within a chapter
- Create a sense of urgency by dropping bits of information one by one, forcing the reader to keep reading

Whether you go long or short depends on your own stylistic preferences. Just keep in mind that length affects pacing as you decide what kind of flow you want for your manuscript.

SCENE BEGINNINGS, MIDDLES, AND ENDINGS

Each scene needs to have its own beginning, middle, and end. The following three chapters will pare the scene down to these three basic sections. The beginning should be vivid and memorable, and help immediately draw your reader into the scene. Scene middles are the vast territory where the stakes must be raised, characters get caught in conflict, and consequences follow that keep your plot interesting. Scene endings, of course, set the stage for the scenes that follow, and leave a feeling or taste with the reader that should be unforgettable. When all three sections of a scene are handled well, the result is an incredibly vivid reading experience. The remaining chapters of part one will help you address these important structural elements of the scene.

2
STRONG SCENE LAUNCHES

All great novels and stories start out with a mere idea. Maybe it's a large idea that spans centuries and crosses continents, like the idea of the origins of the real Dracula; or maybe it's an idea for a surreal short story in which a man has keys for fingers. No matter how grand or minute, strange or beguiling your idea, you must take it through an alchemical process that transforms it into story. How do you do that? This is the function of the scene; it is your story-maker. Inside each scene, the vivid details, information, and action breathe life into your flat idea and round it out into something a reader participates in.

Any story or novel is, in essence, a series of scenes strung together like beads on a wire, with narrative summary adding texture and color between. A work of fiction will comprise many scenes (the number of scenes varies for each individual project). And each one of these individual scenes must be built with a structure most easily described as having a beginning, middle, and end. The beginning of each scene is what this chapter will address. (Chapters twelve and twenty-one, respectively, will discuss how to write the first scene and the final scene in a story.)

The word *beginning* is a bit confusing, since some scenes pick up in the middle of action, or continue where other actions left off, so I prefer to use the term *launch*, which more clearly suggests the place where the reader's attention is engaged anew.

Visually, in a manuscript a new scene is usually signified by a break of four lines (called a soft hiatus) between the last paragraph of the previous scene and the first paragraph of the next one, or sometimes by a symbol such as an asterisk or dingbat, to let the reader know that time has passed, and a new scene is beginning.

Each new scene still has a responsibility to the idea or plot you started with, which is to communicate your idea in a way that is vivifying for the reader and that provides an experience, not a lecture. Scene launches, therefore, pave the way for all the robust consequences of the idea or plot to unfurl. Each scene launch is a reintroduction, capturing your reader's attention all over again.

You want to start each scene by asking yourself the following questions:

- Where are my characters in the plot? Where did I leave them and what are they doing now?

- What is the most important piece of information that needs to be revealed in this scene?

Only you and the course of your narrative can decide which kinds of launches will work best for each scene, and choosing the right launch often takes some experimentation. This section will provide you with techniques for launching with characters, actions, narrative summary, or setting.

CHARACTER LAUNCHES

It's generally a good idea to get your characters on the page sooner rather than later. And, depending on how many points of view you use, the majority of scenes should involve your *main* character(s) (although there may be scenes from which your main character needs to be excluded, for the sake of your plot). If you write fantasy or science fiction, your characters may not be people, but dragons, elves, robots, or any of a vast miscellany of other life-forms; just be sure the reader knows who and what your characters are. The edict is still the same—bring your character into the scene as soon as possible. (Part three will elaborate on how to do this.)

Remember, if your scene launch goes on for too many paragraphs in passive description or narrated ideas without characters coming into play, the reader might begin to feel lectured to, or impatient for something to happen and someone for it to happen to. If your character isn't present by the second paragraph in any given scene, you're in danger of losing the reader.

SET SCENE INTENTIONS FOR CHARACTERS

For every scene, you must establish a purpose, goal, or intention for the character who stars in it. While scene intention is discussed in detail in chapter eleven, it's worth mentioning here, because you need to know your characters' intentions at the launch of every scene so you can reveal, follow, and build upon the intention. To set scene intentions, you must decide:

- What the most immediate desires of the characters are

- When your characters will achieve their intention or encounter some type of opposition

- Whether the intention makes sense to your plot

- Who will help your characters achieve their goal, and who will oppose them

Scene intentions ought to involve some kind of conflict or plot avenue. It does not matter what your character's intentions are, just that you know them from the beginning of each scene so you can see that they are either enacted, met, or thwarted.

ACTION LAUNCHES

Many writers believe they must explain every bit of action that is going on right from the start of a scene, but narrative summary defeats action. The sooner you start the action in a scene, the more momentum it has to carry the reader forward. If you find yourself explaining an action, then you're not *demonstrating* the action any longer; you're floating in a distant star system known as Nebulous Intellectulus—more commonly known as your head—and so is the reader.

Keep in mind the key elements of action: time and momentum. It takes *time* to plan a murder over late-night whispers; for a drunk character to drop a jar at the grocery; to blackmail a betraying spouse; or to kick a wall in anger. These things don't happen spontaneously, they happen over a period of time. They are sometimes quick, sometimes slow, but once started, they unfold until finished.

The key to creating strong momentum is to start an action without explaining anything.

> Albert leads them all into the dining room and everyone drifts around the large teak table, studying the busily constructed salads at each place setting—salads, which, with their knobs of cheese, jutting chives and little folios of frisée, resemble small Easter hats.
>
> "Do we wear these or eat them?" asks Jack. In his mouth is a piece of gray chewing gum like a rat's brain.

Lorrie Moore plunges her reader into the above scene in the story "Beautiful Grade." Though the action is quiet, there is physical movement and a sense of real time. The lack of explanation for what is happening forces the reader to press on to learn more. The action here gives clues to the reader: The fact that characters are led into a room full of wildly decorated salads that a character is uncertain whether he should eat or wear gives a sense of the environment—probably chic. We get a feeling for Jack—he's got a good sense of humor. Clearly something more is going to happen in this environment, and judging from the tone of the paragraph, we can probably expect irony and humor. Action launches tend to energize the reader's physical senses.

To create an action launch:

- **Get straight to the action.** Don't drag your feet here. "Jimmy jumped off the cliff"; not "Jimmy stared at the water, imagining how cold it would feel when he jumped."

- **Hook the reader with big or surprising actions.** A big or surprising action—outburst, car crash, violent heart attack, public fight—at the launch of a scene allows for more possibilities within the scene.

- **Be sure that the action is true to your character.** Don't have a shy character choose to become suddenly uninhibited at the launch of a scene—save that for scene middles. Do have a bossy character belittle another character in a way that creates conflict.

- **Act first, think later.** If a character is going to think in your action opening, let the action come first. "Elizabeth slapped the Prince. When his face turned pink, horror filled her. *What have I done?* she thought."

NARRATIVE LAUNCHES

Writers often try to include narrative summary, such as descriptions of the history of a place or the backstory of characters, right at the launch of a scene, believing that the reader will not be patient enough to allow actions and dialogue to tell the story. In large doses, narrative summary is to scenes what voice-overs are to movies—a distraction and an interruption.

Yet a scene launch is actually one of the easier places to use a judicious amount of narrative summary (since you've only just gotten the reader's attention), so long as you don't keep the reader captive too long.

Take the opening of an early scene in Amanda Eyre Ward's novel *How to Be Lost.*

> The afternoon before I planned how I would tell her. I would begin with my age and maturity, allude to a new lover, and finish with a bouquet of promises: grandchildren, handwritten letters, boxes from Tiffany sent in time to beat the rush. I sat in my apartment drinking Scotch and planning the words.

The above bit is almost entirely narrative summary, and the only action—drinking Scotch—is described, not demonstrated. There is no real setting, and the only visual cues the reader has are vague and abstract. However, the narrative summary does demonstrate Caroline's nature—she feels she must butter her mother up, bribe her even, in order to ask for something she needs, which turns out to be a relatively small thing. It reflects Caroline's tendency to live in her head, and shows us that Caroline is the kind of person who must prepare herself mentally for difficult things—a theme that recurs throughout the book. It's also useful because Caroline spends a lot of time by herself, cutting herself off from her relationships, and, therefore, it is very true to her personality. In just one short paragraph of narrative summary, the reader learns a lot about Caroline, and Ward gets to action in the next paragraph:

> Georgette stretched lazily on the balcony. An ambulance wailed below. A man with a shopping cart stood underneath my apartment building, eating chicken wings and whistling.

If the entire scene had continued in narrative summary, it most certainly would have had a sedative effect on the reader, and the scene's momentum would have been lost.

Narrative launches should be reserved for the following occasions:

- **When narrative summary can save time.** Sometimes actions will simply take up more time and space in the scene than you would like. A scene beginning needs to move fairly quickly, and on occasion, summary will get the reader there faster.

- **When information needs to be communicated before an action.** Sometimes information needs to be imparted simply in order to set action in motion later in the scene. Consider the following sentences, which could easily lead to actions: "My mother was dead before I arrived." "The war had begun." "The storm left half of the city under water."

- **When a character's thoughts or intentions cannot be revealed in action.** Coma victims, elderly characters, small children, and other characters sometimes cannot speak or act for physical, mental, or emotional reasons; therefore the scene may need to launch with narration to let the reader know what they think and feel.

SETTING LAUNCHES

Sometimes setting details—like a jungle on fire, or moonlight sparkling on a lake—are so important to plot or character development that visual setting must be included at the launch of a scene. This is often the case in books set in unusual, exotic, or challenging locations such as snowy Himalayan mountains, lush islands, or brutal desert climes. If the setting is going to bear dramatically on the characters and the plot, then there is every reason to launch with it.

John Fowles's novel *The Magus* is set mostly on a Greek island that leaves an indelible imprint on the main character, Nicholas. He becomes involved with an eccentric man whose isolated villa in the Greek countryside becomes the stage upon which the major drama of the novel unfolds. Therefore, it makes sense for him to launch a scene in this manner:

> It was a Sunday in late May, blue as a bird's wing. I climbed up the goat-paths to the island's ridge-back, from where the green froth of the pine-tops rolled two miles across to the shadowy wall of mountains on the mainland to the west, a wall that reverberated away south, fifty or sixty miles to the horizon, under the vast bell of the empyrean. It was an azure world, stupendously pure, and always when I stood on the central ridge of the island, and saw it before me, I forgot most of my troubles.

The reader needs to be able to see in detail the empty Greek countryside in which Nicholas becomes so isolated. It sets the scene for something beautiful and strange to happen, and Fowles does not disappoint.

To create an effective scenic launch:

- **Use specific visual details.** If your character is deserted on an island, the reader needs to know the lay of the land. Any fruit trees in sight? What color sand? Are there rocks, shelter, or wild, roaming beasts?

- **Allow scenery to set the tone of the scene.** Say your scene opens in a jungle where your character is going to face danger; you can describe the scenery in language that conveys darkness, fear, and mystery.

- **Use scenery to reflect a character's feelings.** Say you have a sad character walking through a residential neighborhood. The descriptions of the homes can reflect that sadness; houses can be in disrepair, with rotting wood and untended yards. You can use weather in the same way. A bright, powerfully sunny day can reflect a mood of great cheer in a character.

- **Show the impact of the setting on the character.** Say your character is in a prison cell; use the description of the surroundings to show how they shape the character's feelings. "He gazed at his cell: the uncomfortable, flat bed, the walls that squeezed around him, the dull gray color that pervaded everything."

The scene launch happens so quickly and is so soon forgotten that it's easy to rush through it, figuring it doesn't really matter how you get it started. Don't fall prey to that kind of thinking. Take your time with a scene launch. Craft each one as carefully and strategically as you would any other aspect of your scene. Remember that a scene launch is an *invitation* to the reader, beckoning him to come further along with you. Make your invitations as alluring as possible.

3

POWERFUL SCENE MIDDLES

Where, exactly, *is* the middle of a scene? The term *middle* is misleading because scenes vary in length and there is no precise midpoint. The best explanation is to think of each scene's middle as a realm of possibility between the scene opening and its ending, where the major drama and conflict of the scene unfolds.

Be wary, because the middle has a seductive power to tempt writers into narrative side roads and pretty flower beds of words which, like those poppies in *The Wizard of Oz*, make the reader want to drift off to sleep.

If you grabbed the reader's attention with an evocative scene launch, the middle of your scene is the proving ground, the Olympic opportunity to hook the reader and never let her go.

UP THE ANTE: COMPLICATIONS

You are probably a very nice person who loathes the idea of even accidentally causing harm to another person. While this kindness is noble in life, in fiction writing it's a liability. You *must* complicate your characters' lives, and you must do it where the reader can see it—in scenes. Doing so is known as upping the ante. That phrase is most often heard in gambling circles when the initial bet goes up, making the potential win greater, along with the risk. What you must ante up in your scenes are those things your characters stand to lose (or even gain), from pride, to a home, to deep love. When you up the ante, you build anticipation, significance, and suspense that drive the narrative forward and bring the reader along for the ride.

This process is both terrible and wonderful. Terrible, because you must hurt your characters—you must take beloved people and possessions away from them, withhold desires, and sometimes even kill them for the sake of drama or tension. Yet it is also wonderful, because mucking about in your characters' lives will make the reader more emotionally invested in them.

In its simplest form, a traditional fictional narrative, whether story or novel, should address a problem that needs to be resolved or a situation that needs to be understood. Something like these: A young girl finds herself pregnant and abandoned by her family and her lover, so she falls into a life of prostitution on her road to spiritual redemption; a relative dies and leaves all his money to one family member, which launches a family feud; parents turn around at the mall and discover their child missing. The problem or situation must also include or encompass smaller problems (often called plot points) with consequences, which is where scenes come in.

Earlier, I mentioned the need to set scene intentions (see chapter eleven for more on scene intentions). An intention is your direction to yourself as to what aspect of the larger plot problem you will set into play in a given scene. Remember, your scenes transform flat ideas into experiences for the reader.

Let's walk through the nebulous middle of a scene, complicating as we go, using one of the examples above—that of the pregnant girl abandoned and left without resources.

Let's call your pregnant protagonist Britney. Resist the easy way out, which would be to narrate in flat prose that "Britney did some difficult and compromising things to take care of herself." Just get right to the work of revealing her plight in vivid scenes.

Start in a logical place—bereft Britney needs to obtain food and shelter so she can figure out what to do with her life. This will be her scene intention, her motivation. Therefore, she will need to go somewhere and do something to get that need met. Now remember your ingredients from chapter one: Britney, your character, stumbles into a physical setting—a dive bar, which you will be sure to describe in all its grimy, low-lit glory. You will be sure to reveal through her point of view—probably the first or third person—that she has chosen this location because she knows she can garner the attention of men, whom she feels are most likely to help her out. You will hopefully show the surprised responses of the men and the bartender, some parrying dialogue, some cat-calling and general reactions to her presence—all of which is action. Then, as she stands there huddled against a barstool, frightened and unsure, a seedy looking man approaches her—and so your drama begins.

Perhaps this man makes her an indecent proposal—to do something she does not find palatable in return for money—and she is desperate enough to consider it. This is a complication. You have just upped the ante, and she now has something to lose—possibly her health, integrity, or her morality—in order to gain what she needs—money, food, and shelter. The reader will worry for her, which creates suspense and anticipation. The reader will not be able leave this poor girl's side; they will have to know what happens next.

And what will happen next? First, remember that the reader is your omnipresent witness. Don't draw the curtain between yourself and him and then report back passively later. Don't stop the complications either. Though you may want the bar fellow to turn out sweet and help Britney out of the kindness of his heart (because you love your character), the middle of your scene is no place for him to turn out to be a saint. Save that for a surprise ending. Scenes need dramatic tension in order to enact their tugging power on a reader. If he turns out nice, the reader can put down your narrative and sleep easy, and you don't want that!

Consider using a handy little graph that one of my editing clients found useful for working out complications in her scene middles. Make four columns and rows on a page like so (they can be longer rows than these):

Protagonist	Scene Intention(s)	Complication	Result
Britney	To get food/shelter	Goes to a seedy bar	Meets "savior" who wants to help
Britney	To take man's help	Man is really a criminal	Hits man with beer bottle and runs
Britney	To get away from man	She has no car and no $$	She hitchhikes

A scene can unfold in a couple of paragraphs or two dozen pages. As long as Britney is engaged in the action with this seedy stranger in fictional real time—a streamlined series of events without a break in time—and in a single location (the interior of a moving car or other vehicle counts as a single location), your scene can be as long as it needs to be.

You need to make whatever happens to Britney in this scene complicated enough that it compels the reader to go on to the next scene or chapter. And you have the same task ahead of you for future scenes.

TECHNIQUES TO UP THE ANTE

Learning how to torture your characters and complicate their lives takes practice and a bit of a thick skin, which can be built up. A note of warning: While complications build anticipation and drama, you should not make things difficult on characters just because; complications have to reveal character and push your plot forward. It's hard to be cruel, so here are some specific techniques to add complications to your characters' lives in the middle of scenes.

The Withhold

Your characters need goals, desires, and ambitions to appeal to the reader's sensibilities. But to create the juicy tension that keeps a reader turning pages, you must dangle the objects of desire just out of reach at times, using a technique known as withholding.

There are many things you can withhold in scenes, such as emotions, information, and objects. Let's take a closer look at each.

Emotional withholding comes in many forms: A father withholds his approval of his son, no matter what the son does to win him over; a woman withholds her love for her abusive husband, and he abuses her more in the hopes of securing it.

One of literature's most powerful illustrations of emotional withholding is found in the novel *Lolita*, by Vladimir Nabokov. Even after protagonist Humbert Humbert, who has a predilection for nubile young girls, possesses young Lolita by becoming her legal guardian after the death of her mother, Lolita gives him her body but withholds the one thing he truly wants: her love and respect. The entire novel is a series of intense, often difficult, scenes that show Humbert's desperate attempt to finagle the perfect circumstances for Lolita to love him. The act of withholding, which Nabokov employs in one form or another in nearly every scene of the book, makes it possible for the reader to tolerate and even empathize with Humbert and nearly forget what he is: a pedophile.

Here Humbert writes of a time when he merely wanted to hold her, to be loved by Lolita, and of her ultimate denial:

> Sometimes ... I would shed all my pedagogic restraint, dismiss all our quarrels, forget all my masculine pride—and literally crawl on my knees to your chair, my Lolita! You would give me one look—a gray furry question mark of a look: "Oh no, not again" (incredulity, exasperation); for you never deigned to believe that I could, without any specific designs, ever crave to bury my face in your plaid skirt, my darling! ... "Pulease, leave me alone; will you," you would say ...

Emotional withholding is a great way to elicit sympathy, empathy, and concern for otherwise unlikable characters, as well as to build concern and drama around sympathetic characters.

Withholding information is the most common type of withholding you'll find in scenes. Many things can be withheld: the whereabouts of a kidnap victim; the location of a stolen treasure; the address of the apartment where a Jewish person is hiding from the Nazis. Withheld information usually sets up a power struggle, as the person who has the information holds power over the person who wants it. (That is, unless you decide to bring in a torturer, which shifts the power back again.) Every scene should contain some plot information that is withheld, or else you might conclude your narrative too early on and fall into the bad habit of repeating information the reader already knows.

Withholding objects is also an option. You might remember a game from childhood known as monkey in the middle, in which two children toss an object back and forth over the head of a third child, who tries desperately to grab for it. While it looks like a game, it's also a form of torture for the third child.

A person witnessing this scene would want to intervene on behalf of the poor child and grab the coveted item out from the hands of those tossing it.

You can play a form of monkey in the middle with your characters if there is an important object that your character wants, but that he must not gain too soon. This is a great technique when two characters want the same object, whether they are fighting for their lives over a gun on the floor, plotting to steal a precious piece of jewelry, or seeking a locked-up teddy bear that represents comfort. The longer you withhold the object from the person or people who want it, especially during the middle of the scene, the more tension you can build.

The Element Danger

A fantastic way to up the ante in the middle of the scene is to put your protagonist or someone he loves in danger. This can be physical danger—the maiden tied to the railroad tracks—like in Annie Proulx's novel *The Shipping News*. The main character, Quoyle, is a doormat of a man who has terrible self-esteem and who can't swim. His inability to swim is a metaphor for how he navigates the world. When he sees a body bobbing in the harbor, he takes it upon himself to rescue it, capsizing his boat in the process and nearly drowning himself. While clinging to a floating ice chest, Quoyle's life flashes before his eyes, and for the first time, the reader sees that he wants to become a stronger man.

Putting your character in danger is one of the most immediate ways to capture the reader. How your character reacts to danger also reveals something about his true nature. Perhaps your timid character suddenly shows some bravery, or, conversely, a macho character turns out to be quite terrified when his life is at stake.

Then there is emotional danger, such as an encounter with a psychotic person, blackmail that threatens a character's livelihood, or mental abuse such as in this bit of a scene from Jane Smiley's Pulitzer Prize–winning novel *A Thousand Acres*. Here, an abusive father suddenly rages at one of his grown daughters, Ginny, whom he considers disloyal:

He leaned his face toward mine. "You don't have to drive me around any more or cook the goddamned breakfast or clean the goddamned house." His voice modulated into a scream. "Or tell me what I can do and what I can't do. I know all about you, you slut! You've been creeping here and there all your life, making up to this one and that one. But you're not really a woman are you? I don't know what you are."

Those offensive and abusive words are strong enough in their own right, but with the characters' history added into the mix—this man abused his daughters when they were young—they are all the more horrifying. It's a painful but brilliant stroke of emotional danger that keeps the reader riveted.

Don't be afraid to invoke emotional danger in your character's lives; they can take it, and it actually builds both reader empathy and dramatic tension.

In truth, the essence of *any* conflict involves a little danger. While in life people tend to avoid arguments and conflict, in fiction, conflict is a great drama-builder. I recommend that in every story or novel your characters get into at least one heated argument—this is a great way to create a sense of emotional danger without having to give your characters bleak childhoods and painful tragedies.

SCENE STEALER

Noria Jablonski, author of Human Oddities, *discusses delaying anticipation in Vladimir Nabokov's* Lolita.

◎ ◎ ◎

The magic of *Lolita* is that Nabokov seduces the reader into a kind of complicity with Humbert Humbert, and when the scene arises where they are about to consummate their relationship at the Enchanted Hunters hotel, I was guiltily rooting for him. Never mind that he has drugged Lolita and intends to violate her, however lovingly. Never mind the fact that he has neglected to tell Lolita that her mother is dead.

Part of why I wave my foam finger for Humbert is simply the fact that I've known all along that this scene was coming, but it's been delayed for a hundred and thirty pages. He delays the anticipated moment, letting the thrill build and build. What sweet relief—Humbert's and mine—that it is Lolita who ultimately seduces him.

The Unexpected Revelation

Scene middles are a great place for a character to learn that he was adopted, that his wife has cheated on him with his best friend, or that he has been wrongly accused of a crime. Revelations can come via letters found in a dead relative's old chest of drawers, from another character's mouth, from an overheard conversation, or even through a device such as dreams. However they manifest, revelations are transformative pieces of plot information that drive your narrative forward and offer huge potential for drama in the scenes where they are revealed.

The power of a revelation is immense. Who can forget the moment in *Star Wars* when Luke hears those terrible words from Darth Vader—"I am your father"—and how they change everything he knows and believes; or the moment when the title character in Charlotte Brontë's novel *Jane Eyre* learns the terrible truth about the secret past of Mr. Rochester, a truth that forces them to cancel their planned wedding. These revelations come with devastating emphasis.

Revelations can also provide relief and comfort, returning fortune and identity and offering a character a chance where before there was none—like Cinderella learning she has a fairy godmother, or Pip discovering the identity of his wealthy benefactor in Charles Dickens's *Great Expectations*—and if you have tested your characters already, withholding from them and putting them in danger, then you might find it useful to provide a revelation that changes their fate in an instant.

4

SUCCESSFUL
SCENE ENDINGS

Are you more inclined to remember the moment you first fell in love, or the moment when your lover broke your heart and walked out your door for the last time? Most of us tend to remember what happened most recently, and what had the greater emotional impact on us. Scene endings can carry dynamic emotional weight when done right, and can leave the reader wanting more. Endings are by their nature conclusive; sometimes they conclude simple things like conversations or dates. In other cases, they end livelihoods and lives. But some endings are unresolved and leave the reader with more questions. Both kinds are acceptable when writing scenes (see chapter twenty-one for more on final scenes).

The end of a scene is a space for the readers to take a breath and digest all that they have just finished reading. Endings linger in memory because they are where things finally begin to add up and make sense. At the end of a scene, if it has been done well, the reader will have more knowledge of and a greater investment in the plot and characters, and feel more compelled to find out what happens next. In fact, you know you've done your work when the reader reaches the end of a scene and absolutely must press on. For novels, often each chapter is one long scene.

It is helpful to put scene endings in one of two categories: zoom-in endings and zoom-out endings. Just like a camera can zoom in or out on the image captured in its lens, endings should either bring the reader up close or pull back and provide a wider perspective.

ZOOM-IN ENDINGS

Anything that invites intimacy or emotional contact with the characters and their plight at the end of a scene has a zoom-in effect on readers, drawing the readers closer, even uncomfortably close in order to ensure that they have an emotional experience.

Character Summaries

Looking back on the events that have come before, characters can summarize, in the form of interior monologues or simple dialogue, what has just happened in the scene at hand.

"Wow," Snow White might say to one of her bluebird friends, "I can't believe the Queen actually sent the woodcutter to cut out my heart! I was so naïve to trust her!" This summary device is useful when your plot is complex, you have multiple main characters, or there is a mystery involved. The more pieces there are to put together, the more useful end summaries can be. A character summary also helps to show readers where your character is at this final moment before you launch into the next scene.

For instance, in Michael Cunningham's novel *The Hours*, a character named Laura has been debating leaving her family because she feels suffocated. At the end of an important scene, she comes to this decision (told in limited third-person point of view):

> She will not lose hope. She will not mourn her lost possibilities, her unexplored talents (what if she has no talents, after all?). She will remain devoted to her son, her husband, her home and duties, all her gifts. She will want this second child.

This kind of ending gives the reader a way of measuring the character's emotional pulse at the end of the scene. Up until this point, Cunningham has built a great deal of anxiety into Laura's storyline, and for this tiny moment, the readers can rest, feeling sure they know what Laura has decided to do. Of course, this is not the end of this character's story, or her dilemma; that is saved for the end of the book.

You do want to be careful not to provide too many summaries—you'll know if you have done so because the action will start to disappear. If you're getting feedback as you write, too much summary will likely cause your reader to report getting twitchy and bored. Use summary endings for character development, to reveal something more about a character that the reader didn't know before.

Revelatory Dialogue

Revelations create drama and tension in your scenes. In chapter three we discussed how revelations can be used in your scene middles to drive your narrative forward, but they can also be used to end a scene on a note of surprise or intensity, especially in the form of dialogue. The end of a scene is a fantastic place for a sudden and surprising piece of information to come out of the mouth of a character. "I shot her!" the man who is presumed innocent might suddenly proclaim during his trial. Revelation zooms the reader's focus in on the character and builds suspense for the next scene. When the reader meets this man again, she will undoubtedly see the consequences of his actions.

The revelation can be quieter, too, more on an emotional level. "I don't really love you," the new bride might confess to her husband on their honeymoon, changing their fate for the worse on what is supposed to be the happiest night of their lives.

The Cliffhanger Ending

If you really want to be sure that your reader will not stop for breath and press forward, you're best off employing the cliffhanger ending. Cliffhangers can happen in a variety of ways and in almost any scene when you want to leave the reader on the edge, uncertain of the outcome: A character is left in grave peril; an action is cut short at the precipice of an outcome; or the tables are turned completely on your character's perception of reality. What all of those scenarios have in common is suspense. They leave the reader wondering every time.

Take this example from Richard Russo's novel *Empire Falls*, in which Christina "Tick" Robideaux, daughter of protagonist Miles, faces off with an angry, hurt classmate:

> It occurs to Tick that Zack Minty's stupid game has prepared her for this moment. She faces John Voss as bravely as she can, knowing it will all be over soon. Her vision has now narrowed to the point where she can barely make him out, his face bloody, his eyes almost sad... Then he squeezes the trigger, and she hears what she is certain will be the last sound she will ever hear, and feels herself thrust backwards into blackness.

The cliffhanger draws the reader so deeply into the action that there is very little chance she will put down the book at that point, and when you have a dangerous cliffhanger as above, which puts a likable character like Tick in danger, the reader will be desperate to go on to find out what happens to her.

Cliffhangers have a tendency to pump adrenaline into the reader's heart, so you want to be careful not to end every scene on such a note. Cliffhangers can be an integral part of controlling suspense if they are not overused.

ZOOM-OUT ENDINGS

Zoom-out endings pull away from intimacy or immediacy. The reader often needs a bit of emotional relief from an intense scene, and pulling back provides him an opportunity to catch his breath or reflect on all that has just transpired.

Visual Descriptions

There are many reasons why a writer might choose to end a scene with a visual description. Visual passages in general ground the reader concretely in the present moment. A visual description simply shows what is; it isn't trying to be, or suggest, something else. In these instances, you will use more of the senses.

If there has been a lot of action in a scene—running, dancing, or fighting, say—drawing back to let the reader see something in a concrete visual way can be a very effective way to end the scene. If a fight has taken place during the scene, you might end the scene with a visual of the beaten protagonist passed out in the street, leaving the reader to wonder how badly injured he is. Or you might draw back to show the reader something peaceful or hopeful: a cow grazing quietly in the moonlight; a woman brewing tea in her kitchen; a child patting the head of a dog. The key here, of course, is that by using the senses, you leave a physical impression on the reader, an imprint that he will take into the next scene.

Visual endings don't need to give the reader anything to chew on beyond what is right there on the page; they are like palate cleansers between intense scenes, clearing away some of the feelings elicited in the scene to make way for a new one. One of the most masterful short stories ever written, "The Dead," by James Joyce, employs just such cleansing visuals between the end of one scene and the beginning of another:

> The morning was still dark. A dull yellow light brooded over the houses and the river; and the sky seemed to be descending. It was slushy underfoot; and only streaks and patches of snow lay on the roofs, on the parapets of the quay and on the area railings.

The visual ending above provides a gentle transition between the last scene of the party, full of boisterous activity and motion and dialogue, and a quietly emotional, devastating final scene between Gabriel and his wife, in which he realizes that he does not know her as well as he thinks. That simple visual paves the way for a truly powerful next scene.

Philosophical Musings

Since writing is symbolic as well as literal, sometimes an ending can reflect back on the events of a scene (or many scenes) with a philosophical bent that explores the thematic undercurrents of the work. In this example from Jane Hamilton's novel *A Map of the World*, the scene ends with a description of a dip in a swimming pool. But this event also means something more to the character:

At face value it had been a dip on a hot night. But it was something else, too. I could see that now, something on the order of a baptism, a kind of blessing.

Ideas of baptism and blessings are recurring themes in the novel, and they make many appearances. Hamilton's use of these themes to end a scene leaves these ideas in the back of the reader's mind like a curious aftertaste that lingers through the scenes that follow.

The best way to work in a philosophical angle is often through the use of a comparison like a simile or metaphor, often a visual comparison, and always in the point of view of whichever character is most important to the scene. For instance, a character who is struggling to decide on whether or not to keep an unexpected pregnancy might, at the end of a scene, see a mother cat nursing her kittens and feel revulsion, which helps her understand her own maternal instincts. You could have her reflect upon this philosophically: "I was frightened by the babies' hunger, their desperate need. I was a woman, and pregnant, but I knew in that moment a mother was so much more than that. More than I could ever be." Let these musings seep out through the character's point of view, not through yours—the author's.

Philosophical endings tend to work best when:

- You're writing in the first person, since the reader is already inside the mind of the character intimately

- Your character is already prone to philosophical musing (it's better not to try for the philosophical ending if your character is literal or not very introspective)

- Your novel or story has a strong theme (redemption, empowerment, loss) that lends itself to philosophical summaries

- Your novel or story is more character driven than plot or action driven; it's hard to get philosophical when a character is about to fall from a cliff or is running from the police

THE CONCLUSIVE ENDING

There comes a time when a scene simply needs to end without anything fancy to get in the way. In these instances, your ending doesn't need to portend any future event, or lend thematic resonance; its job is just to conclude something that has happened or to tie up a plot point. This might be the place you kill off a character that you know must die. Death is a momentous act, and placing a death at the end of a scene gives the reader time to decide how she feels, and if she is ready to keep reading right away.

There are many other conclusive kinds of endings. You can answer questions that have been posed throughout the scene or the story. Who really *is* Superman, Lois Lane wants to know. At the end of a scene, he can reveal himself as Clark Kent. You can unmask murderers, reveal the results of blood tests, and lay down jail sentences at the end of scenes in as straightforward a fashion as you need in order to get the job done.

A conclusive ending bears a feeling of finality, which will leave the reader with a very different experience than if you end with things hanging in the balance, dangling at the edge of a cliff. Eventually, there will be places in your narrative where one plot avenue or character detail needs to be tied up so that others can be handled.

For instance, in Michelle Richmond's novel *The Year of Fog*, protagonist Abby Mason loses sight of her fiancé's daughter, Emma, for just a brief moment, long enough for the child to disappear. She is not seen again for nearly a year. Even after Emma's father, Jake, gives up searching for his daughter months after her disappearance, Abby keeps up the search on her own. When the child finally is found, that event concludes a major plotline in the novel, but the novel doesn't end there.

> She comes out grimacing, holding her fingers to her nose. It's a nothing gesture, universal among children, and yet I'm strangled with emotion just to do see her doing this thing, this normal thing. Alive.

Because it strikes such a resounding note of conclusion, this terrific scene ending could easily be the end of the novel. That said, there is, in fact, much more for Jake, Abby, and Emma to cope with due to all they've been through over the course of the story.

Conclusive scene endings are not the ultimate end of the story or novel, just conclusions to plotlines or events that were set in motion by the significant situation.

In part three, we'll look at ways to end the many different types of scenes that will compose your narrative. Ultimately, though, you will have to choose each scene's ending individually to ensure that it fits the mood, the pace, and the plot.

PART II

THE CORE ELEMENTS AND THE SCENE

I learned that you should feel when writing, not like Lord Byron on a mountain top, but like a child stringing beads in kindergarten, happy, absorbed, and quietly putting one bead on after another.

—*BRENDA UELAND*

5

SETTING

Imagine entering the chilly, ornate cavern of the Vatican, expecting to be amazed by its historical and artistic beauty, only to find yourself disoriented by all the gilt and marble and the cathedral's sheer size. Imagine you did not know where to look first and immediately got a headache. Unfamiliar surroundings can make us feel unsettled and overwhelmed. This is also true of the fictional surroundings you create in scenes. You must act as the tour guide through each scene, expertly guiding the reader to all the important details, pointing out only what is necessary and what will help the reader understand what he sees.

The purpose of setting, a core element of the scene, is almost always to support and contain the action of the scene, but rarely to be the star. Still, setting requires careful consideration, because you want to ground the reader.

Though we'll discuss the implications of setting in specific scene types in part three, it's good to absorb the essential types of setting and props you'll eventually be using.

The first element of building the stage for any scene is describing what can be *seen*. When you create a physical world in each scene, you provide a solid framework to which to affix all the ineffable details to come, like feelings and thoughts. The more clearly you describe what can be seen, the more likely your reader is to feel right at home.

Humans have a funny tendency to look for verisimilitude—elements of real life—in fiction. Though the fun of fiction is that you can make up the world and the characters to your specifications, even fantasy writers know they must develop a believable and rich culture, history, and physical geography to sell the idea that their fantasy world is real. Place is one of the first things that make your story real to the reader.

SETTING THE STAGE

Settings are as varied in fiction as they are in the world: A humid Southern bayou; icy Norwegian fjords; a crumbling Victorian mansion; a stable, pungent with the stench of animals. These are just a few of the infinite number of places in which you might set your characters. Though they may seem like merely the backdrop to the action and drama of your narrative, they are more like the rich soil in which you plant your seeds. *Do not* forget to set the scene. Unless you have a good reason to set your novel or story in a vacuum, establishing a physical setting is one of the most important and literal ways to ground the reader and keep characters from being floating heads.

There are so many details to consider when writing fiction that setting can seem like the least important, and, therefore, an obligation, something you dread or do only because you have to. Yet you don't have to have the setting perfectly figured out at first. You can begin with a vague idea and flesh it out over further drafts. If you've ever seen or starred in a stage play, you're familiar with the ambiguous visual details that constitute settings and places onstage. Often a vague cut-out outline of a city is meant to represent a sprawling metropolis, or a couple of paper trees, a forest. If you struggle with setting, there is nothing wrong with sketching it out loosely to begin with and then, later, when you have a better feel for it, filling it in.

You can make notes to yourself in your scene, such as: "Set in some kind of park with lots of loud children and a pond," or "They're in some kind of Italian café. Research foods and smells for later."

Setting may not come to you all at once, because there are many layers to it. Just make sure your sets are finished before the final draft. Some of the basic setting types you should keep in mind include general geographic location, nature, and homes and buildings.

Geographic Location and Natural Settings

Do you know where in the world your story is set? Is it a world you've made up, like the planet Rakhat in Mary Doria Russell's novel *The Sparrow*, off in the Alpha Centauri solar system? Or is it Memphis, Tennessee, USA, Earth?

The geographical location is the one thing you need to decide as quickly as possible, as it will have more bearing on your characters than other details of setting. Every location comes with information that is useful to the reader (and to you as a writer) from dialect to politics to climate, and that information bears on the characters who turn up there. A born Southerner, for instance, is likely to feel at home in Alabama, while a character from California might struggle to handle its heat, politics, or racial inequality.

It makes sense for scenes to take place in nature, the most prolific of all natural settings, but remember that cool, snow-piled ski slopes affect characters far differently than scorched desert. If someone takes a drunken spill into a lush garden full of flowers, the results will be different than if that character had tumbled into a wall of cactuses. It is your job to attend to these specifics. The reader cannot be physically transported to the sharp cold of Vail, Colorado, or to the dry heat of the Mojave desert by reading your book, but you want him to *feel* as though he is. On the other hand, you don't want to have to give a lengthy geological explanation for the formation of mesas in Arizona if your goal is simply to have a character leap off one of them.

Author Arundhati Roy uses natural settings in her novel *The God of Small Things*, which is set in India. There, the weather and nature—in particular the constant activity of monsoon rains—have a profound influence on the characters.

> Heaven opened and the water hammered down, reviving the reluctant old well, greenmossing the pigless pigsty, carpet bombing still, tea-colored puddles the way memory bombs still, tea-colored minds. The grass looked wetgreen and pleased. Happy earthworms frolicked purple in the slush.

In this small paragraph, Roy creates a feeling for what it's like to experience a monsoon rain in India (with wonderful descriptions, no less). Imagine having to set your schedule around these torrential rains, and how this might shape your characters' relationship to natural forces, and each other.

Houses, Buildings, and Rooms

In the course of a novel, characters might live in houses, huts, and yurts; they might enter and exit bathrooms, mad scientists' laboratories, and hospitals; they might gather in restaurants, bars, and bedrooms. Rooms and homes must be real, because these are the most essential of living and gathering spaces, and most people are familiar with them, whether they live in shacks or large estates, eat at gourmet establishments or bring home pizza. These spaces are telling and should reveal details about characters.

You've heard the old adage that seeing is believing? Well, how will the reader know for sure that a bedroom bears a woman's touch unless a character in the scene sees perfume and lingerie and lovely flowers on the windowsill? How will he know a home is homey unless he can see the fire burning in the hearth and feel the soft rugs beneath his fingers?

Houses are often representative of the characters that live in them. By describing the state of a house, you can also speak to the soul of a character. Lonely characters often live in lonely quarters. Passionate characters often have a taste for the flamboyant, the colorful, or the warm. Use your rooms, buildings, and houses to add to your scenes, not just to serve as flat backdrops.

SETTING DETAILS

Every setting type comes with its own unique setting details that are just as important as basic physical details for creating a vivid and believable environment in which to situate your protagonist. From the historical period to cultural references, settings are more than just the way things appear—they comprise values and mores that you can work into your narrative to create a truly vivid, believable world for the reader to become deeply involved in.

Time in History

It's important not to forget *when* your novel takes place, because this also has a major influence on your setting. Medieval England will provide a setting completely different from that of 1960s Congo, Africa.

When you pick a particularly memorable time in recent history, say the Free Love and anti-government movement of the 1960s in the United States, remember that there are people out there who lived during these times and who will have strong feelings about the accuracy of your portrayal of that time period. Not only will your details need to be especially accurate, but the time period itself, whether you intend it or not, will make a comment on its people and events.

If you choose a historically benign year or decade (if such a thing is possible), or at least one that has seen fewer dramatic events, you may have more room to sketch details broadly. Depending on how important the time period is to your storyline, you might be able to get away with generalities like "the early nineties," or "the middle of the nineteenth century."

Cultural References

Culture defines how people behave and what their beliefs are; the West Coast of the U.S. differs in many significant ways from the East Coast, from accent and manner of speech to political values. Cultures come with icons of worship, social and religious traditions—or lack thereof—and language patterns. If your characters are living in a culture that you personally have never lived in, you will be in the position of having to do some research to get details right. If it's a culture you know well, then you have the bonus of being able to draw on rich material that will authenticate your scenes.

A good example comes from Michelle Richmond's lyrical novel *Dream of the Blue Room*. In it, protagonist Jenny is on a cruise down the Yangtze River in China in a last-ditch attempt to save her failing marriage and to say good-bye to her deceased friend Amanda Ruth, who wanted her ashes sprinkled there. Richmond builds a gorgeous and surreal mood out of these foreign elements with descriptions and images, but she does so in a way that renders the scene accessible and authentic. It is easy to believe you are there on that boat, cruising down this mysterious river in China:

> In the night the river turns silver, the mountains shine down upon it, the air goes cool and wet. This is the China Amanda Ruth wanted, her moonlit landscape, her Land of the Dragon. The villages we pass become magical

in darkness, carnival-like and throbbing, though in the day they seem filthy, overcrowded, rubbed raw by industry. Apartment rows crouch like creatures gone dumb with hunger, and in the air there is a stench of coal. The mist mingles with black ash and factory smoke. It takes all of my energy just to breathe.

You do not have to become an expert and present a brief history or cultural overview of the territory of your novel or story, but you do need to provide enough information, description, and cultural detail to allow the reader to believe they are really there in that country, even if it is on another planet. When in doubt, try to lean into the senses, rendering the foreign land and its culture visible, audible, and even smellable.

A WHIRLWIND TOUR OF SETTING

For a bird's-eye view of all the elements of setting discussed in this chapter, consider these significant elements pulled from scenes in Patrick Suskind's Perfume: The Story of a Murderer.

Geographic Location and Time Period
The following details set the stage of eighteenth-century Paris, France. Notice how vividly you are drawn into the smells and sights. The main character is anti-hero Grenouille, a man born without a smell of his own who lusts after scents:

> In the period of which we speak, there reigned in the cities a stench barely conceivable to us modern men and women. The streets stank of manure, the courtyards of urine, the stairwells of moldering wood and rat droppings, the kitchens of spoiled cabbage and mutton fat; people stank of sweat and unwashed clothes; from their mouths came the stench of rotting teeth, from their bellies that of onions. ...

> For eight hundred years the dead had been brought here from the Hotel-Dieu and from the surrounding parish churches, for eight hundred years,

day in, day out, corpses by the dozens had been carted here and tossed into long ditches, stacked bone upon bone. ...

Here, then, on the most putrid spot in the whole kingdom, Jean-Baptiste Grenouille was born on July 17, 1738.

Houses and Buildings

Here is the neighborhood where young Grenouille lives in his early years. In short passages of description you get a strong visual image of a claustrophobic little village:

> The adjacent neighborhoods of Saint-Jacques-de-la-Boucherie and Saint-Eustache were a wonderland. In the narrow side streets ... people lived so densely packed, each house so tightly pressed to the next, five, six stories high that you could not see the sky, and the air at ground level formed damp canals where odors congealed.

Suskind gives glimpses into the physical space (rooms) of the perfumer, through Grenouille's fascinated eyes:

> He was touched by the way this worktable looked: everything lay ready, the glass basin for the perfume bath, the glass plate for drying, the mortars for mixing the tincture, pestle and spatula, brush and parer and shears.

Natural Setting

After learning all he needs to know about how to make perfume, and then blowing up his perfume master's shop, Grenouille sets off to divorce himself from other people for long enough to be forgotten. He retreats to the wild:

> For the spot had incalculable advantages: at the end of the tunnel it was pitch-black night even during the day, it was deathly quiet and the air he breathed was moist, salty cool. Grenouille could smell at once that no living creature had ever entered the place. ... He was lying a hundred and fifty feet below the earth, inside the loneliest mountain in France. ... Never in his life had he felt so secure. ...

PURPOSEFUL PLACEMENT: EVERY OBJECT COUNTS

Another aspect of setting is the placement of props, or objects that have significance. Most people who went through public school as children had, at one time, to construct something known as a diorama—a still life representing a book they had read, re-created with tiny props, and presented in a shoe box. You could not possibly fit all the details of a famous novel, for instance, into a diorama, so you would have to pare down to the essentials that were most representative of the book. This is a good way to think about the objects that will show up in your scenes: Imagine that each scene is a diorama. You should strive to add only the props that will bring a scene to life—a mechanic will have his tools, a musician his instrument, perhaps—without imbuing these objects with unnecessary power.

If you make the effort to put an object in a scene, the reader will believe that object has significance. This is not to say that every comb, pack of cigarettes, and cup of tea needs to get up and dance the tango, or that you should keep your settings bare, but remember that the more attention you give to descriptions of objects, the more readers will assign import and meaning to those objects. From art on the walls to cigarettes left burning in an ashtray, objects carry emotional weight and may often appear as clues. This is important to consider if your intention is simply to describe a man's possessions to reveal his character; the reader may assume that a cigar is a lot more than just than a cigar, depending on how much description an object gets.

Mood Objects

Some objects are used to symbolize the narrator's feelings and do not play an important role in the plot; thus they can be considered mood objects. They add to the tone of a narrative and deepen our understanding of a character's feelings.

For example, in his novel *So Long, See You Tomorrow*, William Maxwell uses a multitude of mood objects in the narrative. The narrator in this novel, now an adult, is writing his memoirs in relation to a murder that took place in his small hometown, and he describes his childhood home just after his mother's death:

I have never been inside it since that day, when a great many objects that I remember and would like to be reunited with disappeared without a trace: Victorian walnut sofas and chairs that my fingers had absently traced every knob and scroll of, mahogany tables, worn Oriental rugs, gilt mirrors, pictures, big square books full of photographs that I knew by heart.

These objects in and of themselves do not bear any one particular meaning to the narrator; rather, they add up to a feeling of familiarity, of comfort which he lost when his mother died. The fact that they are very quickly sketched, and lumped together in a list, so that no single item stands out as more important than another, tells us that no specific object is important. Though the reader gets a quick picture of the knobs and scrolls of the mahogany table, these details are passed over just as quickly for the "worn Oriental rugs."

The closest this narrator can come to admitting that he missed his mother is to miss the objects he associated with her. While these details certainly add texture to the scene, they are merely representative, placed to call attention to the feelings and memories they elicit in the narrator.

When you describe objects clumped together like this, remember that you're setting mood more than imbuing an object with symbolic power. This is why it's important to notice how much description you give to any one object. If you want an object to be innocuous, just background dressing, then be brief about it. If you want an object to mean something inside your narrative, then it needs to stand alone, or be given more attention than other objects, as described next.

Significant Objects

Significant objects, on the other hand, should call a certain amount of attention to themselves. What makes an object significant? When it directly affects plot or character development. Let's take a careful look at each type to get a better feel for what makes each unique and meaningful.

Plot-Significant Objects

There are obvious significant objects, such as evidence sought by police in mystery plots, stolen heirlooms, lost Egyptian tombs, and buried treasure, that change your plot once they are introduced or found in a scene.

If your story is about the search for a holy artifact, then it's safe to assume that whichever scenes the object turns up in will involve some sort of drama, danger, or other conflict. Also, whether the protagonist or the antagonist has the artifact is likely to sway the course of your plot. You may in fact tease the reader with a significant object and have it turn up in every scene, but continue to elude those who want it most.

In J.R.R. Tolkien's Lord of the Rings series of books, the significant object is merely a tiny ring, but it holds the power to corrupt good people and ultimately destroys anyone who possesses it for too long. Every time that ring turns up in a scene, everyone's attention is focused on it—character's and the reader's alike—and the balance of power continues to shift as the ring works its diabolical magic on everyone it touches. That's a powerfully significant object, and one that continues to shape the course of the plot from start to finish.

A plot-significant object does not need to be quite as weighty as one that holds the balance between good and evil, but it should have a direct link to your plot. It might be a murder weapon, a stolen piece of jewelry, or an item that incriminates a character for adultery.

Character-Significant Objects

Objects have value to people for sometimes very bizarre and personal reasons. A person cherishes a ratty old jacket because of its sentimental power. People collect items that have meaning only to themselves—figurines, dolls, coins—to satisfy an emotional need in a material form, or for purposes of greed, or to feel safe. People also have talismans—objects that hold religious or spiritual meaning and help them feel loved or lucky.

Character-significant objects do not need to change the course of your plot, but they do need to be described in enough detail that the reader understands their value or importance to the character. If a character always kisses a medallion of St. Christopher before he travels, this will reinforce in the reader's mind that this object means something to him. You might even find it useful to write the scene of when he first obtained this object, and how it became significant to him.

While these objects are indeed important, you can introduce them without a great deal of description so long as you effectively demonstrate a character's relationship to the item.

Avoiding Vague Objects

Would your protagonist buy a "vehicle," or a white Toyota Corolla? If someone opened his cabinets, would he find "aspirin," or Advil? Does your character own a "parrot," or a rainbow macaw? The difference is, of course, in the specifics.

It's very important to avoid the vague. If you lead the reader into a "building," she will wonder if it is a bank, an embassy, or a hotel, and this is already too many options for her to have to hold in mind; it's your job to be the tour guide, remember. If your protagonist carries a gun, the reader deserves to know if it's a tiny derringer or a semi-automatic rifle. What you want the reader to wonder about is what happens next, not where the characters are and what can be seen. If you were a painter and you made some loose charcoal sketches, then displayed your work and told people, "some green paint will go here, and some blue there, and probably a little yellow here," they would have absolutely no idea of the painting you intended to make. So try to avoid making that same mistake in your writing. Be clear and visual.

Your objects are opportunities to reveal information about your characters. Objects are the physical manifestations of characters' personalities and moods. Since you can't spend too much of the text in narrative summary describing a character's personality without losing the reader's attention, these props serve to convey information on the character's behalf.

Tim O'Brien, award-winning author of the short story "The Things They Carried," about Vietnam soldiers, uses objects as if they are biographies of each person.

> Norman Bowker carried a diary. Rat Kiley carried comic books. Kiowa, a devout Baptist, carried an illustrated New Testament that had been presented to him by his father, who taught Sunday school in Oklahoma City, Oklahoma. As a hedge against bad times, however, Kiowa also carried his grandmother's distrust of the white man, his grandfather's old hunting hatchet.

In order to use objects properly, you have to get to know your characters, and in order to do that, you need to ask yourself a series of important questions about who your characters are. What do they love or hate, collect or throw away? What do they like to see around them in their house? Are they art snobs or philistines? These, and many others, are questions that only you can answer.

Remember that great characters and the wild plot actions they undertake need solid ground and meaningful props to support them. Always ask, what needs to be *seen* in this scene?

STRIKING A BALANCE

Setting is where many writers get lost in chunks of narrative summary because it's easy, and even fun, to describe the setting. It's crucial to remember that setting exists mostly to serve as a way of both creating authenticity and grounding the reader in the scene (and story) at hand. If setting begins to take too much precedence, and distracts from your characters or storyline, then it needs to be tamed back.

Here is an example of well-balanced setting description, filtered through the character's perceptions, punctuated by small actions, from Jane Alison's lyrical novel *The Marriage of the Sea*:

> Max landed in New Orleans like a sprinter. His cab barreled over the toxic empty highway into town, the battered streets and battered sidewalks and battered, crooked houses. He'd chosen the most romantic hotel, just beyond the Garden District, lopsided and seedy. Once he'd checked in he ran up the staircase, noting with delight the stained glass promise in the window: *Let my beloved come into his garden and eat his pleasant fruits!* Then he had barely put down his bag, barely phoned Sea & Air to provide a temporary number (should his fur teacup and cookbooks and second-hand Paul Smiths be lost at sea in their nailed, stamped crates), before he washed his hands, looked at his teeth, tried to order his fly-away ringlets, paced once up and down the room, lifted the receiver and dialed.

While a lot of detail is given to setting in this paragraph, it feels intimately connected to Max's perceptions, and sets the stage for the fact that he is setting the stage for the woman he is in love with.

When you describe setting details, in order to strike a nice balance and not overdo it, keep in mind:

- **Setting helps create mood or ambiance that sets a tone for the scene.** In the scene above, there's a sense of preparation, of nesting almost, as Max prepares to see his love.

- **Your protagonist needs to interact with the setting.** This can be through his observations of it or by his physically engaging with it. The reader sees New Orleans through Max's eyes here—words like "romantic" and "battered" reflect his opinion.

- **The setting needs to support your plot.** Max is in New Orleans because he has come to be with a woman—a woman, it turns out, who will break his heart.

- **Small actions help break up setting description.** Because Max is moving around, the reader doesn't feel as though he is looking at a static scene. The scene comes alive.

STAYING CONSISTENT

Once you've done the work of establishing the place in your scenes and fleshing out the settings so the reader is clear on where your characters are, it's important to stay consistent. If there are long tendrils of night-blooming jasmine on the porch in one scene, be sure they don't later turn into wisteria.

Don't forget which way the front door faces as your characters enter and exit. If a character sleeps in a room without windows, don't allow in a sudden, unexpected beam of sunlight.

For anyone who has a complicated setting, I often recommend keeping a notebook with all the small details in it as a kind of reference guide in case you get lost. I recommend this for any amount of significant research. If you have trouble organizing, try to keep your notes ordered into chapters and scenes in a linear fashion.

6

THE SENSES

Before language, humans were like other animals; we came to know our world through our most primary set of tools for understanding and learning—our senses. The senses are as core a scene element as you can get, and are very important in writing fiction because they transform flat words on a page into three-dimensional, realistic scenes. However, many writers overlook senses other than sight and sound. In a scene that takes place in a garden, for instance, you might forget to allow readers the opportunity to *smell* the jasmine and lilacs that drew your character out to the garden in the first place. Or you might show a character eating an entire tin of cookies without telling the reader what flavor they are. No matter *when* you add in sensual details—upon revision or at the start—remember that they are key tools for bringing your written world alive for readers.

AUTHENTICITY OF DETAIL

The sensual experiences that you describe should be realistic and believable. If a character is cooking blackberry pie, but the scent emanating from the oven smells "savory and meaty," you're off base; obviously a blackberry pie would smell sweet.

Also, the senses are a part of everyday life, so they should, in fact, be blended into your scenes as an integral part of the stage you set. If your scene's stage is a meadow in County Cork, Ireland, then there ought to be the nutty smell of grass and the sweet perfume of wildflowers, and possibly the musky scent of animals and mud. There might be birds trilling or sheep baaing or the gentle slicing sound of a scythe cutting hay. Characters will feel the wind on their face and the ropy knots of lavender stems between their fingers. The more seamlessly all these sensual details emerge, so that they are the backdrop to the scene in which a young boy confesses to his angry father that he is leaving Ireland, the more the reader will feel transported to that very spot and time, her own senses activated.

SIGHT

Sight is perhaps the most important, and most ironic, element of scene writing. At no time do you actually draw images or pictures while writing, yet the reader must come away from your wall of text with an experience of *seeing*. He must be able to draw in his mind images of what your characters look like, what the world in which your characters interact looks like, and all the minutiae in between. This means that you must have a pretty good visual idea of the world you're writing about so that you can help provide the appropriate cues that will turn words into pictures in the reader's mind.

All that can be seen in your scenes is the fictional equivalent of evidence provided in a court case. In court, you can't get away with saying, "The bloody knife was about yea long, and imagine a carved wooden handle here, and some speckles of blood here. Trust me, it was a big, nasty-looking knife, and definitely the murder weapon!" The lawyer must provide an *actual* knife that meets those specifications for the jury members to set their eyes upon. So must you provide evidence in your scenes. No matter if the piece of evidence proves that someone's lover was just at the house—a cigarette butt covered in suspicious lipstick still smoldering in the ashtray—or if it's graffiti on the side of a house that gives away a vandal; until the reader can *see* proof, it simply does not exist.

When including details of sight in your story, remember that point of view is not only a vehicle for understanding character, it is also the camera through which the reader sees whatever your characters see. A fictional world takes shape to the reader through the eyes and experiences of your characters. Still, many writers fall into the habit of pointing out that a character sees something—"Jimmy saw a huge cloud of dust rise up on the horizon"—which is a habit I call double vision. The point of view establishes that Jimmy is the one seeing. Therefore, when you tell the reader that Jimmy saw, you are literally calling attention to the act of sight rather than to the huge cloud of dust on the horizon, which is the important point of action in the scene. You are saying to the reader: "Look, Jimmy is seeing!" Rather than, "Look at that huge dust cloud! Wowsers, I wonder what it could be!"

The more you can place readers inside the vision and point of view of your characters and remove the *act* of them seeing, the more directly the reader will interact with the sights, smells, and other senses in the scene.

Blindness

When a character loses sight, or never had it to begin with, the writer is no less obliged to describe the physical world, even though that world no longer exists through the character's eyes. Blindness gives way to all the other senses, which must take over. This is a powerful technique to use, as it not only forces the character to experience the settings in a unique way, it provides you with unique challenges.

José Saramago's stark novel *Blindness* has the entire world going blind in the course of a few days—except for one woman, a doctor's wife. The novel centers on a quarantined ward of people who are among the first to go blind. Chaos soon erupts as the ward fills to overflowing and is eventually abandoned by the government when they, too, go blind.

> You can count me out, said the first blind man, I'm off to another ward, as far away as possible from this crook. ... He picked up his suitcase and, shuffling his feet so as not to trip and groping with his free hand, he went along the aisle separating the two rows of beds, Where are the other wards, he asked, but did not hear the reply if there was one, because suddenly he found himself beneath an onslaught of arms and legs. ...

Saramago relies heavily upon the next sense, touch, to delineate the world for the reader.

What the characters see, the reader sees. Remember to extract yourself, the author, from the picture, so that the reader is looking directly through your characters' eyes like he would through a pair of binoculars focused on a far-off stage.

TOUCH

Though the philosopher René Descartes would have us believe it is our thoughts that make us who we are ("I think, therefore I am"), touch is one of our first ways of knowing. Young babies do not think about their blocks and stuffed animals; they grab and grope, prod and poke their toys (and their parents) to learn about them. Touch is a bodily experience. Every character in your fiction will have a unique relationship to his body and to touch, and as the writer, you will need to determine these zones of comfort and contact and the meanings that are layered in.

Practical Touch

What are practical forms of touch? When a character rubs a piece of beach-weathered glass between his fingertips to feel its surface; touches the rough bark of a tree; inspects the edge of a knife for sharpness; runs his fingers over piano keys; or smooths out a bedspread. These forms of touch aren't necessarily significant to the character or the plot; they are actions taken between dialogue or other actions. However, practical touch is sort of like punctuation—you need a little bit in strategic places, because without it the scene would not be fully formed. But it shouldn't call attention to itself.

Practical touch can come in handy when you have a lot of uninterrupted dialogue between characters. A character could stop to touch the smooth surface of a marble countertop before launching an angry salvo, or grip a beer bottle tightly in his hand before defending his action. People tend to be tactile. When we're nervous, we fidget, fumble, or unconsciously drum our fingers. In fact, a character won't get more than a couple of minutes into a day before he begins to interact with the world by touching things.

Perhaps your character has a phobia of germs and wears gloves or refuses to touch certain things—like doorknobs or glasses. This example still shows details of touch. Whatever you determine for your characters, remember to let their fingers do the walking at least a little in your scenes, and know what kind of "toucher" each of your characters is.

Personal Touch

Personal touch is *a range* of physical contact that expresses information about your characters and relates to how they physically interact with other people. While personal touch refers to contact between characters (from the platonic, to the downright naughty), it also refers to ways that your characters interact with the world—offering readers insight into your characters' personalities. For instance, you might create a character with a form of obsessive-compulsive disorder who cannot stop from touching strangers' noses, light switches, mailboxes, etc. Another character might have an obnoxious habit of gesturing wildly with his hands when he talks, knocking things off shelves. The way your characters touch their physical world is important information about who they are.

When characters touch *each other* (or themselves—for instance, your character might be a "cutter" who wounds herself for emotional release), the reader will also take notice. Touch between people is important because it's a way of communicating with one another. In real life you notice when a stranger puts his hands on your shoulders without permission. Your characters should also pay attention to these forms of touch between each other. A character who was sexually abused may not like to hug or be hugged. Yet another character might come from a culture where close physical proximity is normal and has to learn the hard way that another character does not appreciate this. Remember that when characters touch each other, they are *communicating*, so try to be conscious of this communication and what it means to your scene and your plot.

In chapter seven we'll talk about body language as a way to develop and build characters without even using dialogue.

SMELL

Remember a time when you caught a whiff of the scent of a flower or food, and the smell evoked a childhood memory, making you cry, laugh, or even get embarrassed? It's as if memories are housed inside scents, and once your

Make a Scene

nose gets a whiff, the memory is unlocked and, with it, feelings. The sense of smell—our olfactory sense, as it's known to scientists—has a direct link in the brain to memory and emotion. Since experiencing a scent is one of the most common experiences that people have, your characters need to have these experiences too, and you can use the sense of smell to dramatic effect in scenes.

For a moment, let's classify smells into two basic groups: those that smell good, and those that smell bad. If your scene involves a conflict between a morally good character and morally corrupt character, let us say, but you don't want to rely on any narrative tricks of telling the reader which is which, scent can help you get this distinction across. If Jack, your bad guy, smells of cigar smoke and day-old greasy Chinese food, while Bill, your good guy, smells like juniper and fresh air, who do you think the reader will see as bad or good?

Now I can already hear you saying, "What if I hate the smell of juniper?" Point taken. However, in the world of scents, even an unsophisticated reader is likely to believe that juniper smells better than cigar smoke, and that there is a reason you've gone to the trouble to make Jack smell worse than Bill. Or you might opt for a smell that is generally considered good, like the scent of roses.

Also, a character might use perfume or cologne for sentimental or vanity reasons. A woman might wear Joy perfume because her mother and grandmother wore it; it's a part of her wardrobe, and therefore a part of her character. Or a male character might persist in wearing stinky cologne that keeps women from wanting to get too close to him. There are ingenious ways to use scent to reveal details about your characters.

Have you ever been to the movies or out to dinner and *smelled* a person entering before you saw her because of her perfume? Scent is a fabulous way to demonstrate that a character has arrived on the scene: "The pungent sting of bourbon in the air told Jeannie that Sam had let himself into the house *and* the liquor cabinet."

Finally, harking back to the link between smell and memory, you can invoke scent as a way to transition into a character flashback. If you need to go back in time to a scene from your character's past and you can use the smell of peaches at a grocery store to drop Becky into the peach orchard where she first met Eduardo, the love of her life, by all means use it. Scent is a subtle way to transition that won't jar the reader.

SOUND

Sounds can describe a physical setting almost as effectively as visual descriptions. With eyes closed, you can probably tell the difference between a train station and an airport. The places your characters show up have sound signatures, which you can use to enrich a scene's other details.

In a restaurant, for instance, your character, with eyes closed, can hear dishes, glasses, and silverware clinking, the sounds of wait staff calling out orders to cooks, and taking orders from customers. There is a certain kind of buzz of conversation that goes on in restaurants that is different from the sound of a real estate office, for instance. The more you pay attention to these small details when building a scene, the more real the scene will become.

Here are a few different examples of the way sound creates or enhances atmosphere and contributes to the tone and theme of a story.

In Irène Némirovsky's novel *Suite Française*, set in German-occupied France, 1942, sound marks the contrast with the silence of people hidden away in fear of air raids:

> The streets were empty. People were closing their shops. The metallic shudder of falling iron shutters was the only sound to break the silence, a sound familiar to anyone who has woken in a city threatened by riot or war.

In Anton Chekhov's story "At Sea," the following sound description sets a raucous tone that is appropriate to the story of sailors acting on baser impulses:

> Crowded together in the crew's quarters we, the sailors, were casting lots. Loud, drunken laughter filled the air. One of our comrades was playfully crowing like a cock.

Finally, here is a description of the first time the character Francis Macomber hears the lion that will change his fate, from Ernest Hemingway's story "The Short Happy Life of Francis Macomber":

It had started the night before when he had wakened and heard the lion roaring somewhere up along the river. It was a deep sound and at the end there were sort of coughing grunts that made him seem just outside the tent, and when Francis Macomber woke in the night to hear it he was afraid.

Sounds enhance mood, set tone, and create atmosphere, and should not be forgotten when setting the scene.

TASTE

One of my pet peeves about writing is that you don't very often see characters eating. Food is an important part of life, and, I believe, an important part of a good story too, when it can be factored in. While many of your scenes may have no need to invoke the sense of taste, you might ask yourself if there are places in your story where you could add in the act of tasting something. Taste provides great moments of potential conflict and intimacy, such as:

- A mother asks her a son to taste her soup, which provides an opportunity for him to be honest with her about her terrible cooking, leading to either conflict or unexpected closeness.

- A character who has just learned of a terrible loss might bite into a piece of his favorite cake only to discover that, in his grief, he cannot taste a thing.

- A character hoping to impress his gourmet lover with a home-cooked meal might see her true colors when, in rejecting his cooking, she also rejects his love.

Taste provides a fabulous opportunity for feelings and interactions between your characters to arise. Through the simple act of lifting a fork to mouth, your characters can come to epiphanies, exalt in simple pleasures, and enact conflicts that enliven your scenes.

Though the senses are separated out in this chapter to help you look at them individually, you will probably find that a majority of these sensory details will emerge naturally in combination when you begin writing scenes. Your own observations will deliver themselves up through your muse as you write. But when you go back through to do a revision, ask yourself if you have over-written one of the senses and parsed out another, and take opportunities to add or subtract some for sensory balance.

7

CHARACTER DEVELOPMENT AND MOTIVATION

When you put down a book, what do you remember most? Just think about it for minute. Is it the lovely descriptions of city streets? Or the moody, powerful, potent characters who populate them? I'm sure it comes as no surprise that most of us identify most with the characters. Though passages of pretty scenery or buildings collapsing capture the reader's attention for a moment, maybe two, characters bring scenes to life and are the natural focal point. After all, scenes are the primary vehicles for developing these people, particularly your protagonist (and co-protagonists, when you have more than one).

In every scene, you have to create opportunities for your characters to reveal and enrich themselves, and to drive their stories forward in connection with your plot. You also have to give your characters the chance to evolve and transform—and not by magic.

If your characters are the same at the end of your narrative as they were at the beginning, you most likely didn't provide them enough opportunities to act, react, and change.

While we'll look more at other character-related issues in part three, here we'll discuss the basics of character development, and motivation as a core element of the scene.

CHARACTER DEVELOPMENT

The moment your characters are born in your imagination, you should ask: How do they behave in public? With family? Under pressure? Sometimes people act out when they're with family members; a normally compassionate character might have a prejudice that leads him to behave in a cruel or sadistic fashion around people of certain ethnicities; or your character might always be on his best behavior *only* around his priest or his girlfriend. Your characters won't behave the same in every social situation, and for the purpose of drama, you should try to build in moments where they misbehave, or act in ways that surprise others in response to unusual or unexpected events.

How does your protagonist develop over the course of your narrative? Since you can't invite the reader into his entire history at the beginning of the narrative, you only have the elements of the scene to work with—the scene is sort of like improvisational theater. Look at the following formula.

1. Each scene should provide your character with:

- **At least one plot situation or new piece of information to react or respond to.** (Of course, you can have more than one, if needed.) Whatever you choose, it must drive the story forward and cause your characters to react (see chapter eight for types of plot information).

- **A catalyst or antagonist with whom the protagonist interacts.** Other characters are catalysts—they facilitate change and reaction in your protagonist; or they are antagonists—they thwart, oppose, and delay the intentions of your protagonist. Through the interactions your protagonist has with these other characters comes the necessary leverage to develop them into complex people. When there is no other character in the scene, your protagonist will interact only with himself, or with forces of nature or the world around him, in which case you get contemplative scenes (see chapter fifteen).

2. In every scene your protagonist should be motivated by two things:

- **The protagonist's intention for the scene.** Whatever you decide is the intention for your protagonist in a given scene will fuel his motivation. A scene intention (discussed at length in chapter eleven) must be related to the significant situation of your narrative, but each scene may have different intentions for your protagonist. In one scene the protagonist's intention might be to go into an agency to try to track down his biological mother, for instance, and in another it might be to confront the adoptive mother who withheld that information all his life. We'll discuss how to make sure that a character's intentions add up to a good storyline in chapter twenty-three.

- **The protagonist's personal history.** One other factor will motivate your character in every scene: his backstory. You can show insight into your protagonist's nature or history through reflective flashback scenes or dialogue. You can also use it just as personal background information that helps you decide how your protagonist will behave next.

3. Each situation or interaction should make your plot and its consequences for the protagonist either:

- **More complicated.** When the consequences become more complicated, as described in chapter three, you build dramatic tension, create character conflict, and heighten the energy of the scene. Lean toward building more complications in every scene of the first two parts of your narrative.

- **Or less complicated.** There are a few good cases for making situations less complicated for your protagonist: In the final part of your narrative, when you want to resolve plot threads and lead toward resolution; when you want to pull back on the intensity of a scene; and when you want to lull the reader into a false sense of complacency in order to spring a plot surprise on him.

4. Through these complications, your protagonist should change. They can change beliefs, behaviors, attitudes, allegiances or loyalties, appearances, and motivations.

By narrative's end, your protagonist, thanks to the many opportunities you gave him to develop and change in scenes, will not be in exactly the same place emotionally, or even spiritually, as when you began. He will have changed (see chapter twenty-three).

Now, using that formula from above, let's walk through a scene example from Ann Patchett's novel *Bel Canto*. At a lavish birthday party for a Japanese businessman in South America, at which are present many important diplomats and a famous opera singer, guerilla terrorists have taken the entire assemblage hostage. Over the time of their captivity, the terrorists and the hostages begin to form bonds and become civil. In the snippet of a scene that follows, a select few hostages have been granted the aid of the female terrorists to help them cut food with forbidden knives. It could almost be a domestic scene, except that Patchett ups the ante on the characters, and provides all the ingredients for developing character that are described above. I have labeled the ingredients in italics within the text.

> [*The intention of all the hostages in this scene is to prepare a decent meal, since they're all desperately hungry.*] Ishmael stopped, examined his work, then he held out the butchered vegetable and the knife. He held the blade out to Thibault. [*An interaction between two characters that affects the plot.*] What did he know about kitchen manners? Then Thibault had them both, the knife and the eggplant, one in each hand. Deftly, quickly, he began to peel back the skin. [*Thibault brings a gourmet's knowledge of food to the scene—that is his motivation for taking the knife from Ishmael. But this is also a plot situation—Thibault is now using the knife, which he is not authorized to hold.*]
>
> "Drop it!" Beatriz shouted. On calling out she dropped her own knife, the blade slick with onions. ... She pulled her gun from her belt and raised it up to the Ambassador. [*Things have just gotten more complicated for Thibault and the others in the kitchen.*]
>
> "Jesus," Ruben said.
>
> Thibault did not understand what he had done. ...

"Keep your voice down," Carmen said to Beatriz in Quechua. "You're going to get us all in trouble." [*Worsening consequences—if they've been heard, the male terrorists might storm into the kitchen in a violent fury.*]

"He took the knife."

Thibault raised up his empty hands, showed his smooth palms to the gun.

"I handed him the knife," Ishmael said. "I gave it to him."

"He was only going to peel," Gen said. [*Gen's motivation is to defend Thibault because he has a firm belief in right and wrong.*] He could not recognize a word of this language they spoke to one another.

"He isn't supposed to hold the knife," Beatriz said in Spanish. "The general told us this."...

"What about this?" Thibault began quietly, keeping his hands up. "Everyone can stand away from me and I can show Ishmael how to peel an eggplant. You keep your gun right on me and if it looks like I'm about to do something funny you may shoot me. You may shoot Gen, too, if I do something terrible." [*Thibault responds to the situation by changing, by becoming brave. Earlier he was afraid of these people, now he just wants peace.*]

"I don't think—" Gen started, but no one was paying attention to him. He felt a small, cold hardness in his chest, like the pit of a cherry had slipped into his heart. He did not want to be shot and he did not want to be offered up to be shot. [*Despite his belief in justice, suddenly Gen displays fear in response to the same situation that turned Thibault brave—two different characters are motivated by different things—Thibault by hunger and pride, Gen by fear. Patchett magnificently develops two different characters in two different ways in response to the same situation.*]

Though the scene ends without anyone getting shot, the sense of peace and camaraderie that developed before the knife incident is gone, and a climate of mistrust has returned between hostages and terrorists. This scene sets the stage for further character changes down the road. Will Gen dissolve into a fearful mess? Will Thibault maintain his brave façade? It is necessary to read further scenes to find out.

SCENE STEALER

Sheila Kohler, author of the Bluebird: Or the Invention of Happiness, Crossways, *and other novels, finds that there is nothing more memorable than what she calls "first glimpse scenes" in which main characters see each other for the first time, setting the stage for their relationships to unfold.*

◉ ◉ ◉

There are so many great ones. Almost every great book has a great first glimpse scene when the hero and heroine meet, or the hero/heroine meets an adversary (when Pip first meets Miss Havisham in *Great Expectations*, for example). Others include:

- The first time Charles Bovary sees Emma in Gustave Flaubert's *Madame Bovary*. Charles arrives on his horse that takes fright and stumbles. He is then taken by Emma to her father's bedside (he has broken his leg) where she sews pads for his broken leg and pricks her fingers and sucks them (with all the connotations of such an act). Charles is surprised by the whiteness of her nails in a wonderful moment that will cause him, ultimately, great sorrow.

- The first time the main character Aschenbach sees Tadzio, the young man who captures his mind, in Thomas Mann's novella *Death in Venice*. This is the wonderful scene where Tadzio is seen for the first time contrasted with his sisters, the girls who are so severely dressed, "with almost disfiguring severity" who arrive first; the boy, Tadzio, strolls in late, with all his golden curls, in his English sailor suit and his spoilt exquisite air.

- Anton Chekhov's "Lady With the Dog." "Sitting in Verney's pavilion, he saw, walking on the seafront, a fair-haired lady of medium height, wearing a beret, a white Pomeranian dog was running behind her." It is a brief first description without too many details, which are gradually introduced all through the story, but wonderful.

CHARACTER AND PLOT

Hopefully the illustration above made it clear that plot and character are married to one another. Your protagonist ought to be indelibly caught up in the plot situation and information of every scene, and should bear or participate in the consequences that follow. Similarly, your plot should not be able to advance or get more complicated without the active participation of your protagonist.

With that in mind, when developing your characters you should always be thinking about how the plot situation of a given scene will affect the character, and what it will cause him to do, think, or feel.

In every scene you should ask: What is plot-relevant? What is character-relevant? How are the two related? Your plot should be unable to carry on without your protagonist.

A Note on Character Behavior

If you've ever turned up in the aftermath of an exciting incident like a fight or a police chase, you will probably agree that a bystander's account is never as dramatic as witnessing it for yourself. The same is true of character behavior in scenes; inevitably you'll take shortcuts, hoping the reader will take your word for it that "Charles didn't want to live any longer," or "Frederika had a magnetic personality." Well, okay, both details might be true, but unless the reader gets to witness the plot situation of Charles standing at the edge of the bridge ready to leap off, or, through character interactions, sees multiple characters fall in love with Frederika, the reader has no proof of what you tried to quickly summarize.

If you follow the formula for developing characters set forth in this chapter, your characters will have no choice but to become complex, plot-relevant people who feel vivid and real to the reader.

8

PLOT

Without the human mind and consciousness to give significance to the events that happen to us, life is just a series of events unfolding over time to people everywhere. This randomness is one of the reasons that many people turn to literature—inside the pages of a book you trust that you will be led on a meaningful journey revealing insights and giving your spirits and emotions a jolt. In fiction, this is called a plot.

Some people confuse plot for story and think it is enough to have a sequence of events lined up one after the other. A story is just a string of information about a cast of characters in a given time and place. Boy meets girl. Stranger comes to town. The doctor is found dead.

A plot is the method by which that story takes on tension, energy, and momentum, and urges a reader to keep turning pages. Plot transforms "boy meets girl" into *Romeo and Juliet*—with secret love, wild fighting, and tragic conflicts along the way.

In short, plot is the related string of consequences that follow from the significant situation (often referred to as inciting incident, but I prefer my term because many narratives begin less with one single incident and more with a type of situation) in your narrative, which darn well better get addressed, complicated, and resolved through engaging, well-crafted scenes by the end. Some people refer to this relationship of events as causality, but that's a sterile-sounding word. Here we'll just call them consequences.

In chapter two we discussed how any narrative is a series of scenes strung together like beads on a wire. This chapter will look at what element inside each scene is essential to plot. The simplest answer is information.

Plot is constructed out of crucial bits of information—the consequences of, and explanations for, the significant situation and the characters who must deal with it. Plot is best delivered teasingly to the reader in small bites to keep them hungry for more. In a well-written plot, the reader gets just a little bit smarter, a little bit more clued in, as he reads. Each scene should provide one more clue to the puzzle of your plot.

PLOT INFORMATION BASICS

Most writers are as fond of a beautiful sentence as they are a good plot element. It's fun to write lyrical passages, to wax philosophical, and to create images of beauty. Surely there's no harm if a scene digresses from the plot to meander and muse, right?

Nope!

Sorry to be the plot police, but here's the cold truth: Every scene in your narrative must pertain to your plot. Every single one. Even if a character muses or meanders, that activity must be plot-related. A character under suspicion of murder may drift off into thought, but those thoughts had better be about why he's been wrongfully accused, how he's going to prove his innocence, or who the true murderer is, not random memories of whale-watching or hiking.

Scenes exist in order to make the events in your fictional world real to the reader. You want the reader to be knee-deep in your action and emotional drama, to feel for your characters, to hope and dream and want for them.

Each scene, then, must deliver, at minimum, one piece of new information that speaks to one of the following questions: Who? What? Where? When? Why? How?

Every scene.

You must be thinking, how can I possibly do that? Simple—don't end a scene and begin another one until new information has been provided. Providing information is one of the most important functions of a scene and is the foundation of a plot.

New information has three main responsibilities:

1. It must fill in another piece of the puzzle, so that both the character and the reader get a little bit smarter.

2. It must change the course of your main character's thoughts, feelings, or actions.

3. It must lead to new consequences, actions, or behaviors that carry your plot forward.

Every scene must reveal some piece of new information that enlightens the reader just a little bit more. Here we'll look at the different types of plot information more closely.

Who

Much scene time is devoted to characters, since they are generally the most important element of any fictional narrative. You'll want to include a bit of general character information in your narrative—what kind of work your protagonist does, his religion or lack of one, his habits. Does he, for instance, go to AA meetings twice a week, or sing in a gospel choir? These details tell us who your character is in general, not necessarily who he is in relationship to your plot. Character-related plot information, on the other hand, tends to come up over the course of a narrative, often having to do with identity or hidden origins being revealed; someone's past catching up with him; a dark secret being brought to light; or a surprising change of heart. Here's an example of plot-related character information from Ann Patchett's novel *The Magician's Assistant*, in which the protagonist, Sabine, learns after her husband and partner's death, from his lawyer, that he was not who she thought.

> "Parsifal's name wasn't Petrie. It was Guy Fetters. Guy Fetters has a mother and two sisters in Nebraska. As far as I can tell the father is out of the picture—either dead or gone ..."
>
> "That isn't possible," she said.
>
> "I'm afraid it is."

When it comes to characters and plot, think about how your characters can surprise each other, and the readers, by revealing new information about themselves (and not necessarily after death), about things they have hidden or covered up, or about something that is being denied or protected. Most importantly, when you reveal this character information, you should do it directly, through speech or dialogue if possible. Or, if the person has died, either in the form of correspondence he left behind, or through the mouth of another person. Try to rely as little as possible on the thought bubble—in which a character *thinks* a revelation.

What

What is perhaps the widest possible category of all plot information. It is, in essence, what is often described as your hook—the storyline or angle that makes your narrative unique and from which all other plot events will flow.

In *The Magician's Assistant*, for instance, Parsifal's death is the significant situation of the novel—the first big piece of *what* information—that launches the book. The necessity of sharing the information about Parsifal's death with his family sets the next plot events in motion, and leads to great insight and change in Sabine and the other characters. These two main pieces of information drive the entire plot, and each has its own string of consequences that each scene deals with in one way or another.

In every scene you should ask yourself, literally: What is next? What piece of important information do I need my characters to learn, and my readers to become aware of? Remember that every scene needs a new piece of information, or else there's no point to writing it.

Where

Where is one of those lucky bits of information that does light duty in terms of plot most of the time. Occasionally setting is crucial to your plot, especially if one must trace the steps of a murderer, or revisit a place in order to learn something new, or if your narrative is specific to a geographical location. Most of the time, place serves as a backdrop for the other bits of information. In Sabine's case, she has to travel from Los Angeles to Nebraska, two vastly different worlds. Sabine meets with cultural challenges due to the differences between Nebraska and California ways of life, but the plot does not depend upon much information being imparted about place in every scene.

On the level of the scene, when place does come into play it may serve more as a spoken reference—the maid was found dead in the drawing room; Jacques had last been seen in Cancun before he disappeared; my father had a second family in a small town in Florida.

If place does turn out to be crucial to your plot, remember these points:

- **New details must be revealed in any scene to make it play into your plot.** For instance, a mansion might turn out to be haunted, or a beautiful countryside might also be a Native-American burial ground.

- **The new information about the place must have an effect on your character.** His thoughts, feelings or actions in the scene should all reflect the information given. For instance, say Jack and Jill planned to honeymoon in the mansion. Once Jack learns the mansion is haunted, he refuses to stay, causing a fight with Jill.

- **The actions generated by the new information must lead to other plot-related consequences.** For instance, Jill decides she will stay in the mansion by herself, and he can stay in a motel, causing conflict, and building tension.

When

When, in relation to your plot, is the time at which some important action in your narrative takes place: either time in history, or time of day. *When* tends to be important in mystery plots, to determine when a murder or a crime was committed, to employ alibis, and to figure out how long a victim has been dead. Time as a form of information often comes into play in reference to when a crucial plot action takes place. For instance, a man may learn that his wife got pregnant during a time when he was in the army, and therefore, the baby can't be his. Or a mother may learn that her missing child was actually being held hostage in the neighborhood in the days after she thought he was gone. Or a character's innocence may be called into question when it turns out he does not have an alibi.

When is information that will best serve your plot when it brings to light startling, contradictory, or unexpected results.

Why

Ah, motive, that tricky devil. *Why* is very much at the crux of plot. Betrayal, murder, deception, unusual kindness, obsessive love, and many more facets of human behavior will fill up the pages of many a plot. *Why* is often the very thing the novel or story is seeking to understand. Small explanations will be necessary along the way if the reader is to keep up with your plot.

This type of information often gets tossed into narrative explanations and pace-dragging passages of backstory. It's easier just to tell the reader why than to let actions, dialogue, and even flashback scenes tell the truth for you. Don't fall into the habit of explaining why in narrative summary. If your scene needs to reveal why a character behaved a certain way, committed an action, or kept a great secret, return to the chapters on character development and scene intentions in order to get *why* across.

How

How—the method by which things are done—plays a great role in plot. It's usually the piece of information that ties up the investigation, reveals the missing clues to tragedies, and explains how the impossible really was possible. Law and science often play a role in revealing how something was done. Was the heiress murdered with a gun or a poisoned cup of tea? Was the fire started by arson, or by a cigarette butt tossed carelessly aside?

How is often linked directly to *why*. If a character is plotting revenge, for instance, the method of his crime will probably be specific to the injury he believes he suffered—a spurned boyfriend might try to publicly shame the woman who dumped him by scrawling inflammatory words on her house. An insulted bigot might try to attack a person's race.

How really can't be an afterthought. You need to know how things were done by the time you get to the scene in which it is revealed, and then the information should be imparted in as direct a way as possible, most often as dialogue: the reading of police reports, evidence in court, a deathbed confession, and so on. But you may also choose to use a device like a letter, a message played back from a machine, or an e-mail found on a computer—something that a character stumbles across that contains the answer to *how*.

WHEN TO DOLE IT OUT

How you reveal information is just as important as what that information is. The most tempting way to pass on plot information is to narrate in a rushed, matter-of-fact way. But information is best served like food at a fancy French restaurant—in small, elegantly presented courses that neither stuffs the reader, nor leaves him overly hungry. You want the reader to have room for dessert—which is, of course, the end of your book or story.

Some scenes will involve revealing multiple kinds of information, while others may be all for the purpose of revealing one very important kind of information. There's no way to know what to advise without seeing a specific manuscript, but as long as you know that you must have at least one type of new information in every scene, you're on the right track.

You must always be thinking about the span of your narrative. The length of your narrative, whether it is a ten-page story or a five-hundred-page novel, will affect how soon information is revealed to the reader. A short story has less time to get things across, and often has to drive to a brisk emotional impact with a less complex plotline.

The First Part

I'm fond of dividing a narrative into thirds, which I'll refer to as parts (although they are sometimes referred to as acts). In the scenes of the first part you should do the following:

- Lay the foundation. Introduce only enough information to ground your reader.

- Thrust the reader into the action of the significant situation. Make sure the reader knows what the plot is.

- Create a sense of mystery or suspense by withholding information.

The Middle Part

Drive the plot forward by providing more information than you did in the first part. (However, *don't* give away secrets or crucial plot information, because then what motivation does the reader have to keep reading?)

- Up the ante by throwing in new and surprising information.

- Information should lead to conflict and danger that forces your characters to change or redirect.

- Throw in red herrings, or false leads, that let the reader think you're filling in missing information, or, in the mystery genre, that you're solving the mystery.

The Final Part

The final part of your narrative is in some ways the most difficult because you must use it to successfully tie up all the threads you've started. The reader should not have very many, if any, questions by the time the final part is concluded.

- Answer questions and reveal truths.

- Conclude drama. Don't introduce new information, but you may introduce surprising endings to plot avenues.

- Let characters settle into their changes.

- Lead the reader toward a sense of conclusion by turning down the emotional and dramatic tone of information revealed.

The final part is where many writers discover the holes in their plot—they can't tie up all the threads. If that happens to you, revisit your plot, ask what information is missing, and fill in those holes.

Putting the Plot Pieces Together

Of all the core elements, plot can seem like the most complex element, because it isn't specific to one area of your scene, but must relate to all of them. At root, a plot allows for the reader to experience a sense of mystery, as scenes withhold just the right amount of information for just long enough. The reader can see only one bread crumb at a time in the dimly lit forest of your narrative. Of course, the mystery must be solved eventually, and the plot information must add up to a satisfying whole.

Following are examples from Toni Morrison's acclaimed novel *Beloved*, in which plot information is doled out carefully and builds on itself. A scene in the first part of the book opens with a woman called Beloved walking out of a pond fully dressed. She is soon discovered by Denver, one of the main characters, and taken home to Denver's mother, Sethe—a woman with a past full of dark secrets. Through dialogue, the reader learns that Beloved is not like other people. She has hazy origins and behaves unusually. This information is delivered bit by bit in scenes.

"Something funny 'bout that gal," Paul D said, mostly to himself.

"Funny how?"

"Acts sick, sounds sick, but she don't look sick. Good skin, bright eyes and strong as a bull."

"She's not strong. She can hardly walk without holding on to something."

"That's what I mean. Can't walk, but I seen her pick up a rocker with one hand."

That scene achieves the three responsibilities of new information. One, the reader and the characters get smarter: Under the category of *who*, they learn that Beloved is not like other people—she behaves quite oddly. Two, the reader is led to change his feelings about Beloved. Three, motivation comes into play—*why*. Because the characters now see Beloved differently, they begin to act differently with one another in response to her, and their changed behaviors affect the plot consequences.

In the middle of her narrative, Morrison drops even more plot information about who the mysterious Beloved is, though she does not come out and say it; she lets the readers piece it together:

Beloved closed her eyes. "In the dark my name is Beloved."

Denver scooted in a little closer. "What's it like over there, where you were before? Can you tell me?"

"Dark," said Beloved. "I'm small in that place. I'm like this here." She raised her head off the bed, lay down on her side and curled up.

Denver covered her lips with her fingers. "Were you cold?"

Beloved curled tighter and shook her head. "Hot. Nothing to breathe down there and no room to move in."

What does Beloved's description sound like? A mother's womb. The reader slowly learns of Beloved's origins, which is a crucial piece of plot information, within the context of scenes that build upon the plot and reveal character. This slow build gives Morrison time to create a character that is strange and vivid, who represents the sacrifice that her mother had to make in her journey to freedom. If she gave Beloved's identity away immediately, there would be very little dramatic tension or character-building.

As the book moves toward its close, the plot begins to move into its final stage. No longer do the characters wonder who Beloved is; now they've started to fear her. Beloved has become pregnant and begins to take up all the joy, eat all the food, to consume everything that Sethe and Denver need in the household (which is a fabulous metaphor, incidentally, for how grief works). She absorbs Sethe's attention and time and inspires jealousy and rage in Denver. As the plot comes to a close, the reader begins to root for a terrible end for Beloved, despite that she seemed so needy and frail earlier in the narrative; now she has become a parasite. Either Beloved will have to go, or something terrible is going to happen.

Without giving away the ending, I can say that Morrison brings her plot to a close that makes perfect sense—with all threads tied up.

SCENE STEALER

Gayle Brandeis, author of Self Storage: A Novel, *discusses plot in Amanda Eyre Ward's* Sleep Toward Heaven.

◉ ◉ ◉

Years later I still get goose bumps whenever I think about the ending of Amanda Eyre Ward's novel *Sleep Toward Heaven*. The beautifully written plot braids together the stories of three characters—Celia, whose husband Henry was murdered; Karen, the murderer, who is awaiting her execution on death row; and Franny, the doctor who has been treating Karen for cancer.

Celia is reeling throughout the book, trying to find her place in the world after the senseless death of her husband. In the very final scene, she recounts how, during a meeting in a bar with Franny, Henry's ghost came to her and told her to find Franny's notebook in her purse and write down the code for Karen's morphine machine while Franny was in the restroom. Celia memorizes the code, not knowing why until she visits Karen in the prison. The book ends with Celia saying "The numbers to the machine lined up in my head. I opened my mouth." Giving the woman who murdered her husband the means to end her own suffering without having to endure the spectacle of an execution is such a profound act of forgiveness and compassion. It infuses the entire book with a sense of grace, weaving all the threads of the book into a perfect, deeply moving whole.

SHORING UP YOUR PLOT

If a plot is built out of strong, vivid scenes, then the most logical place to start when writing the next scene is to refer to the last scene first. You create your own blueprints scene by scene. So before you go on to write the next scene, in which you move your plot forward just a little bit more, you must see how far, and from what direction, you've come.

You would be amazed at how often writers repeat information, forgetting that they already revealed it in the last scene. Reviewing sometimes as many as two or three scenes back can be crucial to moving your plot forward.

Once you've reviewed the last scene, or scenes, as you plot your way forward, you will come to a decision point. What happens next? Harking back to earlier chapters of this book, you know that you must up the ante on your characters and keep the action moving forward. Always keep your significant situation in mind, and be sure that there are consequences that get first complicated, then addressed and resolved, and that there is an antagonist of some kind that helps to add conflict. So ask yourself, what is the next bite?

If you find yourself stumped, you can run it through this criteria test. The next bite of plot information should:

- Involve your main character(s)

- Be related to the significant situation or one of its consequences

- Give the readers the impression of having more knowledge or clues, or that they're smarter because some new information is revealed

- Add complications or resolve an earlier complication

9

SUBTEXT

Even if you were never an A student in school, you're probably someone who gives everything your best try; after all, you're reading a book on scene writing. At the very least, you can follow the recipe in chapter one and combine all your ingredients to create a rudimentary scene. So don't get discouraged now when you learn that you can write a competent scene that still falls flat.

Scenes often need depth or subtext, texture that links the scene to the themes and larger plot of your narrative, and fleshes them out. A theme is the underlying message, idea, or moral of the narrative. Building in this subtext may take a second draft or more, because you are bound to know your story and characters far better after you have already written them into being.

Scenes that lack subtext read as if they've been dictated by a court reporter: "Bailiff had to escort the defendant, in pearls and red sweater, out of the room. Sunlight filtered in. Courtroom was quiet."

There is nothing wrong with the details above, but a scene full of sentences like that will be guaranteed to lack dramatic tension and emotional complexity. A good scene should ideally have a surface—all that is visible and palpable, from setting to physical descriptions of characters to heard dialogue—and an underbelly, a subtext, where your characters' emotional baggage, agendas, painful secrets, and unconscious motivations lie.

TECHNIQUES FOR CREATING SUBTEXT

Think about the deeper layers of your scenes. The subtext is the layer that contains unconscious information, clues to behavior, even elements of backstory. You can use several different techniques to draw out your story's subtext.

Thematic Imagery or Symbols

In order to work with thematic imagery, naturally you need to know the theme of your book or story. A theme can be thought of as the overall message or large idea of the narrative, as opposed to the plot, which refers to specific events and new pieces of information that take place or are dropped in the narrative. For many writers, theme is determined after the first draft is done. Thematic imagery, then, is images that metaphorically and symbolically conjure your theme.

Some thematic imagery will find its way into your narrative through the magic of the unconscious without you realizing it, but most of it will require conscious application upon revision.

Mary Gaitskill's award-winning novel *Veronica* deals with some dark subjects involving the sordid life of a young model, Alison, and her friend, Veronica, who contracted AIDS in the 1980s. Yet the book is also about redemption and healing. Gaitskill uses images interspersed throughout the book to add subtext to her scenes, like this:

> There were small flowers sprouting on bushes growing alongside the path. They were a flat tough red that paled as their petals extended out, changing into a color that was oddly fleshy, like the underside of a tongue.

Comparing the flowers to a human tongue creates an appropriate subtext for the scene they appear in, in which Alison is facing the reality of her friend's illness. The flowers represent Veronica, who is tough and tender but also only human. And they represent Alison, who is known to most people as a glamorous model, but who is also just human, and suffering under the pressure to be beautiful.

Images can also be simple, just tiny highlights in your larger scene: A tree in the night could suddenly look like a face, portending danger; a character who longs to be pregnant could see the faces of babies in her mashed potatoes, and so on.

Of course, you can always opt to work with the more abstract world of symbols. The great mythologist Joseph Campbell said, "The function of symbols is to give you a sense of 'A ha! Yes. I know what it is, it's myself.'"

Symbols elicit meaning without having to be explained; they add a subtle touch of texture to your narrative.

The Argentinean writer Jorge Luis Borges was very fond of using symbols—like labyrinths, hexagrams, and even a book itself—to represent the complexities of human thought and spiritual mystery.

If your theme is about finding peace, you might plant a dove in the eaves outside a scene, or use an olive branch or a white flag somewhere along the way. The key is to plant your symbols subtly so that the reader doesn't feel as though this subtext is being waved in his face in an obvious manner. You don't need your character to say, "Look, a dove, that makes me think of peace!" A symbol could just turn up as a design on a character's shirt, or on the cover of a book on a desk in someone's office.

Innuendo

It is inevitable that characters in your fiction, as in life, will come across truths that they don't want to admit to themselves or others. Sometimes, this information is obvious to those around them first.

It's important when developing each scene that you plant seeds of things to come later on. Innuendo is a great way to deal with plot developments that haven't come to pass yet; it also helps round out your characters, since innuendo can come in the form of teasing or accusation and usually elicits high emotion.

For instance, say the princess of a medieval kingdom cannot let on that she is in love with a peasant boy because it is a match that can never be. There's nothing more wickedly juicy than a scene in which this piece of information, which she can't accept, is pointed out to her by someone she'd rather not hear it from—perhaps one of her ladies in waiting, who is supposed to keep her opinions in check; or the princess's sister, who will inherit the crown if the princess abdicates it.

"Nice tights," the sister might say to the princess when the peasant boy stops in to deliver a herd of sheep.

The princess, of course, will be shocked and outraged. "As if I'd noticed!" she might say with a rosy hue of indignation on her cheeks.

Innuendo can go further than teasing. You can use it to suggest that someone is responsible for murder or robbery, or to suggest that a character wants another character dead or gone. Innuendo is a way to subtly point fingers so that the reader's attention begins to move just slightly ahead of the scene at hand, layering complication into your scene.

Unconscious or Uncontrollable Behavior

Characters will do all kinds of things intentionally in your scenes, from tenderly caressing an injured animal, to jumping out of flame-engulfed buildings. But there is a whole world of behavior that you can employ in scenes that adds subtext not only to the scene at hand, but to the reader's understanding of the characters and your plot.

A character with a secret history of having been locked in closets for punishment as a child might break into a sweat each time he is in a confined space such as a car or an elevator. Perhaps you don't reveal this detail about the character's past until near the very end of your book, but you can plant seeds in the reader's mind through subtext. If your character sweats each time he's in the car, the elevator, or even a small New York apartment, this registers in the reader's unconscious without having to be plainly stated, thus creating a question that the reader is curious about (why is he sweating?), but does not yet have an answer for.

In Sheila Kohler's psychologically tense novel *Crossways*, protagonist Kate has been forced to leave her life in Paris and return to her childhood home in South Africa due to a tragedy: A car accident has killed her sister, Marian, and left her brother-in-law, Louis, injured and in the hospital.

Louis, a surgeon, is used to being in control of everything in his life—including his wife and their three children. Now that he is injured, and his sister-in-law, Kate, is around to question him, he has a difficult time controlling the rage he usually could suppress publicly.

The nurse leans over his bed. She pats the back of his hand. He has a sudden, strong urge to smack her across her pretty face with it. It is the same urge he had when his wife would ask him what he was doing.

The reader begins to question what it is in Louis's past that causes him to behave so badly toward people less powerful than himself, and of course, the answer is eventually provided and brings with it the final piece of the plot that explains Marion's death.

SCENE STEALER

Elizabeth Cox, author of The Slow Moon, *discusses the use of images in Cormac McCarthy's* Suttree.

My favorite section provides imagery (a spoon, a cup of coffee, or spilled cream with "flies lapping like cats") to deepen tension and to expose the profound sadness felt by Suttree when he learns that his boy is dead.

> As he was going up Gay Street J-Bone stepped from a door and took his arm. Hey Bud, he said.
> How you doin'?
> I was just started down to see you. Come in and have a cup of coffee.
> They sat at the counter at Helm's. J-Bone kept tapping his spoon. When the coffee was set before them he turned to Suttree. Your old man called me, he said. He wanted you to call home.
> People in hell want ice water.
> Hell Bud, it might be something important.
> Suttree tested the cup rim against his lower lip and blew. Like what, he said.
> Well. Something in the family. You know, I think you ought to call.
> He put the cup down. All right, he said. What is it?
> Why don't you call him?
> Why don't you tell me?
> Will you not call?

No.

J-Bone was looking at the spoon in his hand. He blew on it and shook his head, the distorted image of him upside down in the spoon's bowl misting and returning. Well, he said.

Who's dead, Jim?

He didn't look up. Your little boy, he said.

Suttree set his cup down and looked out the window. There was a small pool of spilled cream on the marble countertop at his elbow and flies were crouched about it lapping like cats. He got up and went out.

It was dark when the train left the station. He tried to sleep, his head rolling about on the musty headrest. There was no longer a club car or dining car. No service anymore.

Students, when writing dialogue, focus on patterns of speech and verisimilitude, but often they do not know that dialogue needs to move the action forward, giving information and creating a tension within a particular moment. I tell them to imagine one person saying, "Please, please" and the other saying, "No, no" no matter what is being said. This example offers fast-paced dialogue (even though the moment seems to move in slow-motion). The dialogue carries the action forward as it reveals some new information to a character, and McCarthy produces a true pattern of speech used by the country people that populate the book. The understated quality of McCarthy's dialogue and imagery add clarity and power to the moment described, and give to that moment a dramatic tension of human life happening before our eyes.

Foreground and Background

Scenes can have backgrounds the same way that paintings do, and backgrounds refer to more than just setting. While you draw the reader's attention to what is happening most noticeably in the foreground, you can plant subtle messages and emotional layers in the background through actions. For example, if a couple is about ready to make love in the scene at hand—the foreground—while another couple is fighting in the next room— the background—not only is this a great setup for comedy or drama, but it plants the idea that perhaps the loving couple is moving toward the fate of the fighting couple. You can add suspenseful texture to your scenes without having to resort to narrative summary or intruding into the narrative with statements about how this couple might be destined for failure.

Jane Hamilton's novel *A Map of the World* opens when protagonist Alice, a school nurse, agrees to babysit her neighbor's two little girls. When Lizzy and Audrey arrive, however, Alice's own daughters, Emma and Claire, are giving her such grief that she takes a moment of respite to recollect herself, barely a couple of minutes. It is enough time for young Lizzy, a toddler, to make her way down into the pond and nearly drown.

In the next scene, Alice is at the hospital waiting for Lizzy's family to arrive and for the doctors to tell them of the child's prognosis. She has no idea if Lizzy will live, and if any of their lives will be the same from here on out. Hamilton sets us up for the direction of Alice's (and Lizzy's) fate by throwing this into the scene subtext:

> I remember glancing across the room and noticing Robbie Mackessy's mother. Robbie was a kindergartner at Blackwell Elementary. … He was frequently sick, because of his mother, I thought, because of her negligence. She was leafing through a magazine looking, not at the print, but at me. She was squinting, as if she couldn't stand to have her eyes wide open, to see all of me at once. … It was her ugly mouth, her sneer that made me feel like crying.

The talk of negligence, the details about not being able to "see all of me at once" are all subconscious suggestions of a dark and tragic turn for the worse for both characters.

Each scene is a multidimensional creation. Don't forget the many ways you can deepen and add complexity to it by enriching subtext, a subject that will be addressed in each of the scene types discussed in part three.

10

DRAMATIC
TENSION

Imagine you're watching a game of tug-of-war between two strong men. Between them is a length of rope stretched over a pit full of angry, poisonous vipers. One man pulls the rope his way and the other man teeters on the brink of falling in. Then the teetering man pulls back and soon it's the first man whose life is at risk. This is a visual analogy for the effect of one of the most crucial core scene elements of all: dramatic tension.

Dramatic tension is the *potential* for conflict to happen in a scene. When trouble is brewing, or resolution balances on a pinhead, the reader will be psychologically and even physically tense, and this tension, believe it or not, keeps a reader reading. You couldn't walk away from that tug-of-war match without knowing what's going to happen to both men!

Unlike suspense, which is achieved when information is actually withheld from the reader, dramatic tension relies on the reader knowing that something is about to go down—just not how, and when exactly. Tension keeps the reader waiting with breath held and fists clenched, hoping that the protagonist makes it out of the scene alive, in love, or with his goal achieved (and no viper bites).

As a core element, dramatic tension must be present in every scene on some level. It may take the shape of a prickly feeling of unease your protagonist has when he enters the dark building where the killer was last seen, or an unsettling exchange of dialogue as he wonders if he has just picked an argument with a dangerous man.

Scenes need tension to avoid being mundane or dull. A fiction narrative is a heightened experience of reality in which life is more intense, unusual, and dramatic than real life; else why bother writing about it. Therefore, you want to employ techniques that keep the world inside your narrative from resembling too exactly the quotidian life that most people actually lead. By building a sense of trouble, or the potential for it, into every scene, you will hook the reader. We'll be looking at all of these techniques for building tension in different scene types in part three, but it's useful to have an overview of how tension works first.

Dramatic tension can turn a domestic scene into a nightmare, and it all stems from letting your characters feel uncertain, afraid, and baffled as they wait for the worst and hope for the best.

Most important, tension is what keeps a scene from falling flat, and it's necessary in every scene. To create it you must:

- Thwart your protagonist's goals—delay satisfaction
- Include unexpected changes without immediate explanation
- Shift power back and forth
- Pull the rug out—throw in a piece of plot information that changes or alters your protagonist in some way
- Create a tense atmosphere through setting and senses

EXPOSITION AND TENSION

The language that runs between all the other major scene elements is often referred to as exposition or narrative summary. Just like tendons connect muscle to bone, narrative summary links your scene elements so they don't float, leaving your scene disjointed or weak-kneed. Too much exposition, however, kills the possibility of dramatic tension because it quickly bores the reader. These passages of *telling* prose should be used strategically to build tension or to act as theater ushers, directing the reader's attention on to the important moments in the scene.

Condensing Time

No matter how fascinating your story and how interesting your characters, you can't show every moment of their lives in a single narrative. In order to select the moments to dramatize, you also must select which moments in time to condense, or to summarize. Below is an example from Richard Gwyn's novel *The Color of a Dog Running Away*. Lucas, a translator living in Barcelona, has just begun a love affair with the beautiful and enigmatic Nuria, who he met by following a mysterious invitation to an art gallery. The author has already dramatized the initial throes of attraction and the activities that the newly blissful couple have spent the past few weeks engaged in. Now he needs to speed the plot forward, so he does so with narrative summary:

> In the two weeks that followed, Nuria and I spent every free moment with each other. We ate together, slept together, phoned each other when she was at work, and lived for the evenings and the nights.

Gwyn skillfully collapses two whole weeks into quick summary and then quickly returns to the action:

> One lunchtime I was already on the bench, having spent some time there reading over proofs in the morning sun with a bottle of cold beer. Nuria arrived, exuberant, flushed.

By condensing small passages of irrelevant events in short windows of time, you ensure that your prose won't be flabby and that you can continue to keep tension alive.

Condensing Information

Your characters will be doctors and architects and tradespeople of all kinds. They will weave intricate designs out of silk, build plans for large skyscrapers, and study the flora and fauna of their worlds. What they do as a vocation, a hobby, or for pure survival may be of great interest to you, and may

---

even play a crucial role in your narrative, so you may want to describe the breathtaking minutia of a heart surgery or the drafting of a blueprint because it captures your imagination. Too much description, however—whether in dialogue or through narrative passages—will read like a technical manual and offer no possibility for tension. You want to first digest it, and then filter it through the point of view of your character, offering a condensed version of the facts that gives the reader a taste, a flash, or an insight your characters.

The same is true of information that comes as a result of crime scene investigations, or any mystery that can be solved—from the ancient origins of a sacred relic, to a murder, to how an entire civilization disappeared. Any line of investigation and inquiry will naturally come with lots of clues and information that your characters will need to offer to readers to drive the plot forward and explain things.

Your job is to condense it in a way that adds to the tension and drama of your narrative. For example, in Joanne Harris's novel *Sleep, Pale Sister*, Henry Chester is a painter with a fascination for one model in particular—Effie, a young girl upon whom he projects innocence. He becomes obsessed with her and paints her many times, but rather than showing a bunch of dull sittings, Harris gives the reader an overview of all the sittings in quick, expert lines of exposition that, rather than being boring, add up in their condensed description to an eerie feeling of tension and concern:

> I must have drawn or painted Effie a hundred times: she was Cinderella, she was Mary, she was the young novice in *The Passion Flower*; she was Beatrice in Heaven, Juliet in the tomb, draped with Lilies and trailing convolvulus for Ophelia, in rags for "The Little Beggar Girl." My final portrait of her at that time was The Sleeping Beauty, so like My Sister's Sleep in composition, showing Effie all in white again, like a bride or a novice, lying on the same little girl's bed, her hair, much longer than it had been when she was ten—I had always urged her never to cut it—trailing on to the floor, where a century's worth of dust lingers.

When you condense information like this, try to do so in a way that creates a feeling of trouble brewing. Add up elements that give the reader concern for your protagonist, or suggest a behavior that is a little off-center, or obsessive, or potentially volatile. If the devil is in the details, then use these details strategically to build tension when you tell the reader about the vocation and activities your protagonist (or antagonist) engages in.

OTHER TENSION-BUILDING TRICKS

There really is no good reason not to have dramatic tension in your narrative, because there are so many ways to create it. The next set of techniques can be thought of as tension tools that you can keep in your writer's kit and pull out fairly easily to infuse tension into individual scenes.

Including Foreboding

Foreboding is a feeling that something bad or unpleasant is coming for your protagonist. Unlike foreshadowing, which hints at actual plot events to come, foreboding is purely about mood-setting. It heightens the feeling of tension in a scene but doesn't necessarily indicate that something bad really will happen.

Here's an example from Don DeLillo's novel *White Noise*. In this scene, the young son of Professor Jack Gladney and his wife, Babette, wakes up one day crying and doesn't cease for seven hours straight. Though they can find nothing physically wrong with him, the crying is so abnormal that they take him to the doctor—where they get no answers. His crying instills terror in the family, and it presages a more dramatic situation that is to come later in the book—that of an airborne toxic cloud that descends over their town inexplicably. Notice how something simple like a crying child creates tension and foreboding in the following passage:

> As I started the car I realized his crying had changed in pitch and quality. The rhythmic urgency had given way to a sustained inarticulate and mournful sound. He was keening now. These were expressions of Mideastern lament, of an anguish so accessible that it rushes to overwhelm what immediately caused it. There was something permanent and soul-struck in this crying. It was a sound of inbred desolation.

Since the child is pre-verbal, one gets the feeling that he feels on some level what is to come, and DeLillo conveys this tense, uneasy feeling without dropping any direct plot information. The scene is eerie, tragic, and unnerving, full of dramatic tension as the reader wonders what on earth is going on.

When you create foreboding, remember to think about atmosphere and mood. Invoke the senses. There's something deeply eerie about the sound of a crying child in the previous. Think about how you can use sound—like the plaintive cawing of seagulls; or smell—think of what kind of effect a foul odor will have on a character. Foreboding happens in the moment. You don't have to make good on it the way you do if you use foreshadowing. You're painting an atmosphere to establish a feeling of uneasiness and worry in the reader.

Thwarting Expectation

When a character has an expectation or desire in a scene (and characters always should!), you have a great opportunity to create tension by making the reader (and the character) worry that the expectation will not be met. This can be a large expectation, like the bride waiting at the altar, or something seemingly small, like in this example from Diane Setterfield's novel *The Thirteenth Tale*.

Protagonist Margaret Lea is an amateur biographer and book lover who has been asked to write the biography of the enigmatic and famous writer Vida Winter. In preparation, she begins to read Winter's famous work, concluding with a book of stories called *Thirteen Tales*. Notice how the simple act of expectation—of reading the thirteenth tale—takes on tension as Margaret's expectations are thwarted:

> It was while I was reading "The Mermaid's Tale"—the twelfth tale—that I began to feel stirrings of an anxiety that was unconnected to the story itself. I was distracted: my thumb and right index finger were sending me a message: Not many pages left. The knowledge nagged more insistently until I tilted the book to check. It was true. The thirteenth tale must be a very short one.
>
> I continued my reading, finished tale twelve and turned the page.
> Blank.
> I flicked back, forward again. Nothing.
> There was no thirteenth tale.
> There was a sudden rush in my head, I felt the sick dizziness of the deep-sea diver come too fast to the surface.

This sets up a mood for the rest of the novel. Things are not as they seem. Pieces of the story are missing. It's a brilliant stroke of dramatic tension.

In order to carry this out, you must put something at stake for your protagonist regarding whatever it is he expects, something meaningful to him emotionally, or that has consequences in his life somehow. A man waiting to find out the results of her mother's will, for instance, has a great deal invested in the results. If the lawyer continues over a long period to read out assets that are granted to cousins and relatives less directly tied to his mother, the scene will take on tension. What, if anything, has his mother left your character?

Thwarting expectations is a technique I recommend you use frequently. For if your protagonist gets what she wants or expects in too many scenes, there will be little tension left to keep the reader hooked.

Making Changes Without Explanation

People like to know why things happen, especially when it comes to change. Therefore, if you want to create tension in a scene, you can change something in your protagonist's life without giving him an immediate explanation. The change can be life-altering, or it can be something more befuddling, like in this example from a scene in another of Joanne Harris's novels, *Gentlemen & Players*:

> As the door closed I saw a pile of flat-packed cardboard boxes propped up against the wall.
>
> "Busy day today?" I asked him, indicating the boxes. "What is it? Invading Poland?"
>
> Gerry twitched. "No, ah—just moving a few things around. Ah—to the new departmental office."
>
> I regarded him closely. There was an ominous ring to the phrase. "What new departmental office?"
>
> "Ah—sorry. Must get along. Headmaster's briefing. Can't be late."
>
> That's a joke. Gerry's late to everything. "What new office? Has someone died?"
>
> "Ah—sorry, Roy. Catch you later."

All that has really transpired in this bit of a scene is that Professor Roy Straitley has learned about the creation of a new department at the school where he teaches. Yet it feels tense because Roy is a longtime professor at St. Oswald's School for Boys and it is very atypical for him to be uninformed about a major decision. The reader instantly wants to know why Roy hasn't been informed, and the way that Gerry hems and haws makes it clear that the answer to come will not be pleasing to Roy. Harris could easily have made that a boring scene, or just cut to the chase of Roy finding out, but she creates dramatic tension over the simplest interactions because it sets a tone of intrigue, which she follows through on.

You can do the same thing in your own work by throwing change at your characters that they don't have an explanation for.

It's not useful, however, to throw in change just for the sake of it or out of the blue. Change without explanation must have a basis in your plot. It must motivate your protagonist to learn more, and to take his fate into his hands.

Tension comes from the stakes you set for your characters. If there is little or nothing at stake, there will be little tension.

11

SCENE INTENTIONS

An important way you keep your protagonist from wandering aimlessly about your narrative is to give him an intention in every scene—a job that he wants to carry out that will give purpose to the scene. The intention doesn't come from nowhere—it stems directly from the significant situation of your plot and from your protagonist's personal history. To clarify, an intention is a character's plan to take an action, to do something, whereas a motivation is a series of reasons, from your protagonist's personal history to his mood, that accounts for *why* he plans to take an action. In every scene these intentions will drive the action and consequences; they will help you make each scene relevant to your plot and character development. Intentions are an important way to build drama and conflict into your narrative, too, because as your protagonist pursues his intention, you will oppose it, thwart it, intensify his desire for it, and maybe, only at the end of your narrative, grant him the satisfaction of achieving it.

Every time you begin a scene you want to ask yourself: What does my protagonist want, need, and intend to do? To answer this, you'll need to consider the following:

1. **What are the most immediate desires of the character?** An intention is often a character's desire or plan to do something, whether it's

to rob a bank, propose to a woman, go to the store for cigarettes, or tell off a misbehaving family member.

2. **When will your characters achieve their intention or meet with opposition?** A scene intention should meet with complications to build drama and suspense. Therefore, try not to allow your characters to achieve their intentions right away, or too easily. Know when and where you will complicate or resolve things. Some intentions will have to be achieved, or else your plot will stop cold.

3. **Does the scene intention make sense to your plot?** Be careful not to take tangents and side paths that, while fun to write, don't contribute to the drama already unfolding. Every intention should be related to the significant situation and its consequences.

4. **Who will help your characters achieve their goal?** Who will oppose them? Decide what other characters or conditions will support or thwart your protagonists' intentions, and try to keep some resistance in the scene so that intentions are not achieved too soon, nor delayed beyond what feels realistic.

These basic questions will help direct you when you begin thinking about the actions your characters need to take in a new scene. Now we'll look at the kinds of intentions you'll want to focus on: plot-based, and scene-specific.

PLOT-BASED INTENTIONS

The first imperative any character has in any scene must always be tied back in one way or another to the significant situation of your plot, or else your scenes will feel free-floating, like vignettes. An intention, at its most basic, is a course of action your protagonist plans to take (and sometimes *needs* to take) in the scene that arises first out of the significant situation, and then from the consequences that ensue.

For example, Tess Gerritsen's thriller *Vanish* launches its significant situation when medical examiner Maura Isles prepares to do an autopsy on a Jane Doe—an unidentified female corpse—and the dead woman opens her eyes. No, this isn't a zombie story—the woman is alive, though barely. Maura's overarching plot-based intention, no matter the scene she stars in, is to figure out who this woman is, and what has happened to her—how did she end up in a body bag in the morgue when she wasn't dead! The consequences of the significant situation get underway very quickly, creating new intentions for Maura: For example, the press gets wind of what happened and begins to harass Maura and misquote the medical examiner's office. The nearly dead Jane Doe, once she's in the hospital, turns out to be livid with rage and violent in defending her own life. These are the consequences that spin out from the significant situation, and they drive scene-specific intentions (discussed in the next section).

So, here's an example of Maura Isles engaged in a plot-based intention. Maura is visiting the hospital after Jane Doe has been admitted:

> "I'm here to visit a patient," said Maura. "She was admitted last night, through the ER. I understand she was transferred out of ICU this morning."
>
> "The patient's name?"
>
> Maura hesitated. "I believe she's still registered as Jane Doe. Dr. Cutler told me she's in room four-thirty-one."
>
> The ward clerk's gaze narrowed. "I'm sorry. We've had calls from reporters all day. We can't answer any more questions about that patient."
>
> "I'm not a reporter. I'm Dr. Isles, from the medical examiner's office. I told Dr. Cutler I'd be coming by to check on the patient."
>
> "May I see some identification?"
>
> Maura dug into her purse and placed her ID on the countertop. *This is what I get for showing up without my lab coat*, she thought. She could see the interns cruising down the hall, unimpeded, like a flock of strutting white geese.

So, referring to the points mentioned earlier:

1. **What is Maura Isles most immediate, plot-related intention?** To interview Jane Doe and determine her identity, and discover what, if anything, she remembers of how she came to be left for dead.

---

2. **Will she achieve this intention or be thwarted?** The reader doesn't know when in the scene (or if) Maura will achieve her intention, but Gerritsen does—and in a moment, I'll show you how she complicates this intention unexpectedly, creating drama and action. Though the exchange with the clerk may seem inconsequential, it's quite crucial to building tension. If Maura walked unobstructed into the hospital, which is thronged by press clamoring to get in, and went straight to her patient's room, the scene would lack any element of dramatic tension. Here, the reader wonders if she's even going to get in to see the woman, and since the reader is as curious as Maura as to the identity of Jane Doe, thwarting Maura's intention keeps the reader on his toes. On a larger scale, in the novel, other law enforcement officials will aid Maura, and members of the press and Jane Doe herself will thwart her.

3. **Does the intention make sense to the plot?** Yes, absolutely—naturally Maura will want to speak to the woman who survived death. For the plot to move forward, something new will have to be revealed about Jane Doe.

4. **And finally, who helps Maura achieve her intention?** In this scene, after questioning her and scouring her ID, the clerk lets Maura through, helping her achieve one part of her intention—she gets into the hospital. But will she get to interview Jane Doe? Who will help her? In this scene, as it turns out, no one.

Gerritsen ups the ante on the plot in this scene when Jane Doe, who is more than awake—in fact she's volatile and has to be restrained—gets hold of the guard's gun and shoots him, then takes Maura as her hostage. Afraid of the woman, no hospital personnel want to get involved. Maura ends up relying on her own wits and skills to keep from getting shot.

Complicating intentions is a crucial part of building suspense and tension. Remember that if you allow your characters to achieve their intentions too early in the scene or in the narrative, you dissipate any tension or suspense you might have created.

Plot-related intentions can be demonstrated by the protagonist's direct responses to the significant situation through:

- Interior monologue that shows his thoughts and feelings

- Actions he takes to try to change or influence the outcome of the significant situation

- Dialogue in which he expresses his feelings or thoughts about the plot

SCENE-SPECIFIC INTENTIONS

Now, while your protagonist has an umbrella set of intentions related to the plot that will drive him no matter what is happening in the scene, he will also have more immediate scene-based intentions, like to find shelter after his car has been bombed, or to contact a friend he can trust before the cops find him. These immediate intentions still must relate to the plot, but they are more likely to be related to *consequences*—the many smaller actions and events that stem from the significant situation. Scene-specific intentions keep your characters from being aimless.

Let's look at an example from William Trevor's novel *Felicia's Journey*, about a lower-class Irish girl named Felicia on a trip to England. Her plot situation is that she's pregnant and on a journey to meet up with "a friend" (as she tells customs) who is actually Johnny, the father of her child, with whom she hasn't had any contact since their whirlwind dalliance. She doesn't have his address and he doesn't know she's coming, but Felicia, who is desperate to get out of her small-town life, chooses to believe he is going to marry her when he hears the news.

Now, in an early scene, she has arrived in England. Her plot intention is to get Johnny to marry her and provide a father for her baby. Her scene-specific intention—her most immediate need or desire—is to find the lawn-mower factory where Johnny works:

A man in a Volkswagen showroom is patient with her but doesn't know of a lawn-mower factory in the vicinity. Then an afterthought strikes him as she's leaving and he mentions the name of a town that he says is twenty-five or -six miles off. When it occurs to him that she's bewildered by what he's saying he writes the name down on the edge of a brochure. 'Not the full shilling', is an expression her father uses and 'Nineteen and six in the pound': she wonders if the man is thinking that.

So her intention in the excerpt was to find the lawn-mower factory where Johnny works, but since she doesn't know the town or have an address, she goes to a place that is as close to a lawn-mower factory as she can think of: a car dealership. Driven by her overarching plot intention to be with Johnny, her scene-specific intentions are directed by whatever information she obtains that will help her find him. In this case, she receives for her trouble the name of the town the factory may be in.

Her scene-specific intention then quickly becomes complicated, as the town she needs to go to is twenty-six miles away and she has very little money and no form of transportation. Her next scene intention, therefore, is to find transportation to this city (which, of course, leads to more trouble).

The simplest way to put this is: Scene intentions lead to complications, which lead to new scene intentions, and so on, until you begin to resolve your plot toward the end of your narrative.

Intentions give your protagonist a purpose on a large scale (plot) and on a present-moment scale (scene) so that you get to the action at hand and don't leave the reader wondering what is going to happen next. They help you structure your plot and direct your characters. Then, by complicating the intentions through opposition or some other kind of twist, you build tension, drama, and energy, and create new intentions.

INTENTION OPPOSITION

So now hopefully it's clear that intentions are the stage directions for your characters in every scene. Once your character's intention is established and in motion in a scene, you quickly want to come up with ways to thwart the intentions to build tension and keep a sense of urgency alive for the reader. You can do this by:

- **Preventing the completion of the intention.** Another character intervenes, a rain storm pours down, a car accident happens, etc.

- **Throwing in a twist.** The protagonist learns that what he intends to do is impossible, illegal, or wrong (and he decides to do it anyway, or he gives up completely).

- **Complicating the intentions.** Allow your protagonist to set out with one intention in mind, only to have circumstances beyond his control or awareness intervene and change his course of action.

- **Creating a new intention.** Upon having his original intention thwarted, complicated, or twisted, your protagonist may need to change course altogether and come up with a new intention.

The longer you delay fulfilling your protagonist's desire, the more tension and drama you build. It's useful to delay and oppose intentions for most of a scene, so that the reader is compelled to keep reading to find out when, and how, the intention will finally be achieved—if at all.

INTENTION SUPPORT

Eventually, you will want to provide your protagonist with *some* support of his intentions along the way. You can't delay a desire forever, or your narrative will end feeling unresolved. At certain junctures along the way, then, you need to give your protagonist allies and assistance in achieving his intentions. Whether these come in the form of friends in high places—like headmaster Albus Dumbledore, who always seems to help Harry Potter out of tight fixes—or simply a kind stranger offering shelter to a weary protagonist who is running from a pursuer, these little acts of assistance will keep your character from getting stuck.

If you only thwart intentions, after all, eventually your protagonist will become completely stymied, and the plot will come to a halt.

Keep in mind that no character should be superhuman in his ability to get through difficult trials. In the Lord of the Rings trilogy, Frodo needs his group of companions to get him to Mordor, where he can get rid of the malicious ring for good. Protagonists need friends and supporters, small acts of kindness, insight and clues that lead them on in their journeys.

Ultimately, plot intentions will carry over from scene to scene and will be the main driving force of the narrative's action, and the reason for your narrative's existence. These intentions may change slightly over the course of a narrative, once some aspects of the plot get revealed or wrapped up, but they should inform your characters' actions in every scene. Scene-specific intentions, on the other hand, will be directly related to consequences that unravel from the significant situation and can vary and shift from scene to scene as needed to drive your plot forward and to create various effects—including tension and drama—in your characters' lives.

PART III
SCENE TYPES

Every novel is an equal collaboration between the writer and the reader and it is the only place in the world where two strangers can meet on terms of absolute intimacy.

—*PAUL AUSTER*

12

THE FIRST SCENE

Your first scene is like a window thrown open in a crowded apartment complex at the sound of a scream. Whatever the window opens onto—lovers quarrelling, a murderer fleeing from a body, a strange and beautiful dance—is the significant situation of your plot, and must take place in your first scene (a prologue, by the way, is not your first scene—it's a scene that hints at actions to come).

The first scene in your narrative bears the greatest burden of all, because it must do all of the following:

- Hatch your plot in the form of your significant situation

- Introduce your protagonist and provide a brief glance into his inner or outer struggles

- Establish a distinct, rich setting and subtly evoke the senses without being overbearing

- Set up a feeling of dramatic tension that hints at complications and conflict to come

First scenes are most successful when they begin with an air of mystery, a question or situation that needs an answer, or a crisis from which the protagonist needs to be extricated. The first scene should be compelling enough—with enough action and plot information—that the reader does not need any backstory or expository summary in order to keep reading without getting confused.

Throughout the rest of the narrative, the first scene should resonate in the reader's mind like a haunting tune he can't shake. It is, after all, the point of no return.

INTRODUCING THE SIGNIFICANT SITUATION AND YOUR PROTAGONIST

Burn these words into your consciousness now and forever more: *Plot and character cannot be separated*. Your significant situation is the something bad, difficult, mysterious, or tragic that happens to your protagonist in real-time action—in other words, it feels as though it is happening at the moment the reader reads it because it isn't narrated in exposition and it isn't a flashback scene. The action is happening now! This monumental event is what sets your story in motion, what compels your character to take action, because, after all, the problem belongs to your protagonist first and foremost. Through other plot twists and complications, the significant situation may lead to a whole host of trouble for other characters, but not at page one. The opening scene belongs to your main character.

Your significant situation should happen within the first couple of paragraphs. If you force the reader to wait too long for the event that they hope is coming, you stand to lose them before ever getting to it.

For example, in Lynn Freed's novel *House of Women*, the first scene opens with a beguiling description of a man called only "the Syrian," as seen through the first-person point of view of Thea, a seventeen-year-old girl with a protective mother. It is quickly established, through the lyrical way that Thea describes the man, and then herself, that she is a romantic girl who feels smothered by her mother. The significant situation and the protagonist are introduced simultaneously: The Syrian—a friend of her father's—has come to take her to live with her father against her mother's wishes:

The Syrian stands on the terrace, staring down into the bay. His head and shoulders are caught in the last of the light, massive, like a centaur's. He could be Apollo on his chariot with his hair blown back like that. Or Poseidon. Or Prometheus. He is the darkest white man I have ever seen. It is sort of a gilded darkness, gleaming and beautiful. Even an old man can look like a god, I think.

But of course, he isn't old. He is just older than I am, much older. I am seventeen and a half and have just lost twelve pounds at the slimming salon. My body is curved and firm and brown. Until now, I have been plain, as my mother is plain, but in a different way. My mother is slim and elegant and plain. I have been sallow and lumpy and awkward, and too clever by half, as she says.

Since I lost weight she has become more watchful than ever. If a boy whistles at me on the street, she says he is common rubbish, he wants one thing and one thing only, and if I give in, I will be his forever. The result is that every night I dream of common rubbish. ...

The Syrian turns. He shades his eyes against the sun and smiles. "Join me?" he says, holding up his whiskey and soda.

Thea, being naïve, has no idea of the consequences of what joining him on the terrace will bring. That she will have to marry the much older man, for starters. That she will become a young mother who is isolated and just as trapped in her new life as she felt with her mother.

When you kick off your significant situation, be sure that it directly involves your protagonist and reveals something about her character—whether you only show her actions, or you let us into her interior world. Remember, though, that your situation should challenge your protagonist's status quo. Plot and character are bound together and one without the other will cause your first scene to flop.

In your first scene you aren't going to focus too much on character development; your goal is to introduce your protagonist as quickly and with as much intrigue as possible while getting your story started and hooking the reader. So, what does your first scene need to be successful? The following, for starters:

- **A significant situation that challenges your protagonist's status quo.**
  The Syrian's appearance as the messenger to bring Thea to her father
  is the significant situation that starts the plot and challenges Thea's
  character, future, and innocence.

- **A catalyst with whom the protagonist can interact.** At this point, the
  Syrian is a catalyst—because of him, Thea will take actions she might
  not have otherwise. Though Thea's mother, Nalia, is not present physically in the scene, her mother's wishes for her are, so in this first scene,
  Nalia is the antagonist—the person who wants to thwart Thea's goal of
  leaving. Later on, the Syrian will become an antagonist too.

- **A quick introduction to your protagonist's immediate intentions.**
  Thea's intention is to leave her mother and go to her father. To do this,
  she makes the choice to trust this strange man, the Syrian.

- **A glimpse of your protagonist's personal history and personality,
  which should shed further light on her motivation.** The reader gets
  a quick glimpse into Thea's life: her overprotective mother; her father,
  who has other children and rarely visits; and her repressed curiosity
  about the opposite gender. She feels stifled by her mother, and this
  leads to an urge to change.

- **A course of action or a decision on the part of the protagonist that
  leads immediately to more complications.** Undoubtedly, life gets
  more complicated for Thea by scene's end, as she is now about to leave
  her old life with a questionable stranger.

THE CORE ELEMENTS AND THE FIRST SCENE

Now that we've explored the all-important combination of significant situation and character, let's look at how all the other core elements come into
play. Getting the balance right is crucial, because too much or too little of
any one element can throw off the symmetry of the entire scene. For instance, too much setting description can slow your pace to a crawl, bore the
reader, and stall your story before it's even begun.

Setting

It's tempting to paint a dramatic canvas of setting in the first scene, but be careful not to let setting absorb the attention of your scene. Notice how in the first scene of *House of Women* the setting is elicited by the sparest of physical details. The Syrian "stands on the terrace." He is "staring down into the bay." His head and shoulders are caught "in the last of the light"—so the reader knows that it is nearing evening. In two tiny sentences the reader also gets an image of a porch that overlooks a body of water, and a description of a man who is as charismatic and powerful to look at as a mythical god. By mere suggestion the reader learns that Thea is on the verandah at her mother's home. These are subtle details. The scene is intimate and doesn't require a larger picture with more specific setting. That's a good light touch.

In your first scene, setting should be lightly drawn unless the setting itself is part of your significant situation in some dramatic way (like if your protagonist is lost in a wild jungle or scaling a mountain).

Let's look at how another author infuses her first scene with setting in a manner that also furthers the development of her significant situation. In the novel *The Handmaid's Tale* by Margaret Atwood, the significant situation is a radical shift in government that takes away women's freedom overnight. One day protagonist Offred has a normal life with her husband and daughter, then it is stripped away. In this first scene, she is nothing more than a slave kept by the new ruling class for the sake of reproduction. Atwood uses setting to create tension and unease from the very first sentence. She describes a familiar setting—that of a high school gymnasium—but there's something wrong with the whole picture. Why are the protagonist and these others sleeping there in the first place? Who are these "Aunts" that patrol the room with "cattle prods slung on thongs from leather belts"?

Though Atwood has a matter-of-fact style of writing, by using a normal setting in an abnormal way, she creates an aura of fear and uncertainty that immediately drives her plot forward.

> We slept in what had once been the gymnasium. The floor was of var-
> nished wood, with stripes and circles painted on it, for the games that

were formerly played there; the hoops for the basketball nets were still in place, though the nets were gone. A balcony ran around the room, for the spectators, and I thought I could smell, faintly like an afterimage, the pungent scent of sweat, shot through with the sweet taint of chewing gum and perfume from the watching girls, felt-skirted as I knew from pictures, later in miniskirts, then pants, then in one earring, spiky green-streaked hair. ...

We had flannelette sheets, like children's, and army-issue blankets, old ones that still said U.S. We folded our clothes neatly and laid them on the stools at the ends of the beds. The lights were turned down but not out. Aunt Sara and Aunt Elizabeth patrolled; they had electric cattle prods slung on thongs from their leather belts.

Notice how the first line makes you feel nervous and curious and how the careful descriptions of a gymnasium and the characters' few belongings—"flannelette sheets, like children's, and army-issue blankets"—add up to a feeling that something bad has happened and that worse things (complications!) are to come. The protagonist also describes the setting with a keen note of nostalgia, suggesting that this familiar place is no longer used for a normal or familiar activity. Atwood unbalances our sense of what is normal.

You too can unbalance the reader's sense of normalcy in your writing by having your significant situation take place in a familiar setting in an *unexpected* way. For instance, a murder could take place in a domestically cozy little cottage; or against the backdrop of a dingy back alley where homeless people sleep, a man could propose marriage to a woman.

Unbalancing normalcy with setting is a great way to start your scene off with a visual and emotional pitch.

Subtext and Dramatic Tension

Subtext, as discussed earlier, foreshadows aspects of your plot through the strategic placement of thematic imagery, subtle indications of character behavior, and by showing parallel actions in the background of the scene. Not all genres need as much subtext. Action-driven narratives such as thrillers and mysteries, for example, often bypass the subtle for action, while literary fiction often relies upon more subtext, since the genre emphasizes lyrical language, slower pacing, and richer character development.

Freed does not disappoint when it comes to subtext. Looking back to our earlier *House of Women* example, there's an undeniably erotic subtext to the first scene. Thea describes the Syrian as "gleaming and beautiful"—terms of admiration bordering on the sexual. Thea desires him, or something from him, and as the text points out, her mother has made a point to warn her that boys only want "one thing and one thing only" from her. At seventeen, she is of an age to be naturally curious about men, and without using any telling language, the subtext points to this.

Her subtext also points to the theme of the inequality between men and women. Comparing the Syrian to mythical gods like Prometheus and Apollo makes him larger than life. Thea has been taught to see men as strange and powerful, since she has never lived with her father, and been raised only by her mother. This is an important subtext for how naïve Thea is to the ways of men, because if she better understood them, she would probably not have gone with the Syrian.

The subtext in your first scene sets a tone for the rest of the narrative and creates a trail of bread crumbs leading the reader to believe that a certain direction is in store for your protagonist. In your first scene's subtext you want to develop a mood, foreshadow your protagonist's plot direction, and plant thematic images in the reader's mind.

Whether or not your first scene has a subtext, it needs to have dramatic tension. Dramatic tension is the feeling that something could go wrong for your protagonist, whether by forces working against him, or by ill-advised or unwise choices he makes on his own. You want to be sure that your significant situation immediately gives the reader cause to worry about your protagonist.

Once your significant situation is underway, you'll want to be sure that you keep the tension alive throughout the scene. You'll notice how Freed's first scene is positively dripping with the potential for conflict or consequence. Here is a young woman, kept naïve to men by her mother, out on a clandestine visit at night with a much older man. The reader knows that something is going to happen, and that it will probably go against Thea's mother's wishes and Thea's own expectations.

Pacing

Pace should match the emotional content of your scene. First scenes should get going with an emotional bang—start big or dramatic, ratchet up the suspense or lay on the fear, since you're capturing the reader here.

In Philip Pullman's young adult fantasy novel *The Golden Compass*, the first scene opens with an air of nervous anticipation, and the quick pace mirrors that feeling. Protagonist Lyra, a ten-year-old girl, and her animal daemon Pantalaimon live at Jordan College in Oxford, England. In the first scene, Lyra is snooping in the chamber of the Master of the college despite Pantalaimon's warnings that she will get in trouble. The action is quick and the exposition and reflection kept to a minimum.

> "What d'you think they talk about?" Lyra said, or began to say, because before she'd finished the question she heard voices outside the door.
>
> "Behind the chair—quick!" whispered Pantalaimon, and in a flash Lyra was out of the armchair and crouching behind it. It wasn't the very best one for hiding behind: she'd chosen one in the very center of the room, and unless she kept very quiet. ...
>
> The door opened, and the light changed in the room; one of the incomers was carrying a lamp, which he put down on the sideboard. Lyra could see his legs, in their dark green trousers and shiny black shoes. It was a servant.
>
> Then a deep voice said, "Has Lord Asriel arrived yet?"
>
> It was the Master.

Within a few paragraphs of quickly paced action and brief description, Lyra finds herself in the midst of her significant situation: As a result of being where she isn't supposed to be, she sees someone slipping poison into the brandy of their visiting guest, Lord Asriel, and overhears a conversation she isn't meant to that sets the plot in motion. In order to save Lord Asriel's life, she'll have to let on that she was in a forbidden room, and thus face punishment—putting her in quite the dilemma, which is a great way to thrust the reader into a first scene!

Your first scene is like a cold pool—the reader needs to dive in and get moving fast, or he'll be too cold to stay in the water for very long. In other scene types, you'll have more leeway with pacing. In the first scene, however, a quick pace—with more action and less reflection or exposition—will be a better sell.

To keep the pace quick, think in terms of action. What actions can your protagonist take that stem directly from the significant situation? You might want to have your protagonist take a risk, or be surprised in some way. First scenes are great for reactions—that is, characters being caught off guard in one way or another and having to think quickly about what they'll do next.

Ending the First Scene

Eventually, your significant situation will have to taper off to its close. No matter what kind of plot you choose—a quiet, character-driven one, or an action-based one as your genre and writing style demand—end your first scene with a feeling that trouble, conflict, crisis, or a dilemma has only just begun, and you will almost certainly guarantee the reader keeps on going to the next scene. To do this:

- **Leave the consequences of the significant situation unresolved.** A promise of more to come in the next scene keeps the reader turning the page. For example, if your protagonist has just been caught at the scene of a murder, don't let him be arrested or proven innocent before the first scene's end—leave the reader guessing.

- **End the scene before the character makes a major decision.** This also works if you end the scene just after the character makes a bad decision, like Freed did with Thea in *House of Women*.

- **Allow your protagonist to have a disturbing realization that ultimately changes everything in his life.** What could prompt such a dramatic realization? Maybe your protagonist must flee the country, because his wife is a double-agent and an evil nemesis has found them.

- **Let your protagonist have a knee-jerk reaction to the significant situation.** This reaction should make things more complicated for him and help the scene transition go smoother.

Take a look at how Freed wraps up the opening scene of *House of Women*:

> Even as I slipped out of my sandals and crept down the back stairs, stopping at the bottom until Maude had delivered the drinks tray to him—even as I ran along the pantry passage and through the dining room, out onto the verandah, I knew that nothing they could do would stop me now. Not even if they caught me. Not even if they dug their nails into my flesh and screamed for the police.
>
> "I sail tomorrow," he says.
>
> I can hear my mother in her dressing room. She is humming, she is happy. "I've never seen snow," I say, standing up, "I've never even needed a coat."

While you want to taper the action of the significant situation to a close, you don't want it to feel too conclusive. In Thea's case, she has made a decision: "Nothing they could do would stop me now." She's going. But this is only the end of one stage of her life, at home with her mother. And Freed gives us a final, painful image of the mother "humming, she is happy," which the reader suspects will be Nalia's last moment of happiness before she realizes her daughter has gone.

You can also drop a thematic hint at the end of your first scene, as Freed does with this lovely metaphoric line of dialogue, "I've never even needed a coat." The coat symbolizes protection. With her mother as her keeper, Thea has been safe. But now she's entering a new territory without a coat, without protection.

Finally, leave your protagonist in a little bit of trouble, so the reader feels anxious enough to keep reading. Choose whichever path will create the most potential for conflict and change in the character. A shy, fearful character, for instance, might be faced with a big, brave decision at the end of your first scene—hopefully one that is a consequence of his significant situation. Whatever path you take, leave your protagonist's fate up in the air.

FIRST SCENES VS. PROLOGUES

Many writers don't quite understand the distinction between a prologue and a first scene (or chapter). The reason you will not find an entire chapter here on prologues is because they are not a crucial scene type. Most of the scene types you will have to use at least once in a narrative. A prologue is optional, and many novels don't use them at all.

A prologue is a short scene or chapter at the very beginning of a narrative—it is the very first part of the narrative that will be read, and it comes before the first scene and chapter. But here's where it can get confusing: A prologue may actually take place in the future, or even in the distant past. In fact, it may not fit into the linear chronology of the narrative at all, because its purpose is to provide information that the narrative will not or cannot just yet, but that is somehow needed. Some writers use a prologue as a hook—to tempt the reader with information that the plot will not deliver for many more hundreds of pages. I feel that your first scene should successfully provide that hook, and that if you work hard to write an effective, enticing, vivid first scene, you won't need a prologue. You do find prologues often, however, in certain kinds of genre work. Fantasy is a genre very well suited to the prologue, as it's often needed to fill the reader in on some aspect of the fantasy world that couldn't otherwise be known. Some mysteries may also require a bit of setup that is easiest to do in a prologue, to fill the reader in on the details of the case.

In the young-adult fantasy novel *The Alchemyst*, by Michael Scott, the prologue lets the reader know that even though the book is set in the modern day, Nicholas Flamel and his wife, Perenelle, are seven-hundred-year-old wizards in possession of a magic book called the Codex that is the key to their long life. The prologue simply gets the reader up to speed so the story can unfold without confusion when the Codex is stolen and two young kids are drawn into the plot.

The prologue of *The Secret Book of Grazia dei Rossi*, by Jacqueline Park, works because the entire narrative is a first-person account—essentially a series of letters to the protagonist's son—and the reader needs to know this information before the narrative begins.

In *Windfalls*, by Jean Hegland, the prologue works because the novel is a very literary, character-driven novel in which the major conflicts and crises don't happen immediately to the protagonists. But the prologue is full of strange, lyrical, odd images that invoke a sense of danger or tragedy, which remains in the undercurrent of the reading and leaves a sense of worry about what's going to happen to the characters.

If you want to learn how to write a strong prologue, study the novels of Jodi Picoult, particularly *The Tenth Circle*. Picoult has a unique way of framing a piece of plot information in a way that makes you curious and breathless and urgent. I wouldn't say that her books *need* prologues so much as she has just mastered the art of writing them.

FIRST SCENE MUSE POINTS

- Introduce your protagonist and the significant situation simultaneously.

- Match your pace to the emotional content of the scene.

- Use thematic images to foreshadow an outcome. If your protagonist's life is in danger, set an eerie mood, and use setting objects that conjure up images of death or darkness—a knife, a raven, even a shift in light from bright to dark.

- Unbalance the reader's expectations through setting by employing what is not expected, such as featuring a monastery as the site of a violent crime, or a prison as the setting of a surprising revelation of innocence.

- Keep a tight pace—notice if you are using too much exposition or description that drags the pace down; and watch for lengthy, unbroken passages of dialogue or actions that push the pace too quickly.

- End with your protagonist in trouble or with an uncertain fate, setting up the next scene.

13

SUSPENSE SCENES

Suspense, at its most primal, is a state of uncertainty that produces anxiety. In fiction, no matter whether the condition creating the suspense is positive or negative—Will she say yes to the handsome rogue's proposal? Will he be flung off the cliff?—it tends to have the same effect on the reader: the heart races, nerves are tight, and an aura of apprehension hangs over the scene. This is a good thing. The way to get the reader to white-knuckle her way through a suspense scene is by delaying the inevitable outcome of the trouble your characters are in.

Suspense scenes can be found in almost every genre of fiction, though mysteries and thrillers capitalize on these scenes more than romance or literary novels. For a scene to qualify as suspenseful:

- The protagonist must begin in jeopardy or quickly get caught in the middle of trouble or danger
- The emotional, physical, or spiritual stakes for the character must become more complicated during the scene
- The emotional intensity must increase for the protagonist, and must not let up until the end
- The events of the scene, or fellow characters, must exert pressure on the protagonist to change or act in some way

Use suspense scenes to add emotional voltage to your narrative, to up the emotional ante for your protagonist, and to add complications to your plot that will require new solutions (half the fun of reading is following a protagonist as he gets into and out of and then back into trouble again). A good place for suspense scenes is after a contemplative scene or a dialogue-driven scene whose main purpose is to provide plot information; in those instances a suspense scene will get the reader excited again, and provide your protagonist with new challenges. Suspense scenes also have a feeling of pressing urgently forward, so consider using them before an epiphany scene, because they'll help drive your characters toward big conclusions and realizations.

Pacing obviously plays a large role in the success or failure of a suspenseful scene. When building to painful realizations or inevitable outcomes, it's good to slow down the pace by focusing on small details in a scene or by using a few well-placed lines of exposition or interior monologue. Part of what creates suspense is the agony of not knowing what is going to happen next. Of course, a fast-paced scene can often add that much-needed surge of adrenaline that propels the reader forward. Generally, though, suspense is built upon slow and carefully measured action that builds and holds tension.

Suspense can get lost if you try to rush into it. Think of how nerve-racking it is to watch a ghost-story type movie in which a character is walking slowly down a darkened hall toward a room where he has heard a noise. If he runs down that hall, there's no time for suspense. But by walking slowly and fearfully, he allows the viewers to feel his anxiety. The same technique works to build suspense in your narrative—the more time the reader has to feel nervous, the more effective the scene will be.

OPENING A SUSPENSE SCENE

Suspense scenes should open in a way that gives the reader immediate concern for the protagonist. While your protagonist doesn't need to be dangling from scaffolding just yet, he might be starting the climb. Or you can create a more subtle uneasiness—the protagonist can simply feel that something is not quite right about the unusual silence or overly bright lights of a house or building. In a suspense scene, you want to give the reader an *uh-oh* feeling, a sense of trouble, which should begin to mount and reach a crescendo of pressure toward the end.

Let's look at a suspense scene from Paul Auster's novel *The Book of Illusions*. Though his novel is literary, he works in suspense masterfully. David Zimmer, a translator who is still trying to recover from the loss of his wife and two sons in a plane crash over a year before, has just arrived home after a harrowing drive and a minor accident in the rain. The significant situation of the plot was a letter he received, inviting him to meet Hector Mann, the elusive silent-screen comedian thought to be dead, about whom David wrote a book. David is not convinced of the veracity of the letter, and has written back demanding proof that Mann is actually alive. His proof shows up in the form of a mysterious woman, Alma Grund, sent to fetch him back to New Mexico. Notice how the scene begins fairly benignly, but causes a prickle of anxiety:

> We found the keys with her flashlight and when I opened the door and stepped into the house, I flicked on the lights in the living room. Alma Grund came in after me—a short woman in her mid- to late thirties, dressed in a blue silk blouse and tailored gray pants.

The fact that the strange woman comes in after him is cause for concern. The scene takes on more suspense when, within a couple of paragraphs, David begins to act irrationally though Alma has done nothing threatening. (Auster does not use quotation marks in his dialogue, so I have added them for clarity's sake):

> "Just give me five minutes," she said. "I can explain everything."
> "I don't like it when people trespass on my property," I said, "And I don't like it when people jump out at me in the middle of the night. You don't want me to have to throw you out of here, do you?"
> She looked up at me then, surprised by my vehemence, frightened by the undertow of rage in my voice. "I thought you wanted to see Hector," she said and as she spoke those words she took a few more steps into the house, removing herself from the vicinity of the door in case I was planning to carry out my threat.

Here's the brilliant moment of this scene: the protagonist, David, starts out as the aggressor—the reader isn't afraid *for* him, but afraid he's going to do harm to this poor woman. But subtly, with a slight shift, Auster turns the tables when Alma "took a few more steps into the house." Those few steps are full of suspense. What does she want? Why isn't she afraid of him? Suddenly, Alma has taken the power. And the suspense has only just begun. David still isn't afraid, but the readers is, and rightfully so, for when David comes back downstairs from his bath and finds that Alma is still in his house, after trying unsuccessfully to convince him with words, she takes desperate action:

> The gun was in her hand. It was a small silver-plated revolver with a pearl handle, no more than half the size of the cap guns I had played with as a boy. As she turned in my direction and lifted her arm, I could see that the hand at the end of her arm was shaking.
>
> "This isn't me," she said. "I don't do things like this. Ask me to put it away, and I will. But we have to go now."

To build suspense, you don't need to throw in a gun or a physical altercation, though those will work. Suspense can be created by shifting the power back and forth between characters, letting the reader wonder if your protagonist is going to grab the ancient treasure out of the enemy's hands, or if he's going to fall into the burning pit of magma.

David later wrests the gun out of Alma's hands and shocks them both by putting it to his own head, jacking up the emotional intensity—the stakes—more and more until David finally pulls the trigger.

To create suspense at the beginning of a scene you can:

- **Introduce a catalyst or antagonist whose intentions seem suspect to the protagonist.** David, and consequently the reader, does not trust Alma from the very start because of the manner of her arrival—suddenly, without notice, and in the middle of the night.

- **Allow your protagonist to feel threatened or pressured by another character or event, and to resist the ensuing demand or request.** David is tired, wet, upset, and just wants a bath. Alma's presence and her demand that he fly to New Mexico with her puts pressure on him—his family died in a plane crash, remember, and he's emotionally unstable.

- **Allow your protagonist, under pressure, to react or act out in a way that causes unexpected conflict.** David becomes emotionally volatile with Alma. If he had just let her talk in the first place, it's likely she would not have used the gun.

Remember that suspense is about *delay*. The longer the anxiety-producing event goes on, and the more pressure you can put on your character in the scene, the more suspense you'll build.

MOOD, SETTING, AND SENSORY DETAILS

The mood you create also has a large impact on suspense. Mood, of course, is conveyed through the physical conditions, such as setting and weather, that your protagonist finds herself in. In Auster's suspense scene, he zooms the focus down onto the landscape of the characters' bodies—to the exclusion of the physical world around them—which keeps the reader's attention uncomfortably planted where the action is, in the distance between David and Alma.

Other authors very purposefully use the senses to create a suspenseful mood, as in this example from Harper Lee's novel *To Kill a Mockingbird*. Atticus Finch's two young children, Jem and Scout, are walking home alone after a play on a very dark night, without a flashlight. What informs this scene is that their father, an attorney involved in a heated, racially divided court case in town, has developed some eager enemies. As they walk, the children hear what sounds like a person following them. At first Jem tries to convince Scout that it's nothing, but soon it becomes clear he's scared, too.

> "Be quiet," he said, and I knew he was not joking.
>
> The night was still. I could hear his breath coming easily beside me. Occasionally there was a sudden breeze that hit my bare legs, but it was all that remained of a promised windy night. This was the stillness before a thunderstorm. We listened.
>
> "Heard an old dog just then," I said.
>
> "It's not that," Jem answered.

Notice how the simple use of the sensory details that come after Jem warns his sister to "be quiet" add up to a feeling that trouble is brewing, and build the suspense. The "sudden breeze" on Scout's bare legs. Her brother's breath coming "easily" beside her, and that eerie "stillness" before the storm allow the reader to enter right into the suspenseful moment. Sure enough, trouble comes soon after, in the form of a man intent on harming the children to send a message to Atticus.

Sensory details are tailor-made for suspense, because they lend themselves to metaphor and mood well, and through them, you can affect the reader's senses; sensory details help bring authenticity to the scene. A terrible odor, or the creepy slickness of a dank cellar, can turn an otherwise normal scene into a suspenseful one.

Some great suspense-building setting and sensory techniques include:

- **Weather.** Using dramatic weather, such as storms, blizzards, or harsh, beating sun, is a great way to create suspense if it imperils your characters, keeps them from their goals, or adds complications. Be mindful that the weather relates to your plot.

- **Decay.** In the physical world, a house or boat or car in a state of decay will inevitably create suspense. Rotting wood, a half-submerged car in a lake, or a trail of faded old clothing will cause the reader to feel concerned that if the protagonist investigates these decayed places or objects, he will meet the same fate as the original owners of the objects.

- **Color and light.** Dark colors lend themselves to dark emotions. Dark fabrics or art pieces can add a note of suspense. Intensely bright lights can cause feelings of pressure—as when a character is being interrogated, or caught in a spotlight, trying to escape.

- **Touch.** There are many subtle ways to use the sense of touch to create suspense, particularly when a character fears he is in danger. Think of the eerie nature of these kinds of touch: the feeling of a hand on the back of a neck; the slippery quality of blood on skin; the light pressure of breath in a person's ear.

The beauty of setting and sensory details is that you can add them in minimally—it doesn't take more than a handful of small, well-placed details to evoke a feeling of suspense.

Of course, you'll want to be thinking of more than just setting in creating suspense. The difference between a suspense scene and other scene types is that you want to infuse uncertainty and anxiety into a suspense scene in every way possible. So don't forget that you must introduce new plot information in a suspenseful way, too.

RAISING THE STAKES

Suspense scenes are fantastic when you are about to take your plot in a new direction by changing your character's fate or adding complications to his story. They dramatize these twists, rather than narrate them in exposition.

In Sarah Waters's novel *Tipping the Velvet*, protagonist Nan King, a waitress in her family's oyster bar, comes alive the day she meets Kitty Butler, a vaudeville actress. She is drawn into Kitty's world, joins her on tour, and quickly becomes a part of the act, performing in nineteenth-century London. They also begin a love affair they can carry on only in secret. Nan takes a long overdue leave of absence to visit her home, and when she returns, full of eagerness to see Kitty, Waters builds suspense by hinting to the reader what Nan's fate will be before Nan realizes it herself.

> Our house, when I gazed up at it from the street, was, as I had hoped, quite dark and shuttered. I walked on tip-toe up the steps, and eased my key into the lock. The passageway was quiet: even our landlady and her husband seemed still abed. I laid down my bags, and took off my coat. There was a cloak already hanging from the hat-stand, and I squinted at it: it was Walter's. How queer, I thought, he must have come here yesterday, and forgotten it!—and soon, creeping up the darkened staircase, I forgot it myself.
>
> I reached Kitty's door, and put my ear to it. I had expected silence, but there was a sound from beyond it—a kind of lapping sound, as of a kitten at a saucer of milk.

Waters strategically slows the pace down to a near crawl, so that the reader's focus is delivered very carefully to the most important clue: Walter's cloak on the hook. She also cleverly calls the door "Kitty's door." It has previously been Nan and Kitty's door, but after this scene, Nan will never live there again. While Nan is curious at the "kind of lapping sound" coming from behind the door, she still doesn't realize that her fate is about to change. By keeping Nan ignorant but cluing in the reader, the author keeps the reader in suspense, waiting for the moment when Nan's heart will be broken and her life (and plot) changed forever.

The longer you can delay the moment of conflict through suspense, the more intense the conflict will be for the reader. When you can also keep your own character ignorant of the conflict that is about to come, you have far more possibility for a dramatic change, which is the goal of good suspense.

PLAYING UP THE UNEXPECTED

Strange or surprising actions that challenge a protagonist's sense of normalcy can drive suspense to a crescendo, adding pressure to anxiety by creating confusion. Here's a quickly paced moment of suspense in Justine Musk's horror novel *BloodAngel*. Musk is a deft and careful writer who doesn't just go in for big, melodramatic horror. Instead she puts her character Lucas Maddox in a very unusual situation and does not give him, or the reader, time to understand what's happening. The effect is disturbingly suspenseful.

> He had been waiting for maybe fifteen, twenty minutes when he caught movement from the corner of his eye.
>
> He turned.
>
> Saw an animal in the yellow grass.
>
> He blinked twice, looked again.
>
> Skittering crab-like on all fours: animal-girl in jeans and stained white T-shirt, sun glinting off her pale hair—
>
> He thought: *No.*
>
> And the girl stood in front of him.
>
> Smiling.

What she does after that smile is pretty gruesome, and the suspenseful buildup lets the reader feel unnerved first.

Even if you don't write horror, challenging a protagonist's sense of normalcy is a useful suspense-building technique. Notice how the way she moves on all fours, like a crab, is creepy and unnatural, and makes the reader—as well as the character—look twice. You can challenge normalcy in many ways. For instance, you might confuse your protagonist. Not quite trusting one's eyes can lead to suspense. Was that man in black following him, or just walking down the same streets? Did he actually see his dead wife in the crowd? You might also use bad weather, loud noises, fatigue, or physical illness to play with your protagonist's (and thus your reader's) sense of reality.

ENDING A SUSPENSE SCENE

Eventually, you must end the suspense, even if only temporarily. Sometimes one kind of suspense can lead to another. For instance, in *The Book of Illusions*, at the final moment of the scene, after suspense has mounted to a terrifying crescendo, David pulls the trigger, and this is what happens:

> I finally saw what the trouble was. The safety catch was on. She hadn't remembered to release it. If not for that mistake, one of those bullets would have been in my head.

The suspense doesn't end when the gun fails to go off; it ends when David reflects on the fact that he just survived his own death by a fluke of luck (this also inserts a powerful symmetry into the subtext when you consider that his wife and sons did not have any luck on their side to survive their plane crash). You might notice the urge to take a breath there, now the sense of imminent danger is over. To break the suspense you must conclude the action and offer a pause—either a literal one, or one of reflection from the character's point of view. For all the reader knows, Alma pulls out another gun in the next scene, but the reader isn't there yet—she's basking in a moment of relief. To conclude suspense, you finally give the reader what you've been withholding throughout the scene.

You can also end a scene of this type by maintaining the suspense right up to the end, leaving the scene on a cliffhanger. In *BloodAngel*, the suspense is kept hanging:

And in the moment before he blacked out, Lucas Maddox seized on the impossible fact that this was not a dream, not a drug.

She had come for him.

By having a character lose consciousness, you end the scene, but maintain the feeling of danger or trouble, hence suspense.

If you leave your scene on a suspenseful ridge like that, however, you have to pick that dangling thread back up in the next scene, which means your next scene will have to open suspensefully, too—so consider whether that is what you want to do. This is one of the details about scene-building that is so important to remember; you must always consider how the current scene will set up the scene that follows it.

One last caveat about suspense scenes. Too many of them in a row can take a toll on the reader. There's no perfect formula, but more than three suspense scenes in a row without relief is going to push the reader toward exhaustion. You might want to throw in a contemplative scene or even just a dramatic, but not suspenseful, scene to temper the intensity.

SUSPENSE SCENE MUSE POINTS

- Open your scene in an uneasy or anxiety-provoking way.
- Throw your protagonist quickly into trouble.
- Add emotional intensity to the scene.
- Let events or an antagonist add pressure to your protagonist through opposition.
- Delay conclusions to scene events and thwart character intentions.
- Either break the suspense at the scene's end, or end on a cliffhanger.

14
DRAMATIC SCENES

Dramatic scenes are the vehicle for emotional content in your narrative. When you intend to deliver stunning emotional consequences on either end of the spectrum—from tremendous joy to terrible tragedy—that push your protagonist and his plot into new territory, dramatic scenes will take you there.

What is drama exactly? Director Frank Capra is quoted as saying, "I thought drama was when actors cried. But drama is when the audience cries." Drama's goal is to elicit feelings in the reader, not to show off the writing or the emotional range of your characters. The hallmarks of a dramatic scene, which is often used as a precursor to an epiphany or climax scene, are:

- A focus on emotional intensity
- An emphasis on relationship-oriented interactions (the deepening of connections, or the severing of ties with other characters)
- Actions that facilitate or support the protagonist's access to his inner life or self-awareness
- An indication that the protagonist (and thus the plot) is approaching a turning point

Drama takes many forms—big blowout fights, obsessive love letters, emotionally devastating emotional betrayals—but its main purpose is to drive characters toward change. Through drama, your protagonist will be faced with decisions and complications that cause radical shifts in the way he thinks and acts.

A dramatic scene is effective when it follows a contemplative scene or a dialogue scene in which the protagonist has engaged in an event or reflected upon one and is ready for an emotional confrontation; or it can create an emotional stew that your protagonist will need to process in a contemplative scene to follow.

Because dramatic scenes exist to drive your protagonist toward a point of change, you won't feature as many of this type of scene at the beginning of your narrative as you will toward the middle and the end, when more has happened, and your protagonist has more reason and need to change.

THE BEATS OF A DRAMATIC SCENE

You can comfortably open *and* close your dramatic scene at a slow pace as long as you remember that the hallmark of drama is that the emotional intensity gets higher and higher over the course of the scene, until it reaches some sort of climax. Once you're into the emotional content, the pacing should be fairly quick. Insults are flung back and forth; demands are stated; passion erupts.

The pace of a dramatic scene can follow a three-part formula like this:

1. **Open slow.** Use exposition, setting details, and interior monologue to create a slow-moving beginning.

2. **Speed up pace to match rising emotional intensity.** Strip away exposition; use dialogue, quick actions, and hot emotional content to push the intensity to a crescendo.

3. **Slow down to allow for reflection.** Return to interior monologue or exposition to pull back from the intensity.

In this passage from Ellen Meister's novel *Secret Confessions of the Applewood PTA*, notice how quickly the dialogue moves, and how the emotions flip from anger to sorrow to tenderness:

Paul pushed his chair from his desk and swiveled to face Ruth directly. "I spoke to my priest.

Ruth leaned back and exhaled, deflated. "You *didn't*."

"We can't keep *doing* this, Ruth, it isn't right."

"Why not?"

"You took a covenant before God. Keith is your husband, for better or worse, in sickness and in health."

"Tell me something I don't know!" Ruth stood, growing agitated. "Do you see me abandoning him? Am I walking out the door? No I'm staying. I'm staying to take care of a man who will never be healthy. Will never be normal. Will never be a real husband to me. I deserve *something*, Paul." She started to cry. "So don't give me this sanctimonious crap, okay? Because your wife died. You're free. I'm stuck. This is my forever." She dissolved into sobs.

Paul's eyes filled with tears. He stood and embraced her.

In that passage, the emotional content is hot and intense and the author matches the pace of the scene to that intensity—the conversation moves quickly, emotions are on full throttle, and there is very little narrative summary of any kind to distract from the intensity. Remember that drama always has a quality of urgency—it becomes dramatic through mounting energy, which you can convey through a swift pace and limited narrative summary.

Hot and Cold Emotions

Since drama centers so much on emotional content, here is a quick shorthand for the ways that emotions are exhibited. When emotions are hot (think passion, rage, betrayal), they tend to erupt and spill over. They lean toward the lurid and the melodramatic; they're big and loud. Too much hot emotional content in a dramatic scene will lead to melodrama (we'll explore melodrama in greater detail later in this chapter).

When emotions are cold (think shock, hurt, internalized grief), the drama seems quieter. The character handles the emotional intensity by clamping down, clenching, withdrawing, walking away. When your emotional content is too cool, however, the scene can lose power or fall flat. In every dramatic scene you want to strive to keep a balance of hot and cold.

OPENING A DRAMATIC SCENE

As we just saw, dramatic scenes do not have to launch into intense emotions right at the opening. You have some latitude in starting a scene of this kind, but it never hurts to build slowly towards the drama in order to make it more believable. While it is possible for your protagonist to open his front door and engage in a fight within a few sentences, you want to build plausibility, because these scenes are pivotal in changing your protagonist, and affecting his plotline.

Below is an example of a dramatic scene that opens slowly. *The Confessions of Max Tivoli*, by Andrew Sean Greer, is a literary novel with a fantastical twist: Its protagonist, Max Tivoli (alias Asgar) is born an old man who is doomed to get younger and younger until his death. The only thing that has ever mattered to him is his love for a young girl named Alice who, eventually, through subterfuge and complex arrangements, he manages to marry when she is much older. Of course, he must hide his condition and the truth from Alice, but one day, after she stumbles across a clue, he makes a fatal mistake and tells her the truth. She doesn't take it very well, calling him insane. Notice how, while the scene opens with Max in emotional trouble, it doesn't feel emotionally hot quite yet. But there's a sense of drama about to brew:

> It was early evening, still light, and the curtains were open. Alice lay on the other bed, fully clothed in violet plissé crepe, net frill at her neckline, gloves on her stomach as if she had spent the day out. Her coat and hat lay on the foot of the bed. Whiskey on the table, two glasses, both nearly empty; apparently I had been drinking. I came to and she was talking:
>
> "I don't want anything that's here."
>
> "Alice," I said. "I'm not myself today. There's something I could say right now that would make all the difference, isn't there? You would stay if I said it, Alice. But I'm not thinking well, I'm in a kind of cloud, so you have to think of it. Help me, Alice, what could I say? Let's think. I know it's about ten words, and not big ones. What are they?"

Your hand was on your hat. "We are strangers, Asgar. There's nothing to say."

While Greer's dramatic scene opens slowly with seemingly benign details, such as Alice's clothing, there is a definite sense of foreboding and tension. Quickly the reader realizes that the details add up to something being not right—the empty glasses, and his lack of memory, suggest he's been heavily drinking; the way Alice is dressed as if she "spent the day out"—these details establish that drama is coming.

Dramatic tension, remember, is the *potential* for things to go wrong and the feeling that conflict is still to come in a scene. A dramatic scene, therefore, should achieve a lessening of one kind of tension as the drama plays out, while also creating new tension that comes as a result of new consequences.

When Max finally tells Alice the truth about his condition, it comes with a kind of relief—the reader has been waiting a long time for him to confess. But now a new set of circumstances has evolved: Alice thinks he's crazy and wants nothing more to do with him, provoking him to desperation and despair—here comes the new tension. Ultimately, in trying to keep her from leaving him, he forces himself upon her—and ultimately fathers their only child in the act.

In a dramatic scene, you want to conclude the tension set up by earlier scenes and establish new tension for future scenes. When you open a dramatic scene you are setting the stage for an emotional interaction to follow. Therefore, you want to narrow the focus down to the characters. It's hard to pull off emotional drama if the scene has a lot of background actions or descriptions of scenery, for instance. Dramatic scenes should open with:

• Small actions

• A sense of foreboding

• An emotional intention for your protagonist—remember that drama is about feelings

• An interaction between your protagonist and at least one other character

• An interaction between your protagonist and a larger force of opposition that threatens her intentions

DRIVING YOUR PROTAGONIST (AND THE PLOT) TOWARD CHANGE

After you've opened a dramatic scene, the rest of the scene should involve a series of escalating events and interactions that intensify your protagonist's feelings through emotional complications, thus driving your character toward change. Dramatic scenes put the pressure on your character to transform so that your plot can move forward.

You can create emotional complications in a number of ways, but here are some sure-fire examples:

- **Confrontations.** Many dramatic scenes revolve around a confrontation of some kind. The abused child confronts the parent; the betrayed lover confronts the mistress; the activist confronts the politician.

- **Reunions.** Drama doesn't always have to revolve around conflict, but it should include a quality of tension. When people who have been kept apart (long-lost siblings, lovers) come together again, there is great potential for high emotion.

- **Borrowed time.** When characters have a limited amount of time together, they often react differently—say what they really feel; act more impulsively—thus creating more drama.

- **Crushed expectations.** More often than not, a character's emotional intensity comes from not getting what she wanted or expected.

- **Threat of bodily harm or death.** The specter of intense pain or death has an uncanny way of forcing characters to change, and to have emotional reactions.

Sometimes the change your protagonist undergoes is good for him—the old adage that what doesn't kill you, makes you stronger. Other times, the emotional drama that led your character to this moment of change might also equal his destruction—your particular writing style and your story's theme will dictate which kind of change your protagonist makes. One of the greatest examples of tragic character change brought on by emotional drama comes from Gustave Flaubert's novel *Madame Bovary*.

Fanciful and petulant Emma Bovary is a romantic with a wild fantasy life and a penchant for the finer things in life. She is never satisfied with what she has—she is always striving after something better. She marries Charles Bovary, a doctor, but quickly becomes bored by him and takes a lover named Rodolphe. Their affair is tempestuous, and Rodolphe is arrogant and impatient. He strings Emma along. Meanwhile, in order to cater to her image of how her life should be, Emma gets herself (and her unwitting husband) into deep debt by buying fancy clothing and fine furniture. When her creditors come calling and she cannot pay, she turns to Rodolphe to save her, and the scene that follows, which is full of hot emotional drama, drives her toward a devastating change:

"You have been crying," he said. "Why is that?"

She broke into sobs.

Rodolphe interpreted the spasm as one of love that could no longer be controlled. She made no answer to his question and he took her silence for modesty entrenched within its last defenses.

"Forgive me!" he exclaimed. "No other woman can delight me as you do! I have been a fool, a villain! I love you, and will love you for ever. What is the matter? Tell me!"

He fell on his knees.

"It's just ... that I am facing ruin, Rodolphe. You *will* lend me three thousand francs, won't you?"

"But ... but ..." he said slowly, getting to his feet, while his face assumed a serious expression.

"You know," she hurried on, "that my husband had entrusted the whole of his fortune to a lawyer. Well, the lawyer has run away. We've borrowed. The patients weren't paying up and we haven't been able to realize all our property. ..."

Ah, thought Rodolphe, who had suddenly gone very pale. So *that's* the reason for this visit.

Without the slightest show of emotion, he said: "Dear lady, I haven't got such a sum."

He wasn't lying. Had the money been at hand, he would doubtless have given it to her, unpleasant though such fine gestures usually are. ...

For a moment or two she just looked at him.

"You haven't got it?"

Several times she repeated the same words.

"You haven't got it! ... I might have spared myself this final humiliation. You never really loved me. You are just like all the others!"

All of Emma's hopes are dashed. She is finally confronted with the truth—she has gotten herself into a trouble so deep that none of her usual saviors can get her out. This scene is the pivotal moment in her storyline—she marches straight for her husband's pharmacy and eats a handful of arsenic powder, effectively committing suicide. Tragedy at its finest, heightened by drama along the way.

While drama often comes with negative emotional consequences—someone gets hurt, another gets betrayed or abandoned—your protagonist may also change for the better. When faced with the painful truth, a character may finally let go of an unhealthy relationship, or fit the missing piece into the puzzle of her tragic history. Drama can force a character to exhibit bravery and selflessness and a host of other positive qualities. What matters most is that at the end of a dramatic scene, your protagonist has had a new or enlightening emotional experience that causes her to behave, think, or feel differently.

By keeping in mind that character and plot are indelibly linked, when you drive your character toward change in a dramatic scene, you can also drive your plot to its next step. Dramatic scenes should never be gratuitous—the reason for intense emotional conflicts that change your character is to push the story forward, and get on to the next event and set of consequences.

So, when you write a dramatic scene, you also want to consider the plot consequences that will result. What will happen after a stunning revelation that your protagonist is not who he thinks he is? Where will he go when, after a dramatic fight, his mother kicks him out of the house? Remember: The emotional intensity you establish in your dramatic scene *must* lead to change, and thus consequences for your plot.

CLOSING A DRAMATIC SCENE

Because the nature of drama is to elicit emotional intensity, you don't need to end a dramatic scene with a pulse-pounding cliffhanger. You want to leave your protagonist in a sort of daze or moment of reflection. A lot has just happened to him—now he needs a beat to reflect or just pause, and so does the reader.

The scene in *Madame Bovary* that reaches such a dramatic crescendo that Emma is driven to eat arsenic powder ends like this:

> She went home in a mood of sudden peace, almost like somebody with a calm sense of duty done.

And the dramatic scene where Max Tivoli reveals himself and forces himself upon Alice ends like this:

> She simply stood there facing the door. In my nightmares, I work endlessly on a statue of my wife in just that pose, her back to me. I will never get to carve her face. Then, without turning, she walked out the door to meet her new life, and I had lost her forever this time.

Both scenes end with exposition, which distances the reader from the intensity. Unless your plan is to keep the drama high for more than one scene in a row (in which case you'll end the scene before the drama has concluded), you will want to cool down the intensity. To do this you can use exposition, as above, or end with a character's interior monologue about what has just happened, or employ scenic description of the setting that metaphorically or thematically addresses the content of the scene.

Dramatic scenes are also great precursors to epiphany scenes, for now your protagonist will need to assess what has just happened to her, or because of her.

SCENE STEALER

Leora Skolkin-Smith, author of the novel Edges, *discusses restraint in the work of Alice Munro.*

◎ ◎ ◎

Alice Munro, more than any other writer working today, has presented an enigma that directs and guides me every time I set out to write another novel. Munro is straightforward, a naturalistic realism stylist. But how she can cast spells on her readers! She can astound and amaze and move. Her gentle, sure narrative touch paradoxically creates more power and intensity in her stories, not less.

Here are two examples (and there are many) where her technique appears to be the most evident. The story I chose to select from is called "Royal Beatings," from the collection *Selected Stories*. A daughter is in a kitchen, anticipating a terrible beating from her father because her stepmother told on her and made him predictably enraged. From "Royal Beatings":

> "All right," he says, meaning that's enough, more than enough, this part is over, things can proceed. He starts to loosen his belt.
>
> Flo has stopped anyway. She has the same difficulty Rose does, a difficulty in believing that what you know must happen really will happen, then there comes a time when you can't draw back. ...
>
> At the first or maybe the second crack of pain, she draws back. She will not accept it. She runs around the room, she tries to get to the door. Her father blocks her off. Not an ounce of courage, or of stoicism in her, it would seem. She runs, she screams, she implores. Her father is after her, cracking the belt at her when he can, then abandoning it and using his hands. Bang over the ear, bang over the other ear. Back and forth, her head ringing. Bang in the face. Up against the wall and bang in the face. He shakes her and hits her against the wall, he kicks her legs. She is incoherent, insane, shrieking: Forgive me, Oh please, forgive me! Not yet, he throws her down. ...

Later, Munro adds:

> And just as there is a moment, when you are drugged, in which you feel perfectly safe, sure, unreachable, and then without warning and right next to it a moment in which you know the whole protection has

fatally cracked, though it is still pretending to hold soundly, so there is a moment now—the moment in fact, when Rose hears Flo step on the stairs—that contains for her both present peace and freedom and a sure knowledge of the whole spiraling course of events from now on.

In the hands of a lesser writer this scene might have been overplayed, far too awful and overwhelming for the reader to fully digest; it might have even felt clichéd. A beating from an abusive father is often a tired theme, used so many times in stories it's lost its power. But here Munro seamlessly, invisibly, and deftly keeps flipping the narrative point of view, penetrating the skin of her character, pulling away, distancing, and then moving inside her character once again.

By alternately stepping in and out of her character's immediate feelings in order to weave in a deep, complex analysis of the smallest moments possible, she offers a telling that permits her reader a distance long enough to integrate what is happening.

Munro teaches us, above all else, the value of narrative restraint—the lessons in knowing that each moment, no matter how tiny, contains infinite sources of seduction and meaning.

MELODRAMA

Now let's take a look at where you don't want your dramatic scenes to go—into the territory of melodrama. Author Charles Baxter writes in his book of essays, *Burning Down the House*, that melodramatic writing enacts a kind of "emotional violence against the reader." He goes on to say, "One often feels bullied in its presence, pushed around."

The reason for this bullied feeling is that melodrama contains over-the-top or excessive emotional intensity, or it shifts too quickly to be plausible. You'll recognize melodrama when the emotional content of a scene is so hot it is almost embarrassing, or so hollowly sentimental that the reader feels his intelligence has been insulted. Melodrama lacks nuance. It slams a feeling or a weak character or a theme into the reader's face without doing any deep, foundational work. In essence, melodrama *tells*—loudly, with explosions and screaming ladies—it does not show.

Less Is More: The Art of Subtlety

Have you ever seen a real gross-out, gory horror movie like *A Nightmare on Elm Street* or one of the new slasher films that seem to come out every year? The drama is all very in-your-face, with pretty young victims screaming bloody murder as they're sawed in half (for no apparent reason), and the mangled villain jumping out of the shadows with tools of violence (with no apparent motive). There is nothing subtle about that kind of horror. Subtlety—or cool emotions—goes a long way toward building drama.

In Vendela Vida's novel *Let the Northern Lights Erase Your Name*, protagonist Clarissa has undertaken a search for her mother, Olivia, who left her fourteen years before. In a powerful moment, shown in the scene below, Clarissa finally makes contact with her mother. There's plenty of opportunity for melodrama—an abandoned daughter has a lot to be angry about. But with so much at stake for the protagonist, Vida takes the quieter path:

> "I have something to tell you," I said.
> "Yes I know," she said. "You're my daughter."
> I nodded.
> "I knew the second you walked in the door," she said. The corners of her mouth turned upward. I believed she might hug me.
> "I knew this might happen one day … I thought it was Richard who would track me down. …"
> She traced a flower, transforming the line into a stem. "I don't have anything to say to him, and I don't have anything to say to you. If I had, I could have written you a letter."

The characters don't cry and fight and yell at each other. There is a delicate pause after the sentence "I believed she might hug me" in which no hug follows, and the reader suddenly knows what's going to come. Olivia is not about to stand up and become a loving mother. Clarissa is devastated, and the reader feels this devastation for her without any need for Clarissa to get emotionally loud. Her pain is evident in the silence, in the lack of tenderness from her mother. The reader can feel her grief in the previous paragraph, and in her actions that follow, without any need for melodrama.

With subtlety, you let the reader figure certain things out for himself. You let the impact of information hit in its own time, without ramming it down the reader's throat. You deliver hints and images, rather than swooning ladies and strutting saviors.

The Traits of Melodrama

Believe it or not, you can still have wild situations with large and exciting actions and not go sliding off into melodrama. The most common traits of melodrama are:

- **Sentimentality.** Think of the kinds of sentiments written in greeting cards for lovers. Think of cliché, trite, or corny dialogue. "'You are my everything,' he said passionately to her." "'The Earth wouldn't turn if I couldn't be with you,' she said to him."

- **Hysterics.** Think crying, screaming, arguing that gets too loud, too emotional, or too angry. Allowing hysterics to go on for too long is a sure-fire way to lose your readers.

- **Grand or unrealistic gestures.** These are often found at the end of sappy romance movies, in which the changed man arranges for something utterly implausible, like hiring a famous football team to serenade his love. Big gestures may work for Hollywood, but they rarely fly in writing.

- **Affected speech.** Be careful that your characters don't sound like divas and English barons (unless they are), dropping phrases that real people wouldn't likely utter. Often what seems melodramatic in a character is just a bad affectation, or poorly crafted dialogue.

- **Knee-jerk reactions.** When a character changes his mind or behavior too suddenly, flip-flopping from meek to brave, from kind to villainous, the scene can read as melodrama.

- **Descriptor overload.** On the technical level, remember that an overuse of adverbs or adjectives can often lead to a feeling of melodrama. Often just cutting them away will solve the problem.

How to Cut Melodrama

The kindest thing you can do for your writing—and the reader—is to cut the heart right out of your melodramatic passages using these techniques:

- **Check the emotional intensity.** Your first order of business is to go through your scenes looking specifically at the emotional content. Are people fist-fighting and launching soap-opera style accusations at each other? Are lovers a little too profuse in their expressions? Are your characters saying too much about their feelings rather than demonstrating them? Try to take the temperature of the emotional content of a scene. If it feels too hot, bring it down.

- **Retool dialogue.** Go over your dialogue with the finest-tooth comb around, read it aloud—heck, read it to someone else—until it sounds like things people might actually say to each other (dialogue can still be stylized, but it should not make the reader want to gag or feel insulted).

- **Smooth out character behavior.** Take the diva or the preening prince out of your characters. Get to know who they really are so that their behavior stems from true motivations, not affected or empty behavior.

- **Ground gestures in reality.** Your characters can be bold and passionate, but think twice about having them do things that are too implausible or over the top if you want them to be believed.

- **Equalize characters.** Try not to make one character so much larger than life that he seems out of proportion to the others. Villains often get very colorful in first drafts, since villainy is so much fun to write. But if your bad guy outshines your good guy in his speech and behavior, the scene will feel off kilter, and the reader will become confused about which character to pledge allegiance to.

DRAMATIC SCENE MUSE POINTS

- Dramatic scenes should focus on characters' feelings.

- Drama should reach an emotional climax and drive the protagonist toward change.

- The focus should be on character relationships and interactions.

- Character reactions should be intense, but not melodramatic.

- Dramatic scenes make for good precursors to epiphany and contemplative scenes.

15

CONTEMPLATIVE SCENES

Contemplation—the act of careful consideration or examination of thoughts and feelings and smaller details—is the antithesis of action. When a character contemplates, time slows down, or even disappears, and the scene zooms in tightly and intimately onto the character's perceptions. Outside of traditional literary fiction, contemplative scenes tend to be used sparingly. However, as you'll see throughout this chapter, for some genres and styles contemplative scenes play a crucial role.

A well-crafted contemplative scene typically:

- Has a higher percentage of interior monologue (thought) than action or dialogue

- Moves at a slower pace to allow the reader to get a deeper, more intimate look into the protagonist's inner life

- Shows the protagonist interacting with himself and the setting more than with other characters

- Allows the protagonist time to digest actions, events, and epiphanies that have come before, and to decide how to act next

- Gives pause before or after an intense scene so that the character can reflect and the reader can catch her breath

A contemplative scene rarely acts as an opening scene. Such scenes also tend not to appear too soon in a narrative, as they work best following plot events and dramatic interactions that are worthy of being digested or reflected upon. Too many of these scenes in a row create a sense of drag, and so scenes that involve some action should be interspersed among contemplative scenes. Contemplative scenes contain more thoughts, considerations, and reflections on events than actions.

INTERIOR MONOLOGUE

The defining characteristic of a contemplative scene is that your character spends more time thinking than he does in action or speech. These passages of thought are referred to as interior monologue (since they happen inside the character's mind), and are meant to reveal something to the reader. These thoughts will be overheard by the reader, and therefore have bearing on plot and character development in each scene.

While the old convention was to set off thoughts by putting them in italics, I'm more of a fan of embedding thoughts within the narrative voice as simple, elegant exposition.

For example, in Martha Sherrill's novel *The Ruins of California*, young Inez Ruin, who goes back and forth between her divorced parents, thinks about her father in passages of interior monologue:

> During the lull between his calls and letters, it's not that my father was dead in my mind, exactly. He was kept on hold, cinematic freeze frame — the pause button not released until I picked up the phone or stepped off the plane.

Interior monologue is not time-based, which is why it tends to feel slow. There's no action involved. Notice how Inez's thoughts feel free-floating. You don't get a sense of when or where, but a general feeling for what she thinks about her father. Still, it evokes feelings and sets a tone and helps the readers better understand the protagonist.

Here's a passage of interior monologue from José Saramago's novel *Blindness*, in which it's a little more obvious what the point-of-view character, the doctor's wife—the only character in the narrative who has not gone blind—is thinking:

> Now, with her eyes fixed on the scissors hanging on the wall, the doctor's wife was asking herself, What use is my eyesight? It had exposed her to greater horror than she could ever have imagined. It had convinced her that she would rather be blind, nothing else.

Notice how her thought "What use is my eyesight?" is in first person, so the reader knows these are her thoughts. But the exposition that follows is still coming from her point of view and can also be considered her thoughts.

Interior monologue is very intimate and allows readers to temporarily step inside the mind of your character. Characters really only have a few ways of reflecting in a narrative in a way that invites the reader in to experience it. Your protagonist can speak his thoughts to another character; he can write his thoughts down; or, through interior monologue, he can think important reflections. Dialogue fails as a contemplative technique because most of us don't reflect aloud—we quietly ruminate.

Since interior monologue naturally slows down the pace of your prose, use it sparingly in other scenes. Contemplative scenes, however, are your opportunity to delve into the world of thoughts, and that is why these scenes need to be strategically placed in your narrative. You want to purposely use a contemplative scene to slow things down and to shed insight on your character that dialogue and action simply can't convey.

OPENING CONTEMPLATIVE SCENES

In the aftermath of an action, suspense, or dramatic scene in which big plot events and emotional extremes were central, you want to signal to the reader that a slowdown is taking place from the very beginning of the scene by getting to the contemplation early. If you open a contemplative scene with a lot of action, for instance, the reader may feel unfairly detoured by the contemplation that follows. Some of the most common ways to open a contemplative scene include opening with interior monologue, setting description, or transitional action.

Opening With Interior Monologue

The main requirement for opening your contemplative scene with interior monologue is that the character's thoughts be related to the scene that came before. Don't force the readers to guess what your protagonist is reflecting on—make it clear.

In Charles Dickens's novel *Great Expectations*, protagonist Pip—a young boy who lives with his older sister and her husband—is accosted one morning by an escaped convict who demands that Pip bring him food and drink. Out of terror, Pip does so at great risk to himself. The next scene, which also happens to be the first scene of chapter four, opens with Pip reflecting on the fact that he has not been arrested or punished for what he's done:

> I fully expected to find a Constable in the kitchen, waiting to take me up. But not only was there no Constable there, but no discovery had yet been made of the robbery.

The opening lines let the reader know that this is going to be a scene in which Pip is reflecting on his actions. A couple of lines is enough to let the reader know there will be thinking going on, but the interior monologue can go on for much longer if needed. Back to our *Great Expectations* example: Though the scene includes some small actions, for much of the remaining scene, Pip can barely pay attention to what is happening around him, he's so busy focused on his inner experience, worrying about the trouble he's sure to get in:

> Joe and I going to church, therefore, must have been a moving spectacle for compassionate minds. Yet, what I suffered outside was nothing to what I underwent within. The terrors that had assailed me whenever Mrs. Joe had gone near the pantry, or out of the room, were only to be equaled by the remorse with which my mind dwelt on what my hands had done.

When you open with interior monologue, you signal the reader that the character has something on his mind and that there may be a lot more interior monologue to come within the scene. It's just a nice, fluid way to transition into a contemplative scene.

The key to remember here is that thoughts are slow and timeless, so pages and pages of them will start to drag your pace down to a crawl. You want to make sure that the emphasis of a contemplative scene is on thoughts, but that they are not the sole content of the scene.

Opening With Setting Description

Setting description is a nice way to open a scene because it grounds the reader in physical reality first—the reader can see where the protagonist is before she delves into his inner turmoil. But this technique works especially well when you can use the setting as a kind of reflective surface off which the character can bounce or form his thoughts, like in the example below from Jill McCorkle's novel *Carolina Moon*.

Mack's wife, Sarah, has been in a coma for years, though he still feels the need to be faithful to her. Yet he's falling for another woman, June, and in the very bedroom where Sarah's sleeping body lies, June and he embraced. In the next scene, he's deeply reflective and concerned.

McCorkle opens with a description of the setting that evokes images of family—which Mack no longer has—and uses it as a segue into Mack's internal world:

Mack sits on the porch and watches the lights go out in the houses around him. The house to his left has long been dark, the children who run screaming all afternoon tucked into their beds and sleeping peacefully. He imagines the tired mama with her feet propped up, belly swollen, dim lamp swaying overhead. Even the college kids have turned in for the night, the only window lit being the stark white bathroom that glares in full view. Sarah used to wonder why they didn't get a shade, a curtain; instead, there was an all-day parade of young men with their backs turned to the world outside.

Notice how Mack's thoughts are stirred up in relationship to the environment he shared with his wife—a very natural and realistic way for a character to begin reflecting on events. As he looks around their neighborhood, there's no way to avoid thinking about her, and thus his guilt over falling for June, so the setting is effectively used as a way to get his thoughts on the subject of his wife. The scene could have opened something like this: "Mack felt guilty about kissing June in front of Sarah," but that's a narrative technique with no emotional weight. The way McCorkle does it, the reader sees the world that Mack shared with Sarah and understands his complex thoughts and feelings on the subject better. The scene has a more dramatic impact.

When you use setting details to elicit a character's thoughts and feelings, your character's emotional responses will feel more natural, and the details will give the illusion of action, which a contemplative scene is going to be scarce on. As Mack's thoughts interact with his environment, readers get a sense of action, even though really there isn't any. It's important to keep the energy from falling completely flat in a contemplative scene, and a great way to keep it alive is by having the character's thoughts interact with the setting.

Opening With Transitional Action

Sometimes a contemplative scene is, in essence, the continuation of the scene that came before, so you may begin by concluding the action of the prior scene. For example, at the end of a cliffhanger scene, a woman may have just watched her home erupt in flames. In the next scene, she may be standing by, watching the firemen who are putting out the flames, and reflecting on how her life is now going to change.

Ending a scene before an action is resolved—a suspense or cliffhanger ending—is actually a good technique to use because it keeps the reader worried about the character. If you're coming off a scene with a cliffhanger ending, you have many opportunities to open a contemplative scene by concluding the actions of the previous scene.

When you do this, don't worry about keeping that same cliffhanger energy alive; when you move into contemplative scenes, it's okay to bring the tension and the energy down—in fact, that's the point. Keep the actions small, to a minimum, and let them quickly lead to contemplation.

For example, in Steven Sherrill's wonderful allegorical novel *The Minotaur Takes a Cigarette Break*, the protagonist is M—an immortal Minotaur (half man, half bull) working as a line cook in a Southern restaurant. He's lonely and awkward and has trouble making friends, but a fellow waitress,

Kelly, has steadily been making overtures to him for months. In one scene they wind up making love, but midway through, Kelly has an epileptic seizure. Afraid and unsure of how to deal with human afflictions, M flees the scene, and neither M nor the reader knows if Kelly is okay or not; for all the reader knows, he has consigned her to death. The next scene concludes his flight as M is driving away from the scene:

> Pulling to a stop at the traffic light where Independence Boulevard goes from four narrow lanes to six narrow lanes, the Vega stalls and the Minotaur has to pump the throttle to restart it. He hates this stretch of road. David, a font of useless knowledge, says it's the busiest and most dangerous five miles of asphalt in the entire state.

Notice Sherrill's careful choice of actions here—M is fleeing the scene of Kelly's seizure. The actions at the opening of the next scene serve mainly to let the reader know where M is in relationship to the last scene (and also to offer a metaphor for where he is in his life: stalled and possibly in danger if Kelly is dead). Despite the fact that Kelly might be in mortal jeopardy, M is not a human man who knows to call 911, and the reader is wondering what he's going to do next and how he could just leave her like that. Notice how Sherrill shifts gears and moves quickly into the realm of thoughts.

Make sure in a contemplative scene that opens with transitional action that the action relates to or concludes the action from the prior scene, offers some thematic or metaphoric subtext, and then move quickly into the realm of your characters' thoughts.

CHARACTER AND PLOT

Now that you've got an idea of how to open a contemplative scene, it's important to keep in mind the fundamental purpose of this type of scene: to get as intimate as possible with your protagonist as he experiences the consequences of the significant situation introduced in that very first scene. You want to use these reflective scenes to move into his most inner thoughts and reflections. When you focus on your protagonist's thoughts for a prolonged period of time, the reader gets a very intimate experience of his feelings and perceptions. Because of their inherent slowed quality, you don't need many of these scenes—only a few—and usually, as noted earlier, after your character has undergone something intense, dramatic, or painful. You want to create a realistic pause for him—and the reader—to process what he's experienced.

In order to keep the contemplation relevant to your plot, you want to be sure that your protagonist:

- Has realistic and appropriate responses to a plot event

- Grapples with something that has recently happened in the narrative (the prior scene is ideal), or that is about to happen

- Uses the contemplation scene to make a plan of action, weigh his options, or make some sort of decision related to plot events

Contemplative scenes are not a time for drama—this is where the protagonist tries to make sense of the tragedy, wild success, or unexpected turn that has just taken place in his life.

Let's look at these three points in a scene from Walker Percy's novel *The Moviegoer*. In it, playboy Binx Bolling keeps falling for the wrong women—those who don't love him, and those he doesn't truly love. When he unwittingly falls for Kate Cutrer, a suicidal beauty (and also his cousin), nobody is pleased about it, especially not Kate's mother, his aunt. Yet their relationship offers the two unlikely lovers a kind of redemption, and after spending a weekend together at Carnivale in New Orleans, Binx is deeply reflective and worried ... and in love with Kate. Here is a moment mid-scene where he begins to think about what has happened:

> Nothing remains but desire, and desire comes howling down Elysian Fields like a mistral. My search has been abandoned; it is no match for my aunt, her rightness and her despair, her despairing of me and her despairing of herself. Whenever I take leave of my aunt after one of her serious talks, I have to find a girl.
>
> Fifty minutes of waiting for Kate on the ocean wave and I am beside myself. What has happened to her? She has spoken to my aunt and kicked me out. There is nothing to do but call Sharon at the office. The little

pagoda of aluminum and glass, standing in the neutral ground of Elysian Fields at the very heart of the uproar of a public zone, is trim and pretty on the outside but evil-smelling within. Turning slowly around, I take note of the rhymes in pencil and the sad cartoons of solitary lovers; the wire thrills and stops and thrills and in the interval there comes into my ear my own breath as if my very self stood beside me and would not speak. The phone does not answer. Has she quit?

Notice how this scene achieves the points laid out above. First, Binx grapples with his difficult feelings: He's torn between his desire for Kate, his aunt's disapproval, and his own tendency to use women as a distraction from his feelings. Second, he comes to a decision here, too, to call Sharon—he trusts her opinion and wants to run his feelings by someone who will not shame or scold him. Finally, his reactions, while they are emotional, are appropriate—here he finally has fallen in love with someone, with a history of suicidal tendencies, no less—and she hasn't shown up to meet him as she said she would. His fear and anxiety are getting the best of him.

When you slow things down to reveal thoughts and feelings in this kind of a narrative way, you want to be sure that your protagonist works out issues specific to plot events, and that he comes to a point of change or choice as a result. While people contemplate all kinds of things in real life, from the good to the downright dull, in fiction, musings about how great life is tend to get boring, fast. Save contemplation for where it is most needed—on that which is difficult.

DRAMATIC TENSION

In chapter seven we talked about giving your protagonist at least one new plot situation or piece of information to deal with in each scene, and a catalyst or antagonist to interact with. However, a contemplative scene is the one scene type where you're not obligated to do either of those things. What you *must* do, however, is find a way to keep dramatic tension alive without much action and with limited interaction with other characters. How do you do this?

- **Include internal conflict.** The reason for a contemplative scene is to allow the characters and the reader to digest and make sense of complex decisions and actions that have taken place in the plot. So, whether your character is forced to have time to himself—through jail, kidnapping, or just waking up alone one morning—or feels the need to take that time to understand what has happened to him, the main criteria is that in the scene he actively struggles to come to terms with something, like Binx Bolling did. You want to show that there is struggle and fear and worry in your protagonist's mind. He should be thinking about his options and wondering what will happen. He should not know until the scene's end what he wants or needs to do next.

- **Include unspecified danger.** An absence of action or other characters does not necessarily mean that a scene will feel relaxed. People can contemplate in dangerous situations too, so you can keep the tension alive by creating a sense of danger on the horizon or anxiety in the moment. Maybe your protagonist has been kidnapped, but the captors have left him alone for a few hours. Maybe a man's beloved wife has gone missing and you show him walking through his house, fingering her possessions, wondering what has happened to her and if she is okay.

- **Create an eerie or tense atmosphere.** Use the setting to your advantage. We'll discuss this more in the next section, but consider how weather, physical geography, and objects can serve to create an uncomfortable and tense environment for your character to contemplate in. For example, if you want to create a tense contemplative scene, and you are considering whether to set it in the protagonist's sunny, cheerful backyard, or on the side of a road after his car has broken down, consider that the lonely road in the broken down car has far more potential for tension—that is, creating a sense of potential conflict or crisis for the protagonist.

For example, in Camille DeAngelis's novel *Mary Modern*, a blend of the literary and the fantastic, Lucy Morrigan, who is infertile and the daughter of a genetic scientist, is preparing to clone a child through the use of her grandmother's DNA and her own womb. As she searches for a clipping of her grandmother's hair, she ventures into the attic, where she finds the scrap of cloth that bears drops of her grandmother's blood. Through careful description, DeAngelis sets an eerie mood for the act that Lucy is contemplating:

> Most attics are unpleasant places: cobwebs swaying in the breath of stale wind stirred up by the opening of the door, or perhaps a draft through a hole in the roof or a broken windowpane: the smells of mildew and dust and mothballs; the fear that any given thing you touch will fall to pieces in your hands. Even the natural oil on a clean fingertip leaves a stain on old wood. Why come here, why putter through all these material reminders of lives long since lived?

These careful details bring about a feeling of decay and decrepitude. As Lucy contemplates the illegal act of cloning her own kin, these setting and object details create a feeling of tension and foreboding, which causes the reader to worry about the consequences of Lucy's actions.

In a contemplative scene your setting details should act as mirrors for the emotional content of your character's contemplation. A despairing person might best contemplate suicide in a lonely setting—a deserted room, an empty hotel. A person contemplating a rash and violent act, in contrast, could be reflected in a loud, overwhelming setting, such as a carnival, or you might find objects in the setting that speak to a feeling of anger—a lit match or a line of marching red ants.

SETTING

Contemplation scenes rely heavily upon mood and ambiance. In some cases, setting might even be the reason your protagonist has so much time to think; for instance, a protagonist in prison, trapped in a cave, or making a long, slow journey will obviously have a little extra time on his hands to contemplate the state of his life. As your scene progresses, you have an opportunity to focus on the small details that often get passed over in dramatic or action-driven scenes. If your narrative is about a family tragedy, for instance, a contemplative scene should, through the specific setting details you choose, convey a sense of melancholy and sorrow through dark colors, low light, and any significant objects that can help to convey this mood.

More importantly though, since there is very little action in a contemplative scene, you can weave in setting details intermittently with interior monologue to give your protagonist something physical off of which to bounce his thoughts and feelings so that he isn't just sitting in a vacuum.

In this excerpt of a scene from the novel *Cold Mountain*, notice the careful attention Charles Frazier gives to setting details:

> The women stood out in water to their calves, slapping the clothes against smooth stones and rinsing and wringing them, then draping them over nearby bushes to dry. Some talked and laughed, and others hummed snatches of song. They had their skirt tails caught up between their legs and tucked into their waistbands to keep them from the water. To Inman they looked like they were wearing the oriental pantaloons of the Zouave regiments, whose soldiers looked so strangely bright and festive scattered dead across a battlefield.

The use of details like "smooth stones" and the women's "skirt tails caught up between their legs" direct Inman's attention—they become focal points for his thoughts and distractions from his own discomfort—after all, the man has been walking for days. He's tired, dry, and dirty, with no other company than his own mind. His interaction with the setting (in this instance the women are essentially setting objects, since he only observes them, and does not interact with them) also reminds the reader of the central goal of the narrative—that he is walking back to one woman in specific—the love he left behind for the war.

Focusing on specific setting details throughout a contemplative scene—and not just at the beginning, as we saw earlier in this chapter—not only creates a vivid atmosphere and mood, but also keeps the pace from slowing to an absolute drag. Contemplative scenes have far less action or character interaction to keep the reader engaged, remember. Here you can give the reader a chance to literally stop and smell the roses, or recoil at the stench of a battle scene, letting impression sink in and atmosphere build toward decisions that your protagonist will need to make.

ENDING A CONTEMPLATIVE SCENE

Since the pace of a contemplative scene is more like that of a gentle stream than of rushing rapids, when it comes time to end it, you will want to change the energy just slightly in preparation for the next scene.

After contemplation comes action. Once a character has had time to think and reflect, he will need to take some kind of action to get the plot moving forward again.

So, depending on the type of scene you intend to come next, here are some considerations for ending a contemplative scene on an up tempo, to build back toward action:

- **End with an action cliffhanger.** After all that myopic thinking or paying careful attention to his surroundings, your protagonist may suddenly find himself backed into a corner, a gun at his neck, or a cliff at his back. Contemplative scenes often allow other characters to catch up to your protagonist—after all, he's just been sitting around thinking. A cliffhanger ending is great preparation for an action scene to follow.

- **End with a moment of decision.** If your character has been grappling with a dilemma, the ending is a great place to show the reader that he has made a decision. You don't necessarily need to give away what the decision is, but you could, for instance, end a scene in which the protagonist has been debating whether to tell her husband she's been cheating, with her picking up the phone and dialing him; or a man might grab his gun, get in his car, or do something else decisive that lets the reader know something has been decided. The decision should, of course, relate to whatever issue the protagonist has been grappling with in that scene.

- **End with a surprise.** Because contemplative scenes are so quiet and slow, the reader is not focused on the characters or events that are ostensibly taking place outside of the scene. This leaves room for all manner of surprises. While the character is sitting thinking, something outside of his control could happen, and the very end of a contemplative scene is a great place to drop such a surprise in.

- **End with foreshadowing.** Since some contemplative scenes don't naturally lend themselves to action in the scene at hand, you can end the scene with a bit of foreshadowing that tells the reader there will be action, or dialogue, or some kind of pace-quickening, in the next scene.

Here's an example of the end of a contemplative scene from Jeffrey Eugenides' novel *The Virgin Suicides*, about a group of boys captivated by a family of sisters who all meet the same tragic fate as a result of their domineering parents. The contemplative scene ends with the boys reading from the diary of the youngest sister, Cecilia, which they have illicitly obtained:

> Occasional references to this or that conspiracy crop up—the Illuminati, the Military-Industrial complex—but she only feints in that direction, as though the names are so many vague chemical pollutants. From invective she shifts without pause into her poetic reveries again. A couplet about summer from a poem she never finished, is quite nice, we think:
> *The trees like lungs filling with air*
> *My sister, the mean one, pulling my hair*
> The fragment is dated June 26, three days after she returned from the hospital, when we used to see her lying in the front-yard grass.

Cecilia was hospitalized for an attempted suicide before, so harking back to this drops a note of discord that tells us something is coming in the next scene. There is also an air of remembrance about the previous scene. As they recount the details of Cecilia's journey, they also remember her, setting up the readers for the next big action, when Cecilia succeeds at taking her own life:

> Little is known of Cecilia's state of mind on the last day of her life. According to Mr. Lisbon, she seemed pleased about her party. When he went downstairs to check on the preparations, he found Cecilia standing on a chair, tying balloons to the ceiling with red and blue ribbons.

The next scene opens with the harsh reality of Cecilia's fate, moving quickly from exposition into action as the boys revisit the last day of Cecilia's life.

No matter how you choose to end your contemplative scene, you want to keep in mind that you are setting up the next scene, and that action follows contemplation very nicely because it adds energy back to the equation of your narrative. You may choose to use your contemplative scene to lead your character toward change, toward action, toward drama or suspense to suit the demands of your plot. Rarely do you need two contemplative scenes back to back, however, as this may just slow your pace too much.

CONTEMPLATIVE SCENE MUSE POINTS

- Use contemplative scenes to slow down action in the narrative.
- Signal that the contemplative scene has begun as quickly as possible.
- Focus on the protagonist's inner life.
- The protagonist must grapple with a conflict, dilemma, or decision.
- Utilize setting details to create dramatic tension and set a mood.
- Use the end of the scene to shift the energy toward action.

16
DIALOGUE SCENES

Dialogue is one of the most versatile elements of fiction writing because it can achieve multiple effects. When done well, dialogue can even be a scene-stealer. Most of the great lines in literature were *spoken* by characters, not narrated. This chapter will focus on scenes that are composed primarily of dialogue—not scenes with the occasional line of dialogue tossed in.

Dialogue scenes find their way into narratives of all genre types because of the versatility of conversation, so undoubtedly you'll wind up using these scenes. When dialogue is done right, it tends to feel fast, and therefore can be used to pick up the pace and propel your plot and characters forward. Dialogue is a great conflict builder too, as characters can argue, fight, and profess sentiments in words. It's also a wonderful medium for building tension, as characters jockey for power, love, and understanding.

OPENING A DIALOGUE SCENE

Before you start the scene, you'll want to decide if you're going to use dialogue to convey action, or to reveal character, plot, or backstory information. One of the most common errors is the use of dialogue as filler, with characters discussing the time or the weather. Don't make the assumption that dialogue scenes need to open in the middle of a conversation, either—in fact, this is often a confusing way to open a scene. A dialogue scene can open with one of the elements discussed in chapter two—for instance, you can use a scenic launch, or a narrative, action, or character launch—but then move quickly into dialogue. Here are some essential guidelines for opening this type of scene:

- Ground the reader in the setting before the conversation begins.
- Let the conversation begin within the first couple of paragraphs.
- Involve your protagonist in the conversation.
- Make it clear who is speaking to whom.
- Infuse conflict or opposition into the dialogue.

In J.D. Salinger's classic novel, *The Catcher in the Rye*, there are many dialogue scenes between protagonist Holden Caulfield and the minor characters who populate the story, and these serve many of the functions of dialogue as described later in this chapter. Salinger is good at setting up dialogue scenes so that they reveal character without being confusing. Here's an example of one such scene, in which Holden has come back to the dorm late and wants to talk to his roommate, Ackley:

> A tiny bit of light came through the shower curtains and all from our room, and I could see him lying in bed. I knew damn well he was wide awake. "Ackley?" I said. "Y'awake?"
>
> "Yeah."
>
> It was pretty dark and I stepped on somebody's shoe on the floor and damn near fell on my head. Ackley sort of sat up in bed and leaned on his arm. He had a lot of white stuff on his face, for his pimples. He looked sort of spooky in the dark. "What the hellya doing anyway?" I said.
>
> "Wuddya mean what the hell am I doing? I was tryna *sleep* before you guys started making all that noise. What the hell was the fight about, anyhow?"

Notice how the scene meets all the criteria laid out above—we're grounded through the setting, we can see that it takes place in the dorm room. The protagonist, Holden, is the one coming into the room. We know it's him because we're in his point of view, and we know he's talking to Ackley because he calls him by name. The dialogue then begins almost immediately after we know where we are, and it's full of conflict—he's ticked off his roommate by waking him up, so there's potential for the conversation to be fraught with further complication.

Though you want to get into the dialogue fairly quickly, you don't necessarily have to do so in the first sentence—it may even start a few paragraphs in. Remember, grounding the reader in physical details is important so she doesn't get confused, but the details should also reinforce qualities about the protagonist. This is a coming-of-age story, after all, so Salinger invites us in to the dorm-life experience through his choice of details.

DIALOGUE AND BIG REVEALS

Dialogue is a wonderfully versatile technique for giving the reader information necessary to drive the plot forward or deepen character understanding, without resorting to exposition. Through dialogue you can show the reader who your protagonist is, reveal the effect the protagonist has on other characters, and introduce new plot information that drives the narrative forward.

Revealing Character

One of the best ways to express your protagonist's personality, feelings, and perceptions is through his own words, rather than in exposition. Doing so allows the reader to feel as though he is right there in the same place as the character, getting to know him through direct experience. When the purpose of a dialogue scene is to reveal character, you want to:

- **Show the character speaking under pressure or in conflict.** Always avoid mundane conversation.

- **Let your protagonist's true nature come through in words.** Is he brave? Then show him speaking words of hope and courage. Is he seductive? Let him pull out all verbal stops to seduce every woman he meets.

- **Show him expressing his feelings or thoughts about the significant situation or the most recent plot events.** Through the character's internal dialogue and external action, you can show his personality.

In Truman Capote's brilliant novella *Breakfast at Tiffany's*, his main character, Holly Golightly, is revealed to the reader through memorable dialogue. Holly is rash and bold and sexy and girlish all at once, and this is conveyed every time she opens her mouth or appears in a scene.

The first time the narrator meets Holly, it's via an exchange she has with a neighbor:

> The voice that came back, welling up from the bottom of the stairs, was silly-young and self-amused. "Oh darling, I am sorry. I lost the goddamn key."
>
> "You cannot go on ringing my bell. You must please, please have yourself a key made."
>
> "But I lose them all."
>
> "I work. I have to sleep." Mr. Yunioshi shouted. "But always you are ringing my bell. ..."
>
> "Oh, *don't* be angry, you *dear* little man: I won't do it again. And if you promise not to be angry"—her voice was coming nearer, she was climbing the stairs—"I might let you take those pictures we mentioned."

Though the phrase "silly-young and self-amused" tells us about Holly's tone, her words speak for themselves. If she is sorry, as she claims, then why does she refer to it as the "goddamn key"? Clearly, in her worldview, the key is at fault, not she. She calls her neighbor *darling* and *dear* to soften him up, and then promises him a few lines later that if he lets her off the hook she will in turn let him "take those pictures we mentioned."

We suspect that Holly is used to manipulating with her charm and beauty to get her way. Just a few paragraphs into the scene, Holly Golightly makes an impression and demonstrates her personality.

When you use dialogue to reveal character, the dialogue should be stylized and suited specifically to the character. An educated person speaks differently from someone who has never learned grammar. A rude person will say rude things and insult people with her words.

Revealing Plot Information

One of the most important uses of dialogue—and the most necessary in a plot-driven narrative—is to reveal pertinent information that moves the plot forward, changes your protagonist, creates conflict, or leads the protagonist toward an epiphany. I like to think of this as the "Luke, I am your father" technique. The moment at which Darth Vader tells Luke he is not only his sworn nemesis, but also his father, is a huge turning point in the movie's plot and in the development of Luke's character. It forces Luke to choose between good and evil, and tests his ability to resist his own destruction. Now, not all reveals are this epic, but dialogue is one of the best ways to drop these emotional bombs and drive the plot forward.

When using dialogue to reveal plot information, consider the following:

- **The information must be earned.** Avoid *deus ex machina* techniques. (This term comes from the Greek and referred originally to when a god dropped into a play to solve difficult entanglements. In fiction it refers to any overly simple or convenient technique or device that solves difficult problems without any actual effort on the part of the characters.)

- **You need to show your protagonist's emotional reaction to the new information.** The reader needs to see the character exclaim, gasp, shout, speak a word of surprise.

- **You must place the information drop in the middle of the scene or at the end to achieve the greatest emotional impact.** This helps to create a sense of urgency in the reader.

Here's an example of a big revelation from Maryanne Stahl's novel *Forgive the Moon* that both reveals character and drives the plot forward. Amanda Kincaid comes to a Long Island beach resort for an annual family vacation. Her oldest daughter has left for college; her husband is involved with another woman, and their twenty-year marriage is crumbling; and her mother, who suffered from schizophrenia, has recently died in an accident. The scene opens with Amanda's new lover coming to the door while her father is visiting her cottage. Her father doesn't know who the man is, but from the opening of the scene there's discord, a feeling that something is going to come to a head. And it does, but not in one fell swoop—the scene builds slowly and plausibly toward the revelation.

In the exchange of dialogue below, which falls in the middle of the scene, Amanda and her father—who have never been close—begin talking about mundane details, like Amanda's childhood fear of lightning, and segue to more serious topics of the past, such as her mother's illness, then Amanda's accusation that her father retreated not only from his ill wife, but his children. At first her father is shocked, but then he asks her a question that begins the process of his revelation about her piano teacher:

"Were you angry, Amanda, about my relationship with Gloria?"

"What?" Gloria Price had taught me to play the piano, redirecting my adolescent pain and fueling the fire of my nascent passion for music. Eventually, she'd moved away, but not before she'd made me promise to pursue my talent.

Gloria's voice was the first auditory hallucination my mother had ever described to me.

"Gloria," I repeated.

Suddenly, as though I'd been physically struck, I realized what my father was saying. "What do you mean?"

His fingers rubbed the bridge of his nose beneath his glasses, lifting them till I thought they would fall off, but they stayed. He dropped his hands to his lap.

"Gloria and I," he said softly.

My stomach quivered, as though the low, rolling thunder outside had slipped in through the screen and become particles of air. My mouth grew watery, a sign I was going to vomit. I moved to lean toward the sink and as I did, sugar spilled out of the torn packet, pouring across one of my father's shoes. ...

"Amanda," he began, reaching his hand around to my forehead. I slipped away from him.

"It's the tea," I said without looking at him. "The acid."

My father retreated toward the table and sat back in his chair. He began again. "Your mother and I never discussed Gloria," he said, picking up his spoon and dropping it into his empty mug. "Not in any rational way."

I recalled my mother's accusations. Gloria was her enemy, trying to harm her, trying to steal her children: all said to be hallucinations, all dismissed as evidence of illness. Now it turned out my mother had been right after all. She'd been right and she'd been ill, both at the same time.

No one had believed her.

The revelation of her father's affair is doubly devastating as Amanda realizes that, due to her mother's illness, they thought she was just being paranoid. There are a number of elements in this revelation scene that any writer can learn from. First, Stahl starts the scene with her protagonist caught in an unbalanced situation: Amanda is reluctantly spending time with her father, when her lover comes to the door. She uses subtext to create foreshadowing: The lover's appearance points toward the other affair—her father's—that the scene reveals. Then, she uses segues, small transitions between related topics, to create a sense of conversation and a realistically measured pace. The conversation feels natural, like how people really talk. She uses her setting very well too: Two family members jammed into a small space creates a sense of tension, of something waiting to explode. And then there is the weather. In the opening pages of the scene, Amanda's lover says to her, "Feels like a storm," and the author continues to pepper in details about the weather. (Of course, the real storm coming is an emotional one.) Then there's the element of opposition: Amanda has a feeling that her father wants to talk, but she doesn't want to, so she tries a few unsuccessful strategies to urge her father to go to bed so they won't have to, building a tense atmosphere. And then—yes, there's more—the author shows how this information affects the protagonist: Not only does Amanda become physically ill, she curses at her father and then walks down the hallway, where she kicks his shoe in anger.

Revelations are best when they are complex and slowly built toward—so that they are not just two people standing in a room shouting words at each other. Use as many of the core scene elements as you can. Once the revelation comes, it should alter your protagonist in some way; whether her plot changes, or just her feelings, revelations should lead to some kind of shift.

INFUSING YOUR DIALOGUE SCENES WITH TENSION AND SUBTEXT

Now that we've looked at how to use a dialogue scene to reveal important character and plot information, let's look at how to build tension through opposition in an exchange and how to use subtext to keep even your most heated exchanges from turning into meaningless shouting matches. No matter what you want to reveal through your dialogue, infusing it with additional elements ensures a richer, more layered scene.

Creating Tension Through Tug-of-War Exchanges

In a strong fiction narrative, characters should want things from each other—information, affection, favors, material goods, and so on. The act of wanting powers both conflict and drama. When there's something desired, there is the potential for loss and gain—the essence of good drama. Dialogue should be, on some level, an act of bartering in order to keep tension alive during the course of the dialogue. I call this technique tug-of-war. To use this approach in dialogue, it works best to think of each character as both asking for something and withholding something at the same time. Use dialogue tug-of-war when you need to demonstrate differing points of view or illustrate the dynamics of a relationship. This approach also works when your characters are:

- Exchanging insults or arguing over something

- Trying to manipulate another character

- Trying to seduce another character, or resist seduction themselves

- Attempting to convince another character of a painful truth

- Fending off untrue or unjust accusations

Here's an example from Alice Hoffman's novel *The Ice Queen*, in which the unnamed narrator is weighing whether or not to tell her brother Ned a shocking secret she has turned up about his wife. What the conversation reveals is that Ned has a secret too, but in order to learn each other's secrets, they would have to give up their own first, and neither character is willing to do that yet:

"So are you sure you don't want to know any secrets?"

"Do you?"

"You have secrets?" I was surprised. ...

"Unknown truths," my brother joked. "At least to you. Known to me, of course. At least in theory. What I know and what I don't know, I'm not sure I can be the judge of that."

"Oh forget it." I was annoyed.

The tug-of-war style of conversation delays the reader's access to Ned's secret (a piece of plot information, incidentally), thus building tension. Then the tension mounts even more when the narrator keeps *her* secret a little longer. The scene shows the reader that both characters have an investment in keeping secrets, but the reader has to keep going to find out how these secrets will converge, and what effect they'll have when brought to light.

Here's another tug-of-war example, from J.M. Coetzee's Nobel Prize–winning novel, *Disgrace*. In apartheid-fueled South Africa, white professor David Lurie has come to stay with his slightly estranged daughter Lucy to flee scrutiny after a scandal involving an affair with one of his college students. In trying to escape one terrible event, he becomes a part of another, when his daughter and he are attacked by black men in her home as a territorial act. David is badly burned, and Lucy is ostensibly raped—but David doesn't know for sure, since he was not in the room with her and she won't tell him what happened. However, he quickly urges Lucy to press charges against the boy. Lucy has her own political and personal reasons for not wanting to do so. And there is the other, unspoken subtext, that if not for his own bad deeds, he wouldn't even have been there for her at all. Notice the feeling of tug-of-war between them—how they both want something and are resisting something at the same time:

Sitting across the table from him, Lucy draws a deep breath, gathers herself, then breathes out again and shakes her head.

"Can I guess?" he says. "Are you trying to remind me of something?"

"Am I trying to remind you of what?"

"Of what women undergo at the hands of men?"

"Nothing could be farther from my thoughts. This has nothing to do with you, David. You want to know why I have not laid a particular charge with the police? I will tell you, as long as you agree not to raise the subject again. The reason is that, as far as I am concerned, what happened to me is a purely private matter. In another time, in another place it might be held to a public matter. But in this place, at this time, it is not. It is my business, mine alone."

"This place being what?"

"This place being South Africa."

"I don't agree. I don't agree with what you are doing. Do you think that by meekly accepting what happened to you, you can set yourself apart from farmers like Ettinger? Do you think what happened here was an exam: if you come through, you get a diploma and safe conduct into the future, or a sign to paint on the door lintel that will make the plague pass you by? That is not how vengeance works, Lucy. Vengeance is like a fire. The more it devours, the hungrier it gets."

"Stop it, David! I don't want to hear this talk of plagues and fires. I am not just trying to save my skin. If that is what you think, you miss the point entirely."

Notice in both of the previous examples, there's a sense of movement, of action, even though the authors don't provide the reader with any actual physical movements. This has to do with the pace of conversations—the tug-of-war approach gives the exchanges a quality of movement by infusing them with emotional energy. The respective conversations bounce back and forth between characters, and carry with them a sense of change.

Playing Up Subtext

While the tug-of-war technique is excellent for increasing the tension in a dialogue scene, you don't want your exchanges to become a meaningless volley of words. The key to keeping that from happening? Subtext. People don't always say what they really mean; they withhold information and feelings, use language to manipulate and barter and hint at things. Because of this, you have a lot of opportunity to play with your subtext.

Here's an example of a powerful subtext at work in a conversation from David Guterson's novel *Snow Falling on Cedars*. Ishmael Chambers grew up on San Piedro Island, Washington, and as a young teenager had a brief love affair with a Japanese girl named Hatsue. Their relationship was cut short, however, when Hatsue and her family and many more Japanese residents of the island were moved to the internment camp Manzanar after the attack on Pearl Harbor.

Now, years later, Ishmael is back in town to write about a trial in which Hatsue's husband is accused of murdering a local fisherman. Hatsue and Ishmael have not spoken in all these years, and there is lingering resentment and desire between them. In this instance, the subtext comes from their history, which is shown in flashback scenes throughout the book. That history informs every scene in the present moment:

"It's all unfair," she told him bitterly. "Kabuo didn't kill anyone. It isn't in his heart to kill anyone. They brought in that sergeant to say he's a killer—that was just prejudice. Did you hear the things that man was saying? How Kabuo had it in his heart to kill? How horrible he is, a killer? Put it in your paper, about that man's testimony, how all of it was unfair. How the whole trial is unfair."

"I understand what you mean," answered Ishmael. "But I'm not a legal expert. I don't know if the judge should have suppressed Sergeant Maples' testimony. But I hope the jury comes in with the right verdict. I could write a column about that, maybe. How we all hope the justice system does its job. How we hope for an honest result."

"There shouldn't even be a trial," said Hatsue. "The whole thing is wrong, it's wrong."

"I'm bothered, too, when things are unfair," Ishmael said to her. "But sometimes I wonder if unfairness isn't ... part of things. I wonder if we should even expect fairness, if we should assume we have some sort of right to it. Or if—"

"I'm not talking about the whole universe," cut in Hatsue. "I'm talking about people—the sheriff, that prosecutor, that judge, you. People who can do things because they run newspapers or arrest people or convict them or decide about their lives."

There is no way to talk about unfairness without conjuring the fact that Ishmael—who is white—has had a much easier life than Hatsue, who was punished merely for being Japanese. Yet Ishmael suffered too, because he lost her love, and so both characters feel that they have been unfairly treated. This subtext makes their dialogue that much more charged and interesting than it would otherwise be.

When trying to play up subtext in your dialogue scene, you can draw upon historical events as in the example we just saw, or you might try one of these techniques:

- Use body language to say what isn't being spoken in words.

- Use setting details and objects to elicit references to past events.

- Zoom in on symbolic or suggestive objects in the setting.

- Let the conversation dance around an unspoken topic.

To the last point, let's look at an example from Ernest Hemingway's story "Hills Like White Elephants." The story takes place in a bar and features two characters who don't ever leave their seats. Through the course of the conversation, the reader develops a slow, painful realization of what the couple is discussing. Without the dialogue, the story has almost no action.

Hemingway opens with a quick brush of setting describing the hills of the valley, as well as the American and the girl sitting at the bar. Then, within a few more lines, the dialogue begins. Notice how the conversation feels like action because it moves quickly back and forth between these two characters:

"And if I do it you'll be happy and things will be like they were and you'll love me?"

"I love you now. You know I love you."

"I know. But if I do it, then it will be nice again if I say things are like white elephants, and you'll like it?"

"I'll love it. I love it now but I just can't think about it. You know how I get when I worry."

"If I do it you won't ever worry?"

"I won't worry about that because it's perfectly simple."

Even though 99 percent of this story is dialogue, the subtext-laden nature of this tug-of-war exchange creates a sense of movement, of action throughout, allowing the reader to feel as though he is experiencing the events of a narrative himself, while the swiftness of the exchanges allows for emotional distance from the heavy topic of abortion. And even though the characters aren't engaged in a loud argument, even though there is no hot emotional intensity, the tension is palpable. There's real energy here as the reader sees the dynamics of the couple through their strained dance around a topic neither wishes to say outright.

ENDING A DIALOGUE SCENE

A strong dialogue scene includes information that either deepens the reader's understanding of the characters or explains a plot element (thus the big reveals we talked about earlier). In one way or another, dialogue scenes should offer characters a chance to reveal things. These revelations must be well timed. If you give away too much information at the beginning of the scene—say one character tells her married boyfriend that she's pregnant—in the rest of the scene you will use the dialogue to work out their feelings, motivations, fears, and reactions to that information.

But a particularly effective technique is to drop a revelation toward the end of the chapter. This will either force the reader to keep going on to the next chapter, or it will leave the reader with a powerful experience to mull over.

Here's an example of a revelation that comes at the end of a dialogue scene from Richard Russo's novel *Empire Falls*. In this exchange between protagonist Miles and his curmudgeonly screw-up of a father, Max, a piece of information is revealed that tells the reader a lot about the characters and affects the plot.

Miles has never understood why his father never protested his mother's affair with one of the town's wealthy founders, Charlie Whiting—whose family Miles is still in service to as a result. Max has gone missing, disappearing from town with a mentally addled priest and some church funds, and he calls his son on the phone from Florida to let him know he's okay. Max and Miles quickly get into one of their customary arguments, but this time, the argument comes with a revelation:

Why shouldn't he have a little fun? was what Max wanted to know, since they were asking questions. "Old men like to have fun too, you know. Down here, people like old men."

"Why?"

"They don't say," Max admitted. "Tom hears confessions every afternoon at the end of the bar. You should see it."

"That's terrible, Dad."

"Why? Think about it."

"It's sacrilegious."

"Your mother really messed you up, you know that?"

And that was all it took, just the one mention of Grace, and suddenly the question was out before Miles could consider the wisdom of asking it. "How come you never told me about Mom and Charlie Whiting, Dad?"

Max reacted as if he'd been expecting the question for years. "How come you never told *me*, son?"

The spoken revelation here is that not only did Max know about his wife's affair, he knew that Miles also knew. The implications, however, are far greater than a simple revelation of information. Miles has always blamed his father and held a grudge against him for being gone more than he was around. Yet here the reader learns that Miles took his mother's side against his father all those years ago, even knowing his mother was cheating. This exchange helps Miles realize that he has blamed the wrong parent, in essence, thus consigning himself to his fate: running the Empire Grill under the iron fist of Mrs. Whiting.

By letting this come at the end of the scene, not only does Russo catch the reader off-guard, he creates a powerful resting place. The next scene picks up in another character's point of view (the novel is co-narrated by multiple protagonists), so the reader is left mulling over how this information is going to sink in for Miles, and if it will help him to change his behavior and stop the cycle of guilt his mother started, binding her family to the Whiting family.

Some dialogue scenes will end just like that, on a *kerplunk*, with the final spoken word in the scene. If the revelation came earlier, however, such as at the beginning or middle of the scene, then the ending should reflect whatever took place in the scene: The revelation should have a visible, dramatic impact on the character.

In the scene from *Disgrace*, the tug-of-war conversation reveals that Lucy, despite being raped, doesn't see herself as a victim; and yet David—who *elected* to have an affair with his student—*does* see himself as a victim. Coetzee ends the scene with one reflective line of David's thoughts:

Never yet have they been so far and so bitterly apart. He is shaken.

This is a good, destabilized place to leave David in. Since David hasn't been terribly shaken by anything he's done yet, this signals to the reader that he may be able to change after all.

When it comes time to end a dialogue scene, you'll want to leave your protagonist in one of the following places:

- On the final words of a spoken revelation
- Emotionally, mentally, or spiritually destabilized in some way
- Taking an action based on what was revealed
- Caught in a reflective space to muse on what came in the scene

Remember that dialogue should never be used to discuss mundane or quotidian topics, but always to reveal new information about plot and character. Dialogue can be stylized to match the personality of a character, and should sound realistic.

Finally, be careful with too many back-to-back dialogue scenes. Remember that dialogue feels like action to the reader, so you can break up action by following a dialogue-heavy scene with a suspenseful scene, a contemplative scene, or an epiphany scene. Even within a single scene, a lot of dialogue can start to feel rushed after a while, and should be grounded with physical gestures, setting details, or other brief snippets of exposition.

DIALOGUE SCENE MUSE POINTS

- Dialogue should always reveal new information about either the characters or the plot.

- Dialogue feels like action to the reader and can be used to add energy to an otherwise slower-paced scene.

- Balance a dialogue scene with setting details to create foreshadowing, build subtext, and keep the pace even.

- Use dialogue to reveal plot information in a realistic, not convenient, way.

- When a character speaks, her dialogue should reveal intentions

- Use opposing forces, or tug-of-war, in dialogue to keep tension alive.

17

ACTION SCENES

The American action movie has changed the way people think about action, and not necessarily for the better. We're taught to think that buildings must explode, well-muscled men must leap off crumbling scaffolding, and small children must be rescued at the last minute from near death, or it doesn't count as action. Actions can be smaller and more personal—the only requirement of an action scene is that it rely in part upon physical movement through the space you've created, and evoke a sense of time passing. In action scenes, the reader will feel like he is participating in action because:

- The events unfold in "real time," allowing the reader to feel he is participating in the events of the scene
- The pace is quick, and there is some kind of physical movement
- The protagonist is forced to make quick decisions or to react—to run on instinct rather than intellect
- Unexpected consequences for the protagonist heighten the drama

Action scenes are the ones in which your protagonist acts first and thinks later—in a rage, in passion, or with any other motive, she smashes in the windshield of her cheating boyfriend's car, drops that vengeful letter in the mail, or shows up on the doorstep of the father who never wanted her. Action scenes are also those in which forces catch your protagonist by surprise, thrusting her into motion: hurricanes, sinking boats, mistaken identities. An action scene in a literary novel might not seem as dramatic or big, but you will almost always find scenes in any type of fiction in which people move, react, and rely more on the physical aspects of life than they do on thinking or feeling.

Action scenes feel fast and often intense. Since they rely upon character reactions, they work best when there is something unexpected or surprising about the action—and that increases the reader's worry for the protagonist. (However, too many action scenes in a row can leave your reader overwrought.) Action scenes are a natural fit after a suspense scene, since suspense drives characters toward conflict and action. They're also great after an epiphany or contemplative scene in which the protagonist has digested some kind of important information and is now ready to do something about it.

This scene type will certainly drive the reader forward, but be warned that people have a tendency to skim action scenes, driven forward with their urgency, so you will want to balance them with other types of scenes.

OPENING AN ACTION SCENE

An action scene is so named because the majority of the scene is composed of action unfolding. Therefore, even if you want to start out slow and build toward the action, be thinking about how soon you're going to start the action.

Opening Mid-Action

In medias res is Latin for "in the middle of action"; beginning a scene in the middle of the action is a great way to open when you want to bypasses exposition. Opening *in medias res* forces the reader to dive in and read on to figure out what is happening. You might open a scene like this when the scene that came before it ended on a cliffhanger, essentially continuing the action that was left dangling in the scene prior, or you may just choose to use this technique to keep the momentum of your narrative up-tempo.

Here's an example from Neal Stephenson's science-fiction novel *Snow Crash* of a scene that opens with the protagonist already in action. Notice how the pace is quick right from the launch. In this future world, pizza delivery is controlled by the mafia, and delivering a pizza late means unemployment, possibly death. The scene before this one ends with the protagonist, Hiro (known as "the Deliverator") on a cliffhanger of tension: He has just learned that he has to get an already old pizza (not a good thing) twelve miles in a very short period of time. The next scene opens with him in action:

> The Deliverator lets out an involuntary roar and puts the hammer down. His emotions tell him to go back and kill that manager, get his swords out of the trunk, dive in through the little sliding window like a ninja, track him down through the moiling chaos of the microwaved franchise and confront him in a climactic thick-crust apocalypse. But he thinks the same thing when someone cuts him off on the freeway, and he's never done it—yet.
>
> He can handle this. This is doable. He cranks up the orange warning lights to maximum brilliance, puts his headlights on autoflash.

Opening in this manner allows the reader to feel the pressure that is on the protagonist. It also engages the reader's curiosity. What's going on? Why is the protagonist so upset? What would make him want to pull out his swords and kill the manager? The mid-action scene opening forces the reader to carry on and find out.

When you open an action scene mid-action, the reader should be able to follow the essential action. He should know if your protagonist is running down a street, or in the middle of a crime scene investigation. He doesn't have to know *how*, or *why*—but be sure you make *what* as clear as possible.

Opening With Foreshadowing

If your action scene does not open in the midst of action, then it must be set up to deliver action quickly. You can foreshadow the action that is coming through smaller actions or narrative summary without entirely giving it away. Vendela Vida's novel *And Now You Can Go* opens with Ellis, a young grad student in New York, being held at gunpoint by a man. An action scene toward the end of the book opens with foreshadowing of the related action that is about to ensue:

In the elevator, I watch the numbers as we descend. Sarah's standing with her back to the door, her legs planted and her arms out, as though she's protecting me from whatever I'm about to see.

What she's about to see is the man who held her at gunpoint—who was never caught by police. Two of Ellis's friends, including one particularly volatile guy who is itching for a fight, have brought him there for Ellis to identify so they can proceed to beat him up.

That moment in the elevator prepares the reader for the fact that something is coming. The action comes pretty quickly once she gets off.

"El," the ROTC boy says, "tell me if this is your guy, because if it is, he's a dead man." He's holding the man's arms behind his back. Everyone's eyes are on me, including the man's.

When you open an action scene with foreshadowing or narrative summary, try to keep it short, and simply set up the action that is coming with subtle hints—like the image of Ellis's friend protecting her—and then let the action take center stage. Over-preparing the reader for an action to come can suck the energy or surprise right out of the scene.

CHARACTER DEVELOPMENT AND PLOT IN ACTION

In a fiction narrative, action is one of the ways that you show the true nature of your protagonist without any of the dull work of exposition. Every scene should offer your protagonist a chance to interact, react, and change, but action scenes take this further. The circumstances of an action scene should be just a bit more intense than those in other types of scenes, so that your characters can show what they're really made of, and even make mistakes. And the actions should also move your plot forward.

In William Golding's revered novel *Lord of the Flies*, the entire student population of a boys' school is shipwrecked on an island, and the boys must fend for themselves without any adult rules. In the following scene, the boys have splintered off into two factions: Those who follow the rough, violence-prone Jack, who acts more like a little dictator, and those who follow the gentler, consensus-minded Ralph.

Before the following excerpt, which takes place about two-thirds of the way through the book, Jack and Ralph have been butting heads more and more. Jack is tired of doing things civilly—he wants to take control and his desire for dominance infects the entire group of boys. Jack has figured out how to kill for meat, and this alone wins more boys over to him, inflating his already out-of-control sense of power. Now that he knows he can kill food, he realizes that he has a kind of leverage over the group that Ralph does not. He starts the boys in nothing more than a boyish ritual to show off their dominance, but it quickly descends into a frenzy of violence.

> Jack leapt up on the sand.
>
> "Do our dance! Come on! Dance!"
>
> He ran stumbling through the thick sand to the open space of rock beyond the fire. Between the flashes of lightning the air was dark and terrible; and the boys followed him, clamorously. Roger became the pig, grunting and charging at Jack, who side-stepped. The hunters took their spears, the cooks took spits, and the rest clubs of firewood. A circling movement developed and a chant. While Roger mimed the terror of the pig, the littluns ran and jumped on the outside of the circle. Piggy and Ralph, under the threat of the sky, found themselves eager to take a place in this demented but partly secure society. They were glad to touch the brown backs of the fence that hemmed in the terror and made it governable.
>
> "Kill the beast! Cut his throat! Spill his blood!"

Caught up in the energy of the dance, the boys react by killing their class-mate, Simon:

> The beast struggled forward, broke the ring and fell over the steep edge of the rock to the sand by the water. At once the crowd surged after it, poured down the rock, leapt on to the beast, screamed, struck, bit tore.

Ralph is the only one whose conscience is troubled the next day. His only true remaining friend, Piggy, tries to assuage him saying they were scared, but Ralph knows better.

"It was dark. There was that—that bloody dance. There was lightning and thunder and rain. We was scared!"

"I wasn't scared," said Ralph slowly, "I was—I don't know what I was."

Ralph is changed. He knows now that every boy has within him the potential to be both bad and good, and that the hallmark of maturity is learning to choose the right path.

When you write an action scene, consider how you can challenge your protagonist to discover something unexpected about himself that he wouldn't necessarily know through his intellect. All people have instincts, but not many get the opportunity to act on them, so think about how, through actions, you can let your protagonist access his instincts.

In terms of plot, it's also good to have your character engage in actions that he can't take back so that you create new consequences for him to deal with. If your character, who has a fear of looking foolish, engages in the action of riding a horse for the very first time without telling anyone he's a novice, that's not very dramatic and has little room for conflict. But if that same character rides a horse for the first time and takes it down a forbidden path where the horse breaks a leg and must be put down—that can't be taken back, and it comes with consequences.

ENDING AN ACTION SCENE

There are multiple ways to end an action scene, and we'll look at several strong ways to do so in a moment, but no matter which way you select, an action scene's end should convey the following:

- That your protagonist's life has been altered by the action
- That the actions have created consequences the protagonist will have to deal with in future scenes

Endings can fall into three essential categories: those that slow down the pace and offer room for reflection; those that jack up the tension and suspense and leave the scene on a high note of anxiety that forces the reader to press on; and those that come with big revelations that will change your protagonist or the plot (or both).

Slow-Down Endings

After all that action, you may choose to close your scene with a quieter, slower pace to gives the reader an opportunity to breathe. Use exposition or reflection to bring the pace down for a feeling of conclusion. Notice how Neal Stephenson does it at the end of the *Snow Crash* scene. The protagonist—"the Deliverator," whose name is Hiro—did not, in fact, make his delivery, and he must now flee from the scene of his car crash—in a residential neighborhood—for his life. Stephenson uses exposition to bring the pace down, but he leaves the reader with an image that foreshadows how things are likely to get worse for Hiro.

> Dad is emerging from the back door pulling on a jacket. It is a nice family, a safe family in a house full of light, like the family he was part of until thirty seconds ago.

When you taper an action scene to a quiet close, you still want to leave the reader with the feeling that your protagonist will suffer consequences for the actions in the scene. Even though this is not a typical cliffhanger, because the danger Hiro is in isn't immediate, it leaves the feeling of trouble on the horizon. You can use a foreshadowing image like Stephenson did, or you can allow your protagonist to have a thought or feeling in a brief moment of narrative summary.

Cliffhanger or Suspense Endings

If you want to keep the action alive at the end of the scene so that the reader must keep reading on to the next scene, do not conclude the action of the scene, but bring it to a place where it can hang—that is to say, where the action hasn't concluded or run its course. At the end of the scene from *And Now You Can Go*, Ellis's attacker is gagged and held captive in the elevator by her two friends—one who is holding a gun—who are begging her to identify him so they can beat him up.

> I hear a bang. At first I think the gun's been fired.
> "Jesus," Sarah says. She's been standing next to me, and now she grabs my elbow and thrusts her chin in the direction of the glass door to the lobby. The door is locked after 11 P.M. But the representative of the

world is standing outside, in his green coat, knocking. He points to me. "Sorry about Melissa," he mouths. I try to wave him away. He presses his walnut-colored face to the glass and sees the ROTC boy and G.P. holding the man. He knocks on the glass door with a gloved hand. Then he takes off his glove and knocks harder, with his knuckles.

"Should I get rid of that guy?" Danny says, nodding toward the door.

I hear a grunt. The ROTC boy has punched the man from the park in the stomach.

"Should I get rid of him?" Danny says again, thumbing toward the representative.

"Fucking freak," the ROTC boy says, looking at the door.

Now, even though they do punch the guy once—you might argue that's the action—it's only a test punch. The real pummeling they want to give the guy rests on whatever Ellis says. If she says it's him, the reader is pretty sure they'll beat him within an inch of his life, or worse—they do have a gun after all. But Ellis tells them to let him go, unwilling to perpetrate more violence, and the scene ends before the reader knows what happens:

No one knows what to do next. The elevator has stopped on the sixth floor. The only thing moving is the man's gagged mouth.

"Please," I say. "It's not him. Let him go."

The cliffhanger or suspense ending requires only that you delay the conclusion of the action. It's that simple. It works best when you leave the scene literally in the middle of an action; or, if you use some narrative summary, that it reinforces a feeling of tension or drama about to unfold. This moment also shows the reader how Ellis has gone from a person who wanted revenge, who liked the idea of letting this man get his comeuppance, to someone who feels she does not want to be responsible for perpetuating more violence.

Revelation Endings

When you want to convey that your protagonist is changed at the end of an action scene, a revelation ending is a powerful way to do so, and in the process, to set the stage for the next scene. In a revelation ending, you wait until the very final moments of the scene to reveal—to the reader and protagonist both—what the consequences of the action are. In the *Lord of the Flies* scene, the reader finally understands what happened in the wild dance where the boys were shouting "Kill the beast" at the end of the scene. The beast was, in fact, their classmate Simon:

> The great wave of the tide moved farther along the island and the water lifted. Softly, surrounded by a fringe of inquisitive bright creatures, itself a silver shape beneath the steadfast constellations, Simon's dead body moved out toward the open sea.

Harking back to Ralph's earlier comment, in which he says that he wasn't scared, the reader sees that Ralph knew that he'd participated in something awful. What is revealed is that Ralph is the only character with a conscience.

Since action scenes don't leave much room for emotions, you can drop a powerful emotional note through a revelation in that final paragraph or page that will leave the reader reeling, or convey what will be at stake for the protagonist in the next scene. A revelation can come in a moment of reflection, an exchange of dialogue, a description of the carnage after a riot, etc. A revelation can take almost any form—but if you choose to use it, it should carry emotional significance for your protagonist.

ACTION SCENE MUSE POINTS

- The protagonist's focus is on reaction—instinct before intellect.
- Action involves physical movement that conveys a sense of time.
- Action scenes have less need for reflective or emotional content.
- The protagonist and his plot should be changed by the action.
- The actions should have consequences for future scenes.

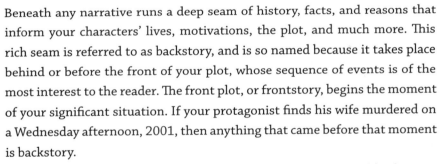

18
FLASHBACK SCENES

Beneath any narrative runs a deep seam of history, facts, and reasons that inform your characters' lives, motivations, the plot, and much more. This rich seam is referred to as backstory, and is so named because it takes place behind or before the front of your plot, whose sequence of events is of the most interest to the reader. The front plot, or frontstory, begins the moment of your significant situation. If your protagonist finds his wife murdered on a Wednesday afternoon, 2001, then anything that came before that moment is backstory.

Backstory is most effective when used in the form of a flashback scene, because then it can be made vivid and allow the reader to participate in it; otherwise, it might drag the prose down to a crawl. A flashback scene still contains all the elements of a scene—setting, action, characters, plot information, dramatic tension—and differs from other kinds of scenes in only one major way: It takes place in the past.

Flashback scenes should:

- Focus on action, information, and character interactions
- Be lean on setting and sensory details, which slow down the pace
- Illustrate or explain a plot or character element in the frontstory

• Enrich the reader's understanding of the protagonist

Note that just because you *can* write flashback scenes does not mean that you should crowd your present-time narrative with them. Flashbacks, even done in the form of a scene, still draw the reader away from the frontstory and run the risk of distracting her. Use flashbacks judiciously, even sparingly. If you use them early in your narrative, be sure to keep them short and quickly paced. And, as in the upcoming example from Neil Gaiman, use them more to drop clues or plot information that will come to bear on the frontstory. You may want to drop one into a contemplative scene that has very little other action, or use one to heighten the tension in a suspense scene. I find that they can get in the way of a dramatic scene—which is all about character interactions in the present—so keep that in mind when writing flashbacks.

TRANSITIONING INTO THE PAST

A flashback is just another kind of scene, but it's important to consider how you transition into and out of one, seamlessly taking the reader from the present narrative into the past. Detours into the past must be constructed carefully if they are to hold the reader's attention and avoid becoming narratively dense. Here are some quick and easy tricks for transitioning:

• **Use the past tense.** Flashbacks often begin with words that conjure the idea of the past, or indicate the past through verb tense. Here are a few examples of transitional sentences that let the reader know she is stepping into the past through the use of the past tense.

From the story "Mothers," by Sylvia Plath:

A few days after they had moved into the house, Tom called her downstairs for a visitor.

From there, Plath quickly drops into a scene where the character Esther meets a Kenyan professor who has an affect on her religious decision.

And from Neil Gaiman's novel *Anansi Boys*:

He had spoken to Mrs. Higgler several years earlier, when his mother was dying.

This memory comes in the middle of a scene in which the protagonist, Fat Charlie, is trying to explain to his fiancée why he doesn't want his father to come to their wedding.

• **Use a specific date or incident to refer to the past.** There's no more direct way to transition into the past than referring to a time or date that the reader know has already passed. Using a date is a nice sturdy way to transition, especially if the date has significance to the protagonist, like in the story "Police Dreams," by Richard Bausch:

> On the morning of the day she left, he woke to find her sitting at her dressing table, staring at herself.

In the frontstory the reader knows that the narrator is divorced. By leading the reader directly back to "the morning of the day she left," the author clearly signals that he is now moving into the past.

• **Use reiteration.** Sometimes you can set up the reader by having a character tell him in words that you will be moving into the past, as in this example from the novel *Carolina Moon*, by Jill McCorkle:

> "Anyway, that old Barry just wouldn't let it rest and kept right on talking; I'll do my best to re-create his exact words. ..."

The reader knows that the speaker is about to move into the past because she's referring to a conversation that has already taken place, which is why she has to "re-create" his words.

• **Use remembrances.** Some writers make it very obvious that a detour into the past is imminent by using specific phrases like "I remembered when," or "She remembered the day." This technique leaves no question that the character is stepping back in time, but is a little less seamless and elegant than some of the other techniques discussed above.

Using the past tense and providing just one transitional sentence between the scene at hand and the flashback is one of the most effective ways to dip into the past without jarring the reader too far out of the present narrative.

HOW TO USE FLASHBACK SCENES

A flashback is still a scene for all practical purposes, but since the scene has already happened, it does not need to do quite as much, and can be a great deal shorter than a typical scene. You don't need to do nearly as much work with the setting, for instance, because setting details slow down the pace and attract the reader's attention; with a flashback, you want to focus on action, information, and character interactions.

In all essential ways you structure a flashback like any other type of scene, except you take into consideration the role of each flashback. Here are reasons to use flashbacks:

• **The past is directly responsible for present plot.** In some narratives, the significant situation of the plot may stem directly from something that happened in the past, and that past event may need to be reopened in order for the reader to understand what happened. Flashback scenes are very useful in this case.

A good example of this comes from Elizabeth Kostova's sprawling gothic novel, *The Historian*, about a father's legacy to his daughter, linked to the existence of the real Dracula. The significant situation occurs when the daughter finds a strange book in her father's study, along with an unusual note. When she asks him about it, he tells her about the night when he first found the book:

> You already know, my father said, that before you were born I was a professor at an American university. Before that, I studied for many years to become a professor. At first I thought I would study literature. Then, however, I realized I loved true stories even better than imaginary ones.

What is masterful about Kostova's transitions into the past is that they are elegant and subtle, so the reader never feels herself moving through time. The scene above opens with the narrator's father talking—*in the frontstory*—to his daughter. Then, slowly, as you can see in the next example, she shifts out of the frontstory with just a few sentences; with the use of the phrase "one spring night" the scene slides into the past, and then very quickly she sets the scene of flashback so quietly with the words "I was in my carrel" that the reader doesn't think about the fact that she's moved into the past—the reader is just immediately drawn there. It's a brilliant technique:

> One spring night when I was still a graduate student, I was in my carrel at the university library, sitting alone very late among rows and rows of books. Looking up from my work, I suddenly realized that someone had left a book whose spine I had never seen before among my own textbooks, which sat on a shelf above my desk. The spine of this new book showed an elegant little dragon, green on pale leather.
>
> I didn't remember ever having seen the book there or anywhere else, so I took it down and looked through it without really thinking. The binding was soft, faded leather, and the pages inside appeared to be quite old. It opened easily to the very center. Across those two pages I saw a great woodcut of a dragon with spread wings and a long looped tail, a beast unfurled and raging, claws outstretched. In the dragon's claws hung a banner on which ran a single word in Gothic lettering: DRAKULYA.

Notice, too, that even though the flashback scene takes place before the significant situation and the narrator's storyline, it still meets the criteria of a scene: There is setting, action, a protagonist, dramatic tension, suspense, and most importantly, a sense of relevance to the narrator's plotline.

The Historian is built on a weaving of past and present, and eventually the two storylines merge. The past catches up with her father—in the narrator's present. When the narrator's father goes missing, she becomes involved in the search for him, Dracula, and the mother she never knew. The flashback scenes prepare the reader for this plot direction.

This type of structure works well when you intend to merge the past and present events—that is, when the events of the past will come into play in your protagonist's life in the present storyline. This is why the flashbacks in *The Historian* begin early on in the narrative—they continue, coming more and more into the recent past, until the past and the present merge.

If you're only going to use flashbacks to illustrate or deepen the reader's understanding of a character, you may want to let a bit more action unfold, getting further into the plot before throwing in a flashback, as flashbacks can slow the pace and lose the reader's interest in the first part of your narrative.

• **You need to create a more suspenseful plot.** When you want to use the past as a way to create suspense in your plot, then you will absolutely need to use flashback scenes to let the reader see the events of the past in limited bites.

For example, in Mary Doria Russell's bold novel *The Sparrow*, Jesuit priest Emilio Sandoz returns in 2059 as the sole survivor of a mission sent more than seventeen years before to make contact with the first known sentient alien life, on the planet Rhakat. All the reader knows early on in the narrative is that Emilio Sandoz—once a respected Jesuit priest—behaved in such a way while there that he is now referred to as a "whore" and "child killer," this based on what little information the rescue team was able to provide. Emilio's hands have also been mutilated beyond use, and he is too traumatized by events to discuss anything.

The front storyline revolves around Sandoz's superiors interrogating him so that they can decide what to do with him and how to punish him. The reputation of the Jesuit priesthood rests heavily on their decision, since media attention is focused on his story.

Through careful flashback scenes of the actual mission in Emilio's point of view, Russell builds suspense as she slowly dips back in time, showing us a man who does not seem capable of being the "child killer" he is accused of being. Here's an excerpt of a scene in which the reader gets to see Sandoz in the past for ourselves:

> Then a juvenile, much smaller than anyone who'd spoken earlier, came forward with another adult, who spoke reassuringly before gently urging the little one to approach Emilio alone.
>
> She was a weedy child, spindly and unpromising. Seeing her advance, scared but determined, Emilio slowly dropped to his knees, so he would not loom over her, as the adult had loomed over him. They were, for the moment, all alone together, the others of their kinds forgotten, their whole attention absorbed. As the little one came closer, Emilio held out one hand, palm up, and said, "Hello."

This Emilio seems like a thoughtful man in the flashbacks, and in the disparity between what his superiors believe of him in the frontstory and what the reader actually sees in the flashbacks, suspense is built.

In order to use flashback scenes to build suspense, you need to dole out plot information slowly and be sure that each flashback provides a new piece of information. In Emilio's case, the reader sees that Emilio is a man who can be patient and kind to a child, which contrasts starkly with being a "child killer." But this is not the end of his story—it's only about halfway through the novel—so there is still a note of uncertainty about what kind of man Emilio is and how events might have changed him. The reader has to keep reading! Withholding crucial plot details keeps the reader engaged and reading on.

- **You need to convey character depth and *death*.** There are plenty of instances in fiction when a character has had an effect on the protagonist but is now either dead or not present in the frontstory. Yet you still want to show the effect this absent character has had on your protagonist. Narrative summary just doesn't cut it when it comes to understanding character depth or motivation. You'll need to use a flashback scene to render the effects visible to readers.

In Neil Gaiman's fantasy novel *Anansi Boys*, protagonist Fat Charlie is planning his wedding to his fiancée, Rosie. In an early scene they have a conversation about how she wants him to invite his estranged father to the wedding, and Fat Charlie wants nothing of the sort. He explains to Rosie that his father was a man who constantly embarrassed him at the most inappropriate times. There is no reason to doubt Fat Charlie, but the reader doesn't really relate to his feelings yet, either, so there's a need for proof of how embarrassing his father really was. So Gaiman takes the reader back in time to offer an experience of Fat Charlie's father. In the excerpt below, Charlie's mother is in the hospital for cancer treatment, and his father shows up out of the blue to visit her in a most unusual manner:

> Coming down the hospital corridor, ignoring the protests of nurses, the stares of patients in pajamas and of their families, was what appeared to be a very small New Orleans jazz band. There was a saxophone and a

sousaphone and a trumpet. There was an enormous man with what looked like a double bass strung around his neck. There was a man with a bass drum, which he banged. And at the head of the pack, in a smart checked suit, wearing a fedora hat and lemon yellow gloves, came Fat Charlie's father. He played no instrument but was doing a soft-shoe-shuffle along the polished linoleum of the hospital floor, lifting his hat to each of the medical staff in turn, shaking hands with anyone who got close enough to talk or attempt to complain.

Fat Charlie bit his lip, and prayed to anyone who might be listening that the earth would open and swallow him up or, failing that, that he might suffer a brief, merciful and entirely fatal heart attack. No such luck. He remained among the living, the brass band kept coming, his father kept dancing and shaking hands and smiling. ...

"Fat Charlie," he said, loudly enough that everyone in the ward—on that floor—in the hospital—was able to comprehend that this was some-one who knew Fat Charlie, "Fat Charlie, get out of the way. Your father is here."

Fat Charlie got out of the way.

The band, led by Fat Charlie's father, snaked their way through the ward to Fat Charlie's mother's bed. She looked up at them as they ap-proached, and she smiled.

The flashback offers us insight into Charlie's father, who is not present in the real-time scene, and who, Charlie learns when he tries to track him down, is recently deceased. Without this insight, Charlie's resistance to having his fa-ther come to the wedding would not have any impact, and the reader would not believe him.

What's crucial about this flashback is its length. When writing flash-backs, you should also strive to make yours brief. It hones in on the mem-ory for not much more than a page and then returns to the present. Re-member to keep your flashbacks short, or else quickly paced so they hold the reader's attention.

Similarly, when a character has a distinct and vivid personality, or per-sonality disorder, for that matter—perhaps he's shy, overly strict, mute, cruel—you may decide to go back in time through a flashback and offer some perspective on this character so he does not seem one-dimensional. For example, in order to understand why Darth Vader was so starkly evil, George Lucas went back in time in his later movies and *showed* young Anakin Skywalker before he became Darth Vader. By witnessing Anakin's pain and loss, the viewers understand him better and develop compassion and sympathy for the character.

When you use a flashback for either of these reasons, be sure to keep the flashbacks short—their purpose is supportive, so you don't want to go too far from the frontstory.

ENDING THE FLASHBACK SCENE

When you end a flashback scene, transition back to the present so the reader is brought full circle to the point where the flashback started, or leave the flashback on a note that will force the reader to keep reading.

In *The Historian*, the goal of the flashback is to set the plot in forward motion. The story piques the narrator's curiosity such that she begins her own investigation into the mysterious Vlad Dracula and her father's past. The flashback also offers insight into the character of her father, who has always been a bit reserved, and hints at details about her absent mother.

The flashback ends by coming back to the present like this:

> "Good Lord," my father said suddenly, looking at his watch. "Why didn't you tell me? It's almost seven o'clock."
>
> I put my cold hands inside my navy jacket. "I didn't know," I said. "But please don't stop the story. Please don't stop there."

The reader shares the narrator's attitude and doesn't want him to stop either—he wants to know what happened next. In this case, since the backstory has a direct effect on the frontstory, the reader and the narrator both have gained new insight that will compel the reader to go forward.

Bringing your flashback back to the present allows the reader to feel as though he has literally traveled back in time and now has a fuller understanding of where he is going.

The example from Russell's *The Sparrow* is structured slightly differently (in fact, all her flashback scenes are). Here, the flashback is its own contained scene; it ends the chapter and does not come back to the present moment. Instead, it leaves the reader with an image of Emilio that's very different from the tortured person shown to the reader at the beginning of the narrative. Her flashbacks serve the role of revealing what happened on the mission to Rhakat slowly and suspensefully. Each flashback fills in more of the puzzle. The reader learns the specifics of the mission in question through Emilio's memories, and through them learn how different Emilio was then from the person he is in the frontstory:

> Emilio Sandoz threw back his head and laughed. "God!" he shouted into the sunshine and leaned down to kiss the top of Askama's head and pull her up into his arms for an embrace that included the whole of creation. "God," he whispered again, eyes closed, with the child settling onto his hip. "I was born for this!"

This back-and-forth quality—a flashback chapter followed by a present-time chapter—gives the narrative a feeling of suspense and plants more and more seeds in the reader's mind that the protagonist might not be so terrible after all.

If you choose this technique for your narrative, you are essentially running two stories side by side, using the flashbacks to build toward a truth that will have to be addressed, answered, and realized in the frontstory.

Finally, in the example from Gaiman's *Anansi Boys*, the flashback ends when Charlie's fiancée, Rosie, with whom he was arguing when he first slipped into the memory, calls his attention back to the present:

> "So," said Rosie, draining her Chardonnay, "you'll call your Mrs. Higgler and give her my mobile number. Tell her about the wedding and the date. ..."

The flashback achieves two crucial functions. First, it shows the reader what Fat Charlie considers embarrassing and inappropriate behavior. He sees his father as a fair-weather man—Charlie resented the fact that his father could just swoop in at the last minute and make his mother happy. (Some might argue that the flashback shows Charlie as selfish, not caring about his mother's happiness, only caring about himself.) Second, it reveals plot information, as the flashback moves to the day of his mother's funeral, where Charlie spotted a stranger who will play a very significant role in the future plot; but the character is merely dropped there as a hint, a piece of foreshadowing.

Structurally, this sort of flashback acts as a detour from the scene at hand—like a slide of the past slipped into someone's photos of a recent vacation. This is a very good use of the flashback for your consideration—it's brief, it adds to the reader's understanding of the characters, and it provides a hint of future plot events to come.

Flashbacks need to feel purposeful, or they lead to the feeling that you've departed from your story, so they should be used as strategically as possible. They should be vividly written and quickly paced, and should leave the reader with the feeling that he has learned something important that he needs to know.

FLASHBACK SCENE MUSE POINTS

- A flashback should focus on all of the following: action, information, and character interaction.
- The information contained in the flashback must have some bearing on the frontstory.
- Always be sure to use flashbacks judiciously so the reader doesn't lose track of the frontstory.
- Use flashbacks when the past directly affects the front plot.
- Use flashbacks when you want to use some element of the past to create suspense in the present.
- Use flashbacks to deepen the reader's understanding of a character.

19
EPIPHANY SCENES

An epiphany is a moment when awareness or a sharp insight dawns suddenly on your protagonist as a result of events and interactions that have driven him to this moment. Epiphany is synonymous with change when it comes to character development. Very often epiphanies come with a cost—characters can be very attached to their perceptions of things and people, and it often hurts when they finally gain awareness. But epiphanies can also bring resurgence in hope or faith that the protagonist believed was lost. By introducing an epiphany, you provide your protagonist with an opportunity to grow, to learn, and to transform.

An epiphany can take place in more than one type of scene—for instance, suspense or drama can build to an epiphany, and an epiphany can also be earned at the end of a contemplative scene. In an epiphany scene:

- The epiphany comes at some kind of cost or it renews hope or faith, or both
- The epiphany rises out of plot events and information—it does not come out of the blue
- Your protagonist gains surprising new insight or breaks through denial
- As a result of the epiphany, the protagonist is forced to make some sort of choice or change

Because epiphanies have a pivotal effect on characters, you don't need to have one in every scene. In fact, one major epiphany in each of your three narrative parts would be plenty. Epiphanies shouldn't happen too early in a narrative either, as they require events and circumstances and emotional information to drive them into being. People don't usually just wake up with insight—it is earned through experience. Very often a dramatic scene (in which hot emotional intensity is elicited), or a suspense scene (in which information has been withheld) comes just before an epiphany scene.

TYPES OF EPIPHANIES

When you write an epiphany scene, you need to take stock of who your character is before the epiphany, what kind of change he needs to undergo, and how you will lead him to this change. Let's look at the kinds of epiphanies a character can undergo.

- **Removing the blinders.** When a character has been in denial but through an act of will decides to learn what the truth is.

- **Realizing a suppressed desire.** This is when a character who has lived his life in a limited way realizes what it is he really wants to do or be— the lawyer who realizes he really wants to work with children; the failed artist who realizes he was only acting out his parents' will for him. These are powerful and usually suggest that the character will have to leave one way of life for another.

- **Accepting the limitations of oneself or others.** Many times a character must realize that the abusive spouse is not going to change; the dead-end job is not going to improve; and that any change he craves will have to be an inside job that nobody else can facilitate.

- **Experiencing identity epiphanies.** These kinds of epiphanies are fairly specific and limited. This is when a person realizes something essential to his being—that she is a lesbian after all; that he wants to embrace his father's African-American culture rather than his mother's Caucasian background; that it's time to convert to Judaism. A character's decision to claim an identity of some kind that he had been resisting or denying can come as the result of an epiphany.

- **Undergoing a rude awakening.** Sometimes a character needs to be forced to change by circumstances or people out of his control. His friends stage an intervention for his drinking; his wife confesses she doesn't really love him.

OPENING AN EPIPHANY SCENE

Now that you have a feeling for the kinds of categories that epiphanies fall into, let's talk about how to open one. What is most important about the opening is that you show the character in conflict of some kind, under pressure, or in some way destabilized. This is the scene in which his old façade is crumbling (or about to), and you want the reader to know that change is on the horizon. Epiphany openings work best when:

- The protagonist is afraid or anxious about the future
- The protagonist is under pressure or stress
- The protagonist takes an unusual action or behaves oddly
- The protagonist expresses conflicted feelings about a given plot event or relationship
- Your setting details or images are symbolic and hint at the kind of epiphany that is to come

Let's take a look at some examples of opening epiphany scenes that show the protagonist unbalanced or en route to an epiphany at the very opening of the scene.

In Michael Cunningham's Pulitzer Prize–winning novel *The Hours,* Laura Brown is a housewife in 1949 with a "perfect" life—a husband with a good job, a healthy son, and a second child on the way. She has a nice house and all the material things she could possibly want, but her true self is stifled; she wants to be more than a mother and a wife, yet there is no way for her to express this in the life she currently leads.

In the scenes prior to this one, the reader sees Laura repress desire, resentment, and her own creative spark, so there's a feeling that some kind of change is on its way in her life, but they don't yet know what it will be (and neither, it seems, does Laura). Two major factors begin to push Laura toward her epiphany. The first is reading Virginia Woolf's book *Mrs. Dalloway*, which boldly emphasizes a woman's right to her feelings. The second is the example of her neighbor, Kitty, who seems, without any angst, to be able to balance all the demands that Laura cannot. One day after a visit, she and Kitty kiss—and though this kiss happens with no premeditation on Laura's part, it further awakens in her a terrible hunger and desire. Soon after that, she has more trouble dealing with the status quo of her life and finds her son's and husband's demands incredibly oppressive.

The epiphany scene opens with her reality in the process of shifting.

> As she pilots her Chevrolet along the Pasadena Freeway, among hills still scorched in places from last year's fire, she feels as if she's dreaming or, more precisely, as if she's remembering this drive from a dream long ago. Everything she sees feels as if it's pinned to the day the way etherized butterflies are pinned to a board.

There are a number of cues that something is different here. The way she feels "as if she's dreaming" and the eerie details of everything feeling "pinned" to the day like "etherized butterflies" are not typical reflections for Laura. The reader feels the tide of change coming. When it is revealed that, in a moment of panic, she left her son with a neighbor and is on her way to rent a motel room, the scene is set for something to happen. Will she kill herself, take a lover, or make some kind of decision about her future and her feelings?

Opening an epiphany scene with a character behaving oddly or under stress or pressure is a very effective technique. It sets the reader up from the get-go to know that in this scene, your protagonist is emotionally volatile—like a fragile chemistry experiment that can all too easily blow up. If you don't immediately open with your protagonist under stress, however, it's good to quickly put pressure on him before too long.

Though character openings are a strong way to begin an epiphany scene, you can also open with strategically chosen setting details or images that foreshadow or set the mood for the epiphany to come. Here's such an example from Janet Fitch's novel *White Oleander*, in which the scene begins with setting and symbolic images.

Seventeen-year-old Astrid—whose poet mother, Ingrid, has been in prison for six years for murdering her lover—has lived through a series of foster homes and undergone terrible traumas. All she has ever wanted was her mother's devoted, unconditional love, which Ingrid has withheld in favor of building Astrid's character. In this scene, Astrid is coming to see her mother after a long absence; her mother is finally up for trial and Astrid is the only witness whose testimony could free her mother. The scene opens with metaphor-laced setting details about fire season in southern California that suggest the trial by fire that Astrid is about to undergo when she sees her mother.

> September came with its skirts of fire. Fire up on the Angeles Crest. Fire in Malibu, Altadena. Fire all along the San Gabriels, in the San Gorgonio wilderness, fire was a flaming hoop the city would have to jump through to reach the blues of October.
>
> It was in the furnace of oleander time that Susan finally called. "I had a trial," she explained. "But we're back on track. I've scheduled you a visit, day after tomorrow."
>
> I was tempted to balk, tell her I wasn't available, make things difficult, but in the end I agreed. I was as ready as I would ever be.

The symbolic image of fire is very powerful here, setting up the idea of someone getting burned in the scene to come. There's also the tension of Astrid considering, for the first time, not going to see her mother—which is a little flash of her steadily growing autonomy. She is "tempted to balk" but ultimately she acquiesces with the line "I was as ready as I would ever be" (suggesting she really isn't ready at all). The reader knows that there is a great deal at stake for Astrid in this scene, and the rest of the scene (which we'll discuss later in this chapter) delivers.

DRIVING YOUR CHARACTER TOWARD EPIPHANY

Once you've set up the scene in which your character is unbalanced and worried about the future, you'll need to up the ante on your character to drive him toward that epiphany. Every character will have a unique set of circumstances that add up to epiphany.

Keep in mind that a character will rarely have the intention to change or see the unvarnished truth. Think about how difficult it is to get a person to change a habit like keeping a messy room, or smoking cigarettes, much less a deeper, more internal behavior or belief. Though you'll have done some of this work toward epiphany already by raising the stakes in previous scenes and complicating your protagonist's life and plot, this scene is the one in which the dam must finally break.

Since epiphanies do not come easily, you will have to exert stress, pressure, and tension upon your protagonist to get him there. Here are some forms of pressure:

- **Threat of loss.** When your protagonist stands to lose something or someone he holds dear, this is a powerfully motivating force for awareness to come in.

- **Incontrovertible evidence.** When a character has been in denial and is finally faced with hard evidence of the truth—a photograph that her husband really is cheating, for example—this can often crack the foundation of denial and let an epiphany shine through.

- **Injuring a loved one.** You'd be amazed at the kind of epiphany your protagonist can come to when confronted with the damage he has unintentionally caused others through his actions.

- **Danger.** Threat is a powerful agent of change. Faced with either death or bodily harm, characters often face their most basic and unvarnished feelings. Your protagonist might suddenly realize the error of his ways, and wish for a second chance, for example, or be surprised to realize that faced with danger, there is only one person he really hopes to see again before he dies.

However you choose to pressure or stress your protagonist into his epiphany, you must be realistic, and you must utilize dramatic tension. Remember that your protagonist must resist the awareness or change just a little, and the epiphany must come with an emotional, physical, or spiritual cost. The goal of epiphany is to force your character to change.

THE MOMENT OF EPIPHANY

While you may stress and pressure your protagonist for the entire scene if you like, I recommend saving the actual moment of epiphany for near the end of a scene because it's good to leave the reader and the protagonist not too long after this sudden dawning of insight. Most people don't take a sudden, spontaneous action after an epiphany—they let it sink in, and so should you. Pausing will also relieve you of the need to try to explain away any tension or emotional weight that the epiphany brought.

In *The Hours*, the moment of epiphany comes for Laura once she is actually alone in a room with nothing but Virginia Woolf's strong voice, and her own silenced desires finally have space to rise into her thoughts. With time to herself, she is able to realize her epiphany:

> It is possible to die. Laura thinks, suddenly, of how she—how anyone—can make a choice like that. It is a reckless, vertiginous thought, slightly disembodied—it announces itself inside her head, faintly but distinctly, like a voice crackling from a distant radio station. She could decide to die. It is an abstract, shimmering notion, not particularly morbid. Hotel rooms are where people do things like that, aren't they? It's possible—perhaps even likely—that someone has ended his or her life right here, in this room, on this bed. Someone said, Enough, no more; someone looked for the last time at these white walls, this smooth white ceiling. By going to a hotel, she sees, you leave the particulars of your own life and enter a neutral zone, a clean white room, where dying does not seem quite so strange.

Laura's epiphany falls into the category of realization of a suppressed desire. She has lived her life in a limited way, and suddenly, this epiphany that she could free herself from her unhappiness through death jars her into a new way of thinking. The epiphany is handled through interior monologue—the reader enters into her thoughts and directly learns what the epiphany is. In many cases, revealing an epiphany through interior monologue is necessary, as it is hard to demonstrate an epiphany through behavior, and even dialogue can be a stretch, because epiphanies are usually quiet, intimate affairs. Laura's epiphany does, in fact, lead to a major change.

In *White Oleander*, Astrid's epiphany is more directly elicited. In her meeting with her mother, Astrid takes a courageous leap and asks something of her mother—challenging her mother's all-powerful hold over her, and begging for some tenderness in the process:

> She shook her head, gazed down at her bare tanned feet. "If I could take it all back, I would, Astrid." She lifted her eyes to mine. "You've got to believe me." Her eyes, glinting in the sun, were exactly the color of the pool we swam in together the summer she was arrested. I wanted to swim there again, to submerge myself in them.
>
> "Then tell me you don't want me to testify," I said. "Tell me you don't want me like this. Tell me you would sacrifice the rest of your life to have me back the way I was."

The reader aches for Astrid as she waits to hear what her mother will say, but at the same time, the reader fears Astrid is about to get burned, as the opening of the scene suggested. Her mother does not reply automatically, which already tells Astrid something—and in the time that she waits for her mother to show up for her, Astrid has her epiphany:

> And suddenly I felt panic. I'd made a mistake, like when I'd played chess with Ray and I knew a second too late I'd made the wrong move. I had asked a question I couldn't afford to know the answer to. It was the thing I didn't want to know. The rock that never should be turned over. I knew what was under there. I didn't need to see it, the hideous eyeless albino creature that lived underneath.
>
> "Listen, forget it. A deal's a deal. Let's leave it at that."

Astrid realizes in that moment, in a removing-the-blinders style of epiphany, that she has lived in terror of learning that her mother doesn't really love her. Her whole life she has lived with this fear. This kind of epiphany usually comes with a kind of resignation for the character—on some level she has known all along who her mother is, but has willed herself not to see it.

The scene doesn't end there, however. By taking the responsibility out of her mother's hands, by agreeing to the deal, Astrid gets the *result* she wants—her mother tells her that she does not have to testify and that she would do anything to have her daughter "partway back." But this all comes at a cost for Astrid, because it was not offered unconditionally. Also, though Astrid is happy to hear those words, the reader still mistrusts Ingrid and isn't sure she means it. By the epiphany's end, Astrid's blinders are fully removed. She sees her mother as she truly is and doesn't have to try to please her anymore.

When you reach it, the moment of epiphany should come with great emotional consequences that either make things better for your protagonist or present him with a difficult emotional choice that he must make. An epiphany can free the protagonist, or it can bind him to a terrible decision. You want to demonstrate the cost of the epiphany—whether through a brief passage of interior monologue or through an action he takes that is clearly derived from the epiphany.

The post-epiphany work of resolving and concluding the events of the epiphany will take place in the next scene or scenes. I encourage you to resist using narrative summary or too much interior monologue to deal with the changes wrought by the epiphany. Character changes are best demonstrated. If your character's epiphany was an identity epiphany, in which he realized that he could not be a doormat any longer, then you will want him to take actions that show him improving upon his self-esteem and confronting people who have treated him carelessly. Epiphanies mark a change of direction and path for your protagonist, and from the point of epiphany on you will want to show how that realization has changed him.

EPIPHANY SCENE MUSE POINTS

• An epiphany should cause a protagonist to change.

- Open this type of scene with your character anxious about the future or under stress.

- Exert pressure and generally up the ante on your protagonist mid-scene to drive him toward epiphany.

- End your scene just after the epiphany to let the reader and the protagonist digest it.

- The epiphany should cause a change in the protagonist's outlook and direction that will be demonstrated in future scenes.

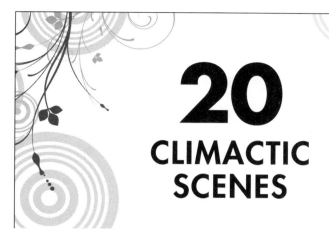

20

CLIMACTIC SCENES

In fiction, the climax is the high point of all the action and drama in your narrative—where the events that began with the significant situation come to a roiling, intense head. The result of the climax events will have the most dramatic impact on character change and will point you toward the ending (often called the denouement) of your narrative. A climactic scene will be one of the most, if not *the* most, intense, dramatic, powerful scenes in your entire narrative. That is the job of the climax.

You should have only one major climactic scene in your narrative, unless you have multiple narrators who each have their own climax to undergo (though you may want your multiple narrators to undergo the same climactic event, and just choose one person's point of view through which to reveal it). This is because once the climax is over, the job of the rest of your narrative is to resolve, tie up, and conclude what has taken place. Crafting the finale of your novel is akin to picking through the wreckage after a fire and figuring out what's left and how to proceed.

A successful climactic scene must have the following:

- Opposing forces must now collide. Your protagonist and antagonist (whether person, natural disaster or other) must meet and clash.

- The climax event must be directly related to the significant situation.

- Confrontation must be central. Your protagonist must confront something or someone (this can be an inner confrontation in a more literary novel) so he can change or be changed.

- The stakes should be very high: life and death, ties about to be severed, kingdoms on the verge of being lost.

- The pace must be swift, but allow room for emotional content.

Remember that the climax is also the point of no return. Once your protagonist arrives here, there is no turning back; character and plot will be changed permanently. Therefore, a climactic scene tends to fall toward the end of your narrative because there is a lot less to do after the climax. In a literary novel, an epiphany scene can serve as the climactic scene—a character's epiphany may be big enough to carry a climax. The narrative will feel less urgent, less intense to the reader as you work to tie up remaining threads.

SETTING UP A CLIMACTIC SCENE

A climactic scene should not come as a total surprise to the reader. If anything, it may come as a relief, because scenes prior to this one should have increased in tension and suspense, and become more emotionally dramatic for your protagonist, clueing the reader in that a terrible collision (literal or figurative) is on its way. If you have created more consequences for your protagonist in the middle of your narrative, he should be under a great deal of obvious stress, and knee-deep in conflict by the time the climactic scene arrives.

You want your climactic scene to open with a clear sense of action and drama about to unfold, and one very powerful way to do that is to leave the scene before it on a note of suspense or tension, or in some other way that suggests conflict is coming.

Robert Heinlein's astonishing science fiction novel *Stranger in a Strange Land* tells the story of Valentine Michael Smith—a human child born on Mars and raised by Martians. When he is brought back to Earth he has a volatile and transformative effect on everyone, and eventually becomes the ringleader of a cult in which everyone is taught to see themselves as God and jealousy, competition, and ambition are abolished. This leads to a blissful commune which, naturally, threatens "civilized" society. Michael's goal is to introduce all of humanity to this way of being, but there are forces against him.

At the end of the scene prior to the climactic scene, Michael—who has been meditating for a long time on how to handle the fact that humans, en masse, don't take too kindly to the kind of ideals he wants to teach them, and consequently want him dead—comes to a decision point:

> Then Mike's eyes opened, he grinned merrily. "You've got me all squared away, Father. I'm ready to show them now—I grok the fullness." The Man from Mars stood up. "Waiting is ended."

While the reader doesn't know exactly *what* he's going to do, his words signal that action is coming in the next scene and that it will be big. And so it is. In the next scene, Mike leaves "the Nest"—the place where his group of followers lives—and goes out into the stormy lynch mob of a crowd that is waiting for him. They stone him and call him names, but he speaks his truth, even though he knows that they want to kill him:

> "*Blasphemer!*" A rock caught him over his left eye and blood welled forth.
> Mike said calmly, "In fighting me, you fight yourself ... for Thou Art God ... and I am God ... and all that groks is God—there is no other."

We'll talk more about how this scene unfolds further in the chapter. First, though we'll look at *two* scene endings prior to the climactic scene of one of the most wonderfully weird, dark, and yet human novels I've ever read, *Geek Love* by Katherine Dunn. This discussion should help you think about how to set up your climactic scene a *few* scenes in advance.

In *Geek Love*, the Binewskis are a carnival family—in order to secure their livelihood, parents Al and Lily make sure that their offspring are suitably carnival-worthy by experimenting with chemicals and drugs during each pregnancy. They wind up with a set of Siamese twins, Elly and Iphy; Arturo the "Aqua Boy," who has flippers instead of limbs; Olympia, or "Oly," a "hunchback albino" dwarf; and Chick, who has telekinetic powers and can make people think whatever he chooses. The novel is written as Oly's memoir—though most of the time, the scenes are so vivid, the reader forgets that all that is happening has in essence already happened.

Despite the horrific and absurd nature of the premise, *Geek Love* is a serious book in which serious things happen to the characters. As the family of freaks grows up, Arturo—who has long been the star of the show—develops a megalomaniacal need for attention and power, and exerts more and more control on all his family members, since there would be no show without him. He develops a following of people who worship him, and he uses his brother Chick's powers to get these people to do as he wants.

At the end of the chapter that precedes the climactic scene, protagonist Oly has been forced to give away her infant daughter, Miranda, because her brother Arty feels she is a "norm" who can't contribute to their act. Because Oly is afraid of him and afraid for her daughter, she kowtows to Arty and does as she is told, but not without resentment. Here is how the scene ends, setting the reader up for the climax to come two scenes later:

> My job was to come back directly, with nothing leaking from beneath my dark glasses, to give Arty his rubdown and then paint him for the next show, nodding cheerfully all the while, never showing anything but attentive care for his muscular wonderfulness. Because he could have killed you. He could have cut off the money that schooled and fed you. He could have erased you so entirely that I never would have had those letters and report cards and photos, or your crayon pictures, or the chance to spy on you, and to love you secretly when everything else was gone.

The statement "when everything else was gone" is the reader's first clue that bad things are coming in the next scene, which takes place a year later in time, though it doesn't feel like it. The next scene is very short and shows Arty at his narcissistic height, with Oly still tending to him in her fear. That scene ends with this strangely foreboding image of Arty:

> When it was set, the final greasing had a sheen of its own and kept the white on even through the final hour under water with Arty squirming his wildest. The white tipping and streaking were new touches. Arty examined himself in the mirror and his wide mouth wriggled from corner to corner.

You get the feeling that this is the last close-up of Arty the reader is going to get. This is Arty at his pinnacle, blind to what is about to happen. There's something about the line "Arty squirming his wildest" that suggests perhaps death throes, or pain. And anytime you end a scene with a narcissistic character admiring himself in the mirror, you're setting up the reader to knock him off his throne. The scene nicely sets the stage for the climax that follows (which comes later in this chapter).

Setting up your climactic scene requires that you lace the ending of the prior scene or two with a sense of impending doom or instability. It needs to be clear to the reader, whether through simple interior monologue, or by some combination of setting detail and action, that change is coming.

THE CLIMACTIC EVENT

The actual opening of your climactic scene can be handled in many ways. Most climactic scenes get quickly to the action—after all, you've held the reader off for a long time already. Don't waste too much time setting up the opening; let things build fast.

The nature of a climactic scene is that it builds quickly and steadily toward the climax, with the pacing of an action scene. This is not a scene where you want to linger in lots of exposition, as what makes a climactic event is that it happens too fast to be stopped. The best climactic scenes have all the elements working together: specific action; dialogue rather than interior monologue to convey what's happening; setting details to balance the action, and to build atmosphere for the climactic event—details are good in a climactic scene because so much is at stake that you don't want the reader to feel he missed anything; and emotional content—the protagonist's feelings should be conveyed in some way, from fear to relief.

Let's look at how these details play out in the *Stranger in a Strange Land* climactic scene. Remember, it opened with Michael walking out to face his foes and being attacked. As the scene progresses, the crowd is getting more aggressive, but Michael doggedly continues to speak his message of love:

"God damn it—let's stop this taking the Name of the Lord in vain!"—"Come on men! Let's finish him!" [*Dramatic tension.*] The mob surged forward, led by one bold with a club; they were on him with rocks and fists, and then with feet as he went down. [*Action.*] He went on talking while they kicked his ribs in and smashed his golden body, broke his bones and tore an ear loose. [*Very specific details.*] At last someone called out, "Back away so we can get the gasoline can on him." [*Dialogue.*]

The mob opened up a little at that warning and the camera zoomed to pick up his face and shoulders. The Man from Mars smiled at his brothers, said once more, softly and clearly, "I love you." [*Emotional content.*] An incautious grasshopper came whirring to a landing on the grass a few inches from his face [*Lovely details deliver a momentary pause before the finale.*]; Mike turned his head, looked at it as it stared back at him. "Thou art God," he said happily and discorporated.

(*Discorporated*, for those who haven't read the book, means that his soul has left his body.)

Notice that the pace is quick due to the action and dialogue, yet through the use of focused details, like the camera zooming in on him, and the landing of the little grasshopper, the pace is slowed just enough so that the action doesn't move too fast to overwhelm the impact of what is happening. The statements "I love you" and "Thou art God" convey an emotional tone—and in contrast to the mob that is tearing him apart, despite that this is his death, Valentine Michael Smith seems at peace. This is a more emotional climactic event.

You may choose an emotional climactic event when the content of your narrative has dealt more with relationships or inner conflict, or any kind of powerful emotional content.

In *Geek Love*'s climactic event, Dunn also utilizes all the elements of a scene for a complex, emotional, detailed, and powerful climax. Unlike Heinlein, she strings together a series of small, terrible events that build more action and intensity into the final moment—there's not a lot of time for the reader to feel anything but a mounting sense of horror. First, Iphy kills her Siamese twin, Elly (a suicide, essentially, as they share organ systems), claiming that Elly killed her baby, Mumpo. That's three tragedies right there in a row. Chick and Oly rush in, and Chick tries to use his mental power to bring them back to life, but of course he cannot. Chick, who was devoted to the twins, is devastated, and decides that it is all Arty's fault; in a brilliant stroke of character, the normally calm, sweet, devoted one finally blows—literally, with this climactic event:

> It came billowing, scorching toward us, and the Chick, in his pain, could not hold himself but reached. I felt him rush through me like a current of love to my cross points, and then draw back. I, with my arms lifted, felt his eyes open into me, and felt their blue flicker of recognition. Then he drew back. ... The flames spouted from him—pale as light—bursting outward from his belly. He did not scream or move but he spread, and my world exploded with him, and I, watching, bit down—bit down and knew it—bit down with a sense of enormous relief, and ground my teeth to powdered shards—and stood singed and grinding at the stumps as they died—my roses—Arty and Al and Chick and the twins—gone dustward as the coals rid themselves of that terrible heat.

Here, the climactic event is a kind of relief for Oly, who never felt that she had any control over what was happening to her. It reveals to her that she *was* powerless, and now it's over before she can stop it.

The goal of the climactic event is to bring significant situation and the resulting plot consequences to a head so that there's some kind of transformation in your protagonist's life or struggle. The climax is the moment where the protagonist is tested, tried, and permanently altered by whatever happens.

A climactic event does not have to be subtle—you can launch into your climax in no uncertain terms; the only real goal is that the events of the action bring your significant situation to a logical head. This next example is from Sara Gruen's novel *Water for Elephants*, set in the prohibition era of the United States, and starring Jacob Janowski, a young man whose dreams of taking over his father's veterinary business are dashed when his parents are killed in a car accident. To escape his grief, he jumps on a random train one night only to find himself an unwitting new part of the Benzini Brothers Circus come morning.

Jacob quickly falls in love with Marlena, the acrobatic star of the circus, who is married to the tempestuous August, a man who takes out his anger on the animals—in particular, a new addition, an elephant named Rosie, who quickly tires of her abuse.

For pages the tension builds between August and Jacob, as well as among the disgruntled circus employees and their employer, "Uncle Al," who often withholds their pay. These many tensions build for the entire novel until one day, when a bunch of men who were "red lighted" (thrown off the train overnight) come back for revenge during a performance with the intention of ruining the circus.

Gruen signals the climactic event in a cacophonous way:

> I reach for it, but before I can pick it up the music crashes to a halt. There's an ungodly collision of brass that finishes with a cymbal's hollow clang. It wavers out of the big top and across the lot, leaving nothing in its wake.
>
> Grady freezes, crouched over his burger.
>
> I look from left to right. No one moves a muscle—all eyes point at the big top. A few wisps of hay swirl lazily across the hard dirt.
>
> "What is it? What's going on?" I ask.
>
> "Shh," Grady says sharply.
>
> The band starts up again, this time playing "Stars and Stripes Forever."
>
> "Oh Christ. Oh shit," Grady jumps up and backward, knocking over the bench.
>
> "What? What is it?"
>
> "The Disaster March!" he shouts, turning and bolting.

The climactic event gets underway with a literal crash of cymbals, and what happens from there is mayhem and chaos—animals and circus-goers fleeing and screaming, people being run over and attacked, all leading up to the penultimate moment (I won't give it away completely, but you'll get the feeling of what's to come):

> My eyes sweep the tent, desperate to the point of panic. *Where are you? Where are you? Where the hell are you?*
>
> I catch sight of pink sequins and my head jerks around. When I see Marlena standing beside Rosie, I cry out in relief.

August is in front of them—of course he is, where else would he be? Marlena's hands cover her mouth. She hasn't seen me yet, but Rosie has. She stares at me long and hard, and something about her expression stops me cold. August is oblivious—red-faced and bellowing, flapping his arms and swinging his cane. His top hat lies in the straw beside him, punctured as though he'd put a foot through it.

Rosie stretches out her trunk, reaching for something.

In this climax, the opposite forces—the innocent elephant and the brutal animal trainer—clash, and the result changes Jacob and Marlena, and even Rosie, for good.

Some climactic moments will test your protagonist directly. He will rise to the challenge and prove himself worthy of something—he will deliver that ring to the fires of Mordor. Some will take things or people away from your protagonist, leaving her to deal with an emotional experience that changes her. Either way, climactic scenes, like epiphanies, are about change; but climactic scenes are about more permanent change. A protagonist can come to an epiphany without reaching the ultimate event of the narrative. But once you arrive at the climactic event, nothing will be the same.

POST-CLIMACTIC EVENT

When the climactic scene is over, your work changes. No longer do you have an imperative to drop in new plot information or create suspense. The scenes that follow a climactic one are about resolutions, sorting through the aftermath of the event and determining where to go next, showing that your protagonist has changed. You do want to be sure that all plot and character questions are answered, however.

In *Stranger in a Strange Land*, Michael's death gives his followers motivation to keep up his work—to turn the world into a better place. In *Geek Love*, the loss of her family and her livelihood forces Olympia to finally become her own person, and it allows her to tell her daughter, Miranda, the truth of her origins. While the climax leads to loss, it also leads to a better future for Miranda. In *Water for Elephants*, Jacob and Marlena can now create a different kind of life for themselves, and those who suffered under brutality of one sort or another are able to get free of it.

Your climactic scene is a big one in the narrative—it is, in essence, the point that the entire narrative is driving towards, the moment of no return, and it should be written with care.

CLIMACTIC SCENE MUSE POINTS

- Use as many of the elements of a scene as possible to build a well-rounded, complex climactic event: action, dialogue, setting details, emotional content, dramatic tension.
- Each protagonist will have only one climactic scene.
- The climax event must be directly related to the significant situation.
- The climax is a point of no return that must change your protagonist permanently in some way.
- Keep the stakes high.
- The climactic scene is the high point of action and drama—all scenes that follow it will be slower and more reflective, and contain less action.

21
THE FINAL SCENE

All good things must end. But as the aphorism goes, the end of one thing is also the beginning of another. Final scenes, then, are the end of one chapter in a protagonist's life. A rare few protagonists will actually die at the end of a narrative, but in general your final scene is the conclusion of the events that your first scene opened with—your significant situation. However, the final scene need not feel completely over and done with. In fact, a final scene may very well feel like a new beginning. This scene should:

- Provide a snapshot of where your protagonist is after the conclusion of your plot
- Be reflective in tone
- Provide a full-circle feeling by recalling the significant situation
- Move at a slower pace

You *may* also save one last surprise, answer, or insight for the final scene, but this isn't something that's necessary.

Though the final scene marks the end of your narrative, in the reader's mind, your characters and settings may very well live on, so you want to put as much work into creating a memorable ending as you did into your captivating beginning.

LEADING UP TO THE FINAL SCENE

Before we go on to look at the structure and content of your final scene, let's discuss the final *scenes*—yes, that's plural—that come before the very final scene of your narrative. The three to five scenes that come before the last scene have the job of supplying answers to outstanding questions that your plot has raised (see chapter eight). Those scenes are where you solve the crime, return the kidnapped child, or bring the lovers back together, thus tying up your plot, decreasing tension, and bringing a sense of resolution to your narrative. The job of the true final scene is to show the reader where your protagonist is now, how he has changed, and what he thinks or feels as a result of the consequences of your significant situation and its offshoots.

Showing Character Transformation

The final scene is the last impression your protagonist will make upon the reader. Unless you have a very, very good reason for your protagonist not to have changed (if, for instance, the plot of your novel was that people were trying to change him through brainwashing, cult activities, or some other form of coercion, then a successful arc would portray your character *resisting* change), your protagonist should not be the same person he was when he started out. The principle areas where your character is most likely to reflect change are in his attitude, job, relationships, and even location. Whether he has a new outlook, a new lifestyle, a new love, or a new sense of self—character change is the defining factor of your final scene.

Concluding the Significant Situation

As a result of your narrative's significant situation, a world of consequences has unraveled for your protagonist, taking him on a complex and interesting journey. That journey eventually has to conclude in a way that makes the storyline feel finished. If the story is a murder investigation, the reader must learn whodunit by the end. If it's a romance, the reader should glimpse the happily ever after. You get the idea—the final scene of your narrative will either be the literal conclusion of the significant situation, or the point in time that comes just after the situation ends.

The final scene is the place where your protagonist reflects upon, deals with, or accepts the consequences of your significant situation.

Final scenes inevitably have a contemplative air about them and may not be as long as other scenes because there's no need to introduce elaborate new actions or plot situations. The final scene is a snapshot of where your protagonist finds himself at the end of his journey, and should offer just a glimpse. Most tension and drama should be concluded or winding down by then. (You rarely leave a narrative on a suspenseful note unless there's definitely a sequel coming.) The ending is a place of reflection, and right from the launch of your final scene, you want to make this clear by slowing down the pace and providing room for reflection or interior monologue.

FINAL SCENES VS. EPILOGUES

Just as there is a difference between a first scene and a prologue, a final scene is not the same as an epilogue. The reason you will not find a chapter on epilogues in this book is because I am not a fan of them. (Without an epilogue you must really do the work of completing your character's journey and transformation. You must come to a satisfying end point.) But many, many writers choose to write them, and they do them quite well. I have read some very successful epilogues. In some books they are even necessary; and you are free to write one. Keep in mind that an epilogue is a scene, or a reflection, that comes sometime in the future after the narrative has concluded. Which means that your epilogue is never your final scene. It is a scene that comes after your final scene.

- The epilogue for *Life of Pi*, by Yann Martel, works because Pi's story—of being trapped with a Bengal tiger in a tiny boat and surviving on the ocean for 227 days—is so wild and fantastical that the epilogue, which takes place outside of Pi's point of view, offers insight the reader could never have gotten from Pi himself.

- The epilogue of *Lolita*, by Vladimir Nabokov, explains why Humbert Humbert, who had no intention of having his behavior

toward Lolita discovered, is confessing. It turns out to be a suggestion by his lawyer, a tactic to make him seem more sympathetic
in court.

- The epilogue of *Sleep, Pale Sister*, by Joanne Harris, works because it allows the reader to see what became of Henry Chester—a character who gets away with some pretty awful behavior
toward his wife in the narrative. Harris gives the reader a satisfying peek into how he gets his comeuppance.

OPENING YOUR FINAL SCENE

Counterpoints and reflective exposition are two popular techniques for
kicking off your final scene because both methods allow you the opportunity
to fully illustrate to the reader just how much the events of the story have
changed your character.

Counterpoints

A fantastic way to show that your character has changed as a result of your
significant situation is to open the final scene with a counterpoint to the
first scene, so that the reader has direct and specific cues about how your
character has changed. What this means is that you set up your final scene
to resemble your first scene, but you change the details to reflect the kind of
change your character has undergone.

For example, in Kate Atkinson's literary mystery novel *Case Histories*,
cop-turned-private-investigator Jackson Brodie's final scene opens with a
distinctly lighthearted tone, with the words (in French) "goodbye sadness."
He has solved his case, accepted that his ex-wife will never take him back,
and found himself attracted to Julia, the quirky woman he met while investigating her sister's death. There's a carefree tone and mood to the scene.
He's driving in his convertible, playing music on the radio, and wishing he
could get rid of Julia's dull sister Amelia so they can flirt more effectively:

Au revoir tristesse. Jackson drove with the top down, the Dixie Chicks playing loudly on the car stereo. He picked them up at Montpelier Airport. They

were dressed ready for the convertible, in chiffon head scarves and sun-glasses, so that Julia looked like a fifties movie star and Amelia didn't. Julia had said on the phone that Amelia was a lot more cheerful these days, but if she was then she was keeping it to herself, sitting in the backseat of his new BMW M3, harrumphing and grunting at everything that Julia said. Jackson suddenly regretted not buying the two-seater BMW Z8 instead—then they could have put Amelia in the boot.

Now contrast that with the Jackson Brodie the reader met at the beginning of the narrative, who was having trouble quitting smoking, dealing with car and work troubles, and fighting with his ex-wife:

Jackson switched on the radio and listened to the reassuring voice of Jenni Murray on *Woman's Hour*. He lit a new cigarette from the stub of the old one because he had run out of matches, and faced with a choice between chain-smoking or abstinence, he'd taken the former option because it felt like there was enough abstinence in his life already. If he got the cigarette lighter on the dashboard fixed he wouldn't have to smoke his way through the packet, but there were a lot of other things that needed fixing on the car and the cigarette lighter wasn't high on the list. Jackson drove a black Alfa Romeo 156 that he'd bought secondhand four years ago for £13,000 and that was now probably worth less than the Emmelle Freedom moun-tain bike he had just given his daughter for her eighth birthday (on the proviso that she didn't cycle on the road until she was at least forty).

Notice how in both scenes he's driving in a car and listening to the radio, yet the feeling of the first scene is tense and cranky—while the final scene is relaxed and free and improved upon. In the final scene, he's driving a new BMW, not a lemon of an Alfa Romeo. He's not worrying about his ex-wife or his daughter, and whereas in the first scene he had "enough abstinence in his life," now he's got the prospect of a relationship with a new woman.

Counterpointing your first scene is a wonderful way to provide a de-finitive sense of closure and change to your narrative. Look back at your first scene and see how you can set up a similar one in terms of the setting and other small details, but change the tone, pace, and interior monologue to show that your protagonist is clearly in a different place from where he started.

Reflective Exposition

Reflective exposition is another strong way to kick off your concluding scene. Since the final scene is a time for reflection—after all, you've just spent a novel or story's worth of time dealing with actions and interactions, putting your protagonist in conflict and danger, and keeping tension and drama alive—interior monologue and exposition can be a natural fit here.

In Janet Fitch's *Paint It Black*, protagonist Josie Tyrell has finally gotten a glimpse into the life and mind of her boyfriend, Michael, who committed suicide at the start of the book. She has driven to the hotel where he did it, read the journal entry he made just before, and come to understand the family he came from. Now she's left to pick up the pieces of her life and carry on:

> Josie sat on the bed in number 4, smoking a ciggie. The sunlight shone bright and cold through the open door. She knew it was time to leave. There was nothing else to do but pack up and head home. And yet, how could she leave this place where he'd made his end? She sat up against the rickety headboard and picked cholla spines out of the bedspread, flicking them into the ashtray. Maybe she should take up knitting. Something quiet and productive. She didn't want to go back home, back to the empty house, as if Michael had fallen through a hole in the ice and just disappeared. But she couldn't drag his raw death through her days like this, like a giant bleeding moose head.

When you open with interior monologue, you can drop the reader directly into the mood, emotion, or thematic state you want him to be in for the finale. If you want to set the stage for redemption, forgiveness, acceptance, or any of the larger themes of literature, interior monologue and exposition allow you to do this quickly and to the point, since final scenes are not often very long—they are merely bookends to your protagonist's journey.

ESTABLISHING THE RIGHT PACE

Your final scene does not need to have the same dramatic structure as all other scenes. Your significant situation is over, and your protagonist has undergone his changes. Your final scene does not require you to set a new intention that must be carried out. It is the place to let your protagonist rest and reflect, and for you to convey a feeling, an image, or a sense of theme to the reader. Therefore, the pace tends to be slower. Actions are small and kept to a minimum, with attention to details that elicit your character's inner life and attitudes, hopes and feelings.

Let's look at a few excerpts from the middles of final scenes. Notice their pacing, how they feel slower, quieter, and more reflective.

Author Louise Erdrich uses setting details to bring her pace down in the final scene of her novel *The Painted Drum*. Protagonist Faye Travers, whose sister died young, has just been through an intense relationship with a local sculptor whose teenage daughter was killed, resurrecting Faye's own grief. The novel has spent a lot of time focusing on the loss of children and on grief—and Faye herself has pushed much of her own grief away. By the end, however, her experiences have softened her, and she's ready to face things as they are. In the final scene she goes to visit her sister's grave:

> My sister's stone marker is very distinctive. It's a carved angel that our mother bought from a church about to be demolished and had engraved with the date and name. Perhaps because the angel was not meant as a memorial in the first place, there is something stealthily alive about her—wings that flare instead of droop, an alert and outwardly directed expression, a hand clutched to her breast not as a gesture of reverence or sorrow, but, I think, breathless delight.

There is little action in this scene—the most Faye does is clear away the debris that has piled up on her sister's headstone—because actions are not necessary. Notice, too, that despite being in a cemetery, at her sister's grave, Faye seems optimistic. You can feel her grief lifting in the way she describes the angel on her sister's marker as being "stealthily alive" and clutching her breast with "breathless delight." This final scene is pointing toward positive change. Faye is freed from her grief, and this is shown to us in the details.

Setting details are powerful when you want to slow down the pace and convey mood. In your final scene, ask yourself how you can direct the reader's focus onto small details in a way that also creates the tone you're shooting for. For example, if your story was about a criminal who finds redemption, in the final scene you could use images that convey freedom and forgiveness—like a bird flying across the expanse of the Grand Canyon, or another character offering your protagonist his hand. These details will help you to bring your pace down to reflect the tone of your narrative.

You can also slow your pacing down in the final scene by dropping into the realm of metaphors, which have a timeless quality. In Margaret Atwood's novel *The Robber Bride*, three women—Tony, Roz, and Charis—have been personally injured by one woman, Zenia, whom they all met in college. Zenia is a masterful manipulator who has always selfishly put herself before others, and who even manages to fake her death and stage a funeral. But she is not dead at all, and she continues to wreak injustice on the three friends until, finally, the women stop her for good.

In the final scene, Tony reflects upon what has happened and who Zenia was in a series of metaphoric reflections that slow the pace and aim for an emotional finish:

> No flowers grow in the furrows of the lake, none in the fields of asphalt. Tony needs a flower, however. A common weed, because wherever else Zenia had been in her life, she had also been at war. An unofficial war, a guerilla war, a war she may not have known she was waging, but a war nevertheless.
>
> Who was the enemy? What past wrong was she seeking to avenge? Where was her battlefield? Not in any one place. It was in the air all around, it was in the texture of the world itself; or it was nowhere visible, it was in among the neurons, the tiny incandescent fires of the brain that flash up and burn out. An electric flower would be the right kind for Zenia, a bright, lethal flower like a short circuit, a thistle of molten steel going to seed in a burst of sparks.

There are images of war and of flowers—two very powerful contrasting metaphors that sum up the themes of the novel nicely. Metaphors often show up in literary novels, but you'll find them even in genre works because they say so much with so few words.

THE FINAL SENTENCES

In the final scene, the last two to three sentences (and especially the last one) are like DNA—they carry the feeling of the entire novel with them, even beyond your narrative. They should leave an emotional flavor that speaks to the entire journey your protagonist has undergone. Here we'll look at final sentences that end with action, reflection, and images.

Final Actions

The reader likes to know that the characters she's come to love will live on. Actions have a way of making characters' lives feel still in motion even after the book or story is over. So you may decide to end your final scene with your protagonist taking a symbolic action or gesture. I stress *symbolic*. If you end on an action, it should suggest a larger action than the mundane—it should conjure a feeling of an action the protagonist is taking in his life.

In *The Robber Bride*, for instance, the action doesn't come until the final sentence. In much of the final scene Tony is outside reflecting on the damage Zenia wrought—she caused her to mistrust other women, to hate them even, at times. The final paragraphs show Tony outside staring at a pottery statue of Zenia, thinking, and then being drawn to the sounds of her friends inside. The scene could easily end at the finish of these paragraphs, reflectively:

> Tony picks her up and turns her over, probes and questions, but the woman with her glazed pottery face does nothing but smile.
>
> From the kitchen she hears laughter, and the clatter of dishes. Charis is setting out the food, Roz is telling a story. That's what they will do, increasingly in their lives: tell stories. Tonight their stories will be about Zenia.
>
> Was she in any way like us? thinks Tony. Or, to put it another way around: Are we in any way like her?

But Atwood has Tony make one last action, a symbolic one:

Then she opens the door, and goes in to join the others.

For Tony, rejoining her friends is an important action that suggests she is ready to open herself again to women friends. That final action crystallizes all of Tony's thoughts and tells the reader that Tony has healed.

Final actions should speak to how your protagonist is going to behave differently in the world now that he has survived the trials of your narrative. Think symbolically. Ask yourself how a small action can convey a larger meaning. Your protagonist could be staring down a dirt road at the end of a narrative in which he has been afraid to make choices. As his final action, he can walk down the unknown road, for example. Symbolic actions carry weight at the end of a narrative and will give your final scene a feeling that there is more to come for your protagonist.

Final Reflections and Thoughts

By the end of the narrative, the reader can tell how the protagonist has changed, but it may still be unclear how the protagonist feels about his changes or about something that took place in the narrative. In this case, a direct expression of feelings is needed.

In Chuck Palahniuk's novel *Invisible Monsters*, a novel about identity and about learning to accept oneself in whatever way possible, the narrator—formerly a fashion model—is shot in the face early in the narrative and must undergo massive facial reconstruction, losing her beauty entirely. While in the hospital, she meets Brandy Alexander, a man in the process of undergoing sex reassignment surgery to become a woman. Brandy's female form looks uncannily like Shannon used to look before her accident. At the end of the novel, the reader isn't quite sure how Shannon feels about herself, now that her beauty is gone. What the reader knows is that she has made some sort of peace with the past and found friendship in an unlikely source—Brandy. The final sentences convey Shannon's feelings on her identity:

> Completely and totally, permanently and without hope, forever and ever I love Brandy Alexander.
> And that's enough.

Brandy represents the self she used to hate—who was pretty on the outside, but tortured within. By admitting her love for Brandy, she does in effect admit to loving herself.

A summary thought or reflection on your narrative works best when it is unclear how the narrator feels at the end, or if there has been some sort of gray area or waffling about feelings. A final thought sums it up so the reader can rest with a sense of understanding.

Final Images

Images resonate with the reader more than actions or interior monologue because they speak the language of the subconscious—they directly trigger emotional responses without an intellectual interpretation.

In Richard Lewis's novel *The Killing Sea*, two teens are affected by the cataclysmic tsunami of 2004 in Indonesia. The life of Sarah, an American girl on vacation with her parents and brother, is changed drastically when her mother is killed in the tsunami strike and her father disappears. In the aftermath of the crisis, struggling to get back to a place where she and her brother can get help, she meets Ruslan, an Indonesian boy, and winds up helping him to find his missing father. All throughout the narrative, Sarah's grief for her mother is tangled. She has always believed that her mother didn't want to have her, and this thought haunts her. In the final scene, Ruslan draws Sarah a picture of her mother as he imagines her:

> And in the simple, graceful lines of her gently smiling face, in the eyes that looked right into her, Sarah saw all the love that her mother had always had for her, and how absolutely, utterly wrong she'd been to ever have doubted it.

While that is a lovely sentiment, the final sentence is the most powerful because it plants an image in the reader's mind, conjuring not only tears, but the waters of the tsunami itself that took her mother and father away:

> Something gave way within her, and the raw waters of grief came rushing in.

I am a fan of images that symbolically and metaphorically speak to the journey the protagonist has undergone. Think about the themes of your narrative. Is it about loss, healing, faith, forgiveness? It helps to make a list of images that come to mind for whatever your themes are, and then from that list, to select or create a final image that speaks to your protagonist's personal journey.

FINAL SCENE MUSE POINTS

- The final scene is a snapshot of your protagonist in the aftermath or at the very end of the significant situation.

- Final scenes should reveal that your protagonist has changed.

- Final scenes are slower and more reflective.

- Final scenes do not require much action.

PART IV

OTHER SCENE CONSIDERATIONS

Only if poets and writers set themselves
tasks that no one else dares imagine will
literature continue to have a function.

—ITALO CALVINO

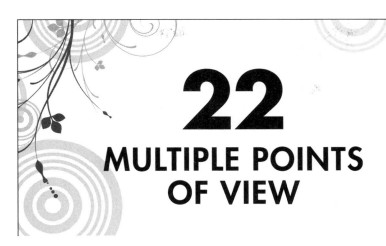

22

MULTIPLE POINTS OF VIEW

In fiction, point of view (POV) is the camera through which the reader enters your protagonist's world, sees what he sees, and shares in his feelings and perceptions. POV has a direct influence on the tone, mood, energy, and pace of a scene (not to mention your overall narrative).

In order to master POV from one scene to the next, you must use it with integrity and consistency, by which I mean that the reader should feel expertly guided at all times throughout your scenes, never confused about whose POV is being presented. If you've shown the scene of a murder through a shocked widow's eyes, for example, you don't want to suddenly leap into the point of view of the vigilante detective who is hunting the murderer down without legitimate reason and careful transition. Otherwise you'll leave the reader a little feeling a little whip lashed and out of sync with your story.

In this chapter, we'll examine the different kinds of POV in relation to what effects they create. We'll also talk about how to make POV leaps and transitions inside scenes, and from scene to scene, so that whatever POV you choose to use works for your scenes, not against them.

CHOOSING YOUR CAMERA

POV is not only the camera that shows what your characters see, it is also what determines how close the reader can get to get to your characters. The distance between your characters and the reader defines the intimacy of the scene or story. The more intimate the POV, the more the reader feels as if he is personally experiencing what the character is. The more distant the POV, the more the reader feels like an objective observer on the sidelines. Your content will motivate your choice of intimacy in part. If you are writing about the lives of women in Afghanistan, like Khaled Hosseini does in his novel *A Thousand Splendid Suns*, then it will work to your advantage to bring the reader in close—through first person or limited third person, in which there is very little separation from the characters. Use this next section to choose the degree of intimacy you want, and the level of objectivity you need to tell your story.

First Person

First-person points of view reach out and grab the reader, like a small child standing in a room screaming "Me, me, me!" You can't help but turn to look. The "I" pronoun is very immediate, and it draws the reader emotionally directly into the characters' experience.

The following example comes from Marilynne Robinson's Pulitzer Prize–winning novel, *Gilead*, in which a dying minister writes down his life story for his young son to read someday. The memoirs are peppered with actual observations of his life as he is dying:

> I must try to be mindful of my condition. I started to lift you up into my arms the other day, the way I used to when you weren't quite so big and I wasn't quite so old. Then I saw your mother watching me with pure apprehension and I realized what a foolish thing to do that was.

If it's intimacy you strive for in creating characters, you can't get much closer than first person. You are literally inside the protagonist's head, which is very useful when you want to put the reader directly into your characters' shoes.

On the same note, the problem with first person is that if your character undergoes tremendous suffering, physical pain, or crisis, first person might be too immediate and painful. To provide objectivity and pull back from the intensity, you can use third-person limited, which we'll look at shortly.

Also, because first person is so immediate, your verb tenses will have a lot more power than in other points of view. The present tense, when conjoined with first person, is probably the most immediate experience you can give the reader: "I hold the gun up to Max's head." Whew ... that gun is liable to go off and poor Max may have only moments left. In the past tense, "I held the gun up to Max's head." Do you see how the past tense offers a tiny beat of distance?

Second Person

Second person is a narrative version of self-talk. The "you" pronoun is coming from the character, aimed back to himself. It is first person turned even more deeply intimate, because the reader is not only inside the person's mind and thoughts, he essentially *becomes* the character.

Here's an example from Aimee Bender's story "The Bowl" in her collection of short stories, *The Girl in the Flammable Skirt*.

> When you open the wrapping (there's no card), you find a bowl, a green bowl with a white interior, a bowl for fruit or mixing. You're puzzled, but obediently put four bananas inside and then go back to whatever you were doing before: a crossword puzzle. You wonder and hope this is from a secret admirer, but if so, you think, why a bowl? What are you to learn and gain from a green and white fruit bowl?

This POV is very intimate. Best used when the intention of the scene is to explore a character's feelings or attitude, or to draw the reader in incredibly close; but not so effective when you have a lot of action or character interaction unfolding in the scene at hand. The "you" second-person point of view plants the reader deeper inside the character's experience until the line between reader and character is blurred.

Second person can seem slightly humorous, even when the subject matter is not, because it's not a tense that we use in actual spoken conversation very often. When was the last time you heard someone refer to himself as "you"? Second person is an exquisitely self-conscious point of view, which can be fascinating and fun when the subject matter or the protagonist is quirky or the style is experimental, but otherwise second person feels as if

---

the reader has just opened a window on a character's mind in the middle of a deeply personal thought process. As a result, it's not used very often.

Third Person

You'll recognize third person by the use of pronouns "she" and "he." There are two main forms of the third-person point of view—omniscient, which is more distant, and limited, which is more intimate. I find that writers have a tendency to interchange the two in confusing ways.

Third-Person Limited

Third-person limited is really one of the most straightforward and practical of all points of view. It provides enough distance, via the "he" and "she" pronouns, that the reader is not riding piggyback with the characters, but it also allows you to develop one character at a time, and never confuses the reader. If the character's point of view is in limited third person, the reader knows, "I am looking out through Snow White's eyes here." There is no guesswork or moving between characters' thoughts.

In the third-person omniscient POV, the camera can move wherever it needs to, into any character's head, to look out upon any facet of the scene at hand. This flexibility offers more options for drama and conflict, and is often employed in an epic or historical novel, where important information needs to be communicated outside of a character's perspective.

Omniscient Continuous

When you can see inside the head of more than one character, and hear multiple characters' thoughts in a back-and-forth kind of fashion, you're in the omniscient continuous, as I like to call it. When the camera pans from Snow White to Dopey, Grumpy, and Doc, and you can hear the thoughts and opinions of each one as they discuss what to do about that nasty old witch, you're smack dab in omniscient.

When you employ omniscient in scenes, it creates a sense of movement because you must jump from character to character, which also creates emotional distance. It's useful to be able to dance back and forth between characters' thoughts when a scene involves multiple characters.

Omniscient Instants

Omniscient instants, on the other hand, are bits of information inserted into third-person limited POV that offer up information in the scene that the characters can't know but which helps clarify details for the reader.

Here's an example in Ingrid Hill's novel of ancestors, *Ursula, Under*, which is a series of linked historical stories that trace back the lineage of a child, Ursula, who has slipped down a mine shaft and is awaiting rescue.

> [Rene Josserand's skull] is still there today, undiscovered, four and a half feet into the rich earth, beneath leaves, grass, and clay, never touched by a gravedigger's hand. There are local post cards, but none of them says, "Paradise, Michigan, home of the tomahawked skull of Rene Josserand," because no one knows.

Since Rene Josserand—one of Ursula's ancestors—is long dead, and "no one knows" about his existence, then technically, there isn't a single person in the narrative who could deliver that information to the reader. Yet Hill chooses to tell it to us, since his story is integral to the life of the protagonist, Ursula, and ties up his storyline for us as best as she can.

Keep in mind that too many omniscient leaps will inevitably pull the reader out of the continuity of his reading. He might stop to ponder, "Hey, I'm not really supposed to know that" or even, "Who exactly is telling me this?"—and you don't want too much of that.

THE STORY ARC OF MULTIPLE PROTAGONISTS

> Once you've decided on each protagonist's POV, and whether you will use multiple scenes per chapter or let each chapter be a stand-alone scene, you must remember one final element: When you have multiple protagonists who each get POV scenes and chapters, you have a burden to give each character a narrative arc—each must undergo change and be connected to the significant situation, and their plotlines must also merge. Co-protagonists must share a journey and come together in the end for the narrative to work.

This means that, following the instructions in chapter twenty-three, each character has an imperative to:

- Respond to the significant situation (your work will be a lot more cohesive if they all share the same significant situation)

- Engage in consequences stemming from the significant situation

- Change as a result of the significant situation

- Merge his individual storyline with those of the other protagonists by narrative's end

Ultimately you want to select points of view that will convey the appropriate intimacy or distance levels you aim to achieve, offer consistency to the reader so that there is no confusion over whose point of view you are in, and devote equal stage time to every protagonist who stars in your narrative.

Books that successfully merge two or more protagonists' storylines: *A Thousand Splendid Suns* by Khaled Hosseini; *My Sister's Keeper* by Jodi Picoult; *Fall on Your Knees* by Ann-Marie MacDonald; *Case Histories* by Kate Atkinson.

USING MULTIPLE POINTS OF VIEW IN SCENES

In order to discuss multiple POVs in scenes, we need to quickly refresh the concept of a scene (at its most distilled): a container of significant action in which a protagonist acts on a scene intention, and in which conflict ensues, leading toward climax and change. POV is the camera through which you choose to show the events in the scene to the reader. If you have one protagonist only, then that is the character who gets the camera. Use the POV descriptions in this chapter to decide what kind of effect you want to achieve, and to choose your POV accordingly.

Choosing POV gets trickier when you have multiple protagonists, or simply multiple points of view that you want to show in a given scene. If you elect to use a limited POV, you will never have to worry about jumping from head to head within a given scene. Your biggest concern will be when and where to switch from narrator to narrator. But if you *do* want to be able to pan the camera through the thoughts of characters A, B, and C as event X unfolds, you will want to pay attention to this next part.

Changing POV Within a Scene

If you have more than one character within a scene whose points of view are relevant, then you'll need to use the omniscient POV. When your narrative tackles large issues: war, culture, race, identity—in which a complex or comprehensive look at a situation is required, omniscient POV is a good choice. Omniscient allows you to go beyond the personal—beyond the intimate experience of a small handful of characters—to include more history, cultural details, or perspectives that will add up to a more cohesive look at a subject.

Omniscient is also useful when you need to show more than one side of a story—and need to be able to jump back and forth between characters to offer alternate takes on events as they're happening, rather than later on in reflection.

However, you must make omniscient clear right away from the first paragraph in the first scene. If the reader believes that he has *only* been able to see inside character A's head, and then you suddenly leap into character B's head, the reader will feel confused and possibly irritated. And a word of warning: Too much jumping back and forth—or between more than three or four people in a given scene—*will* create confusion.

Here's an example of omniscient POV from the novel *Rosie*, by Anne Lamott—the story of a single mother raising her daughter after her husband's death. From the first scene in the book Lamott shows the reader that she is in the omniscient by providing information that comes as if from a god-like source, a source that knows all:

> There were many things about Elizabeth that the people of Bayview disliked. They thought her tall, too thin, too aloof. Her neck was too long and her breasts were too big. The men, who could have lived with the size of her breasts, found her unwilling to flirt and labeled her cold. The women were jealous of how well her clothes hung on her.

Since this information is not being delivered directly through the camera of any one character, the reader is signaled immediately that it is omniscient—the camera can move wherever it needs to go. Lamott maintains this POV throughout all the scenes, dancing effortlessly into the thoughts and feelings of her protagonists, Elizabeth and Rosie. In one paragraph she is in Rosie's POV:

> Rosie Ferguson was four when her father died. As she sat on her mother's lap at the crowded Episcopal service, she knew that her father was dead but kept waiting for him to join them in the first pew, wondering what he would bring her.

Then in the next paragraph in the same scene, we're in Elizabeth's POV:

> Elizabeth held Rosie on her lap, dimly aware that her daughter was trying to take care of her—Rosie kept patting her and smiling bravely—but Elizabeth couldn't concentrate on what was happening. It was too surreal. ...

Once you choose omniscient, you have to commit to it—you can't back down from it within the scene. Notice, too, that Lamott lets each character have a good paragraph of her own—the minimum amount of headspace I recommend you give each character if you're going to hop from head to head. Starting a new paragraph is a good way to signal to the reader that you're moving the camera again. Along those same lines, keep in mind:

- To keep a sense of cohesiveness, change POV at the end of action, not in the middle
- Change POV at the end of a line of dialogue—do not try to weave one character's thoughts into another character's speech
- Change POV when you want to offer another character's reaction to an event in the scene

A word of warning: When you're in the omniscient and can move into any character's head, be selective. The reader doesn't need to hear the thoughts or know the opinions of all minor characters. Stick to the point of view of characters who can contribute to plot information or deepen the reader's understanding of your protagonists.

Changing POV From Scene to Scene

Remember that a scene should largely take place in one location (unless the characters are on a moving vehicle or taking a stroll). Therefore, if you've got a chapter-long scene—that is, you're writing one scene per chapter—you automatically limit the physical location of the chapter.

When you have multiple scenes within a chapter, try to think of each scene within the chapter as a separate square of a quilt, or a piece of a puzzle that must add up to some sort of goal or understanding within the chapter. It's best to use multiple scenes in a given chapter when you want to:

- Look at one issue or topic from multiple angles

- Switch to multiple physical locations or in and out of present time

- Build up new plot information that the current scene won't allow, but that needs to come at that juncture in the story

- Introduce another character within the chapter

Author Jodi Picoult includes multiple scenes per chapter in her books because she writes about subjects that can be viewed from many different angles: suicide, rape, motherhood. Therefore, in a given chapter, when addressing a specific plot angle, she'll often give multiple characters a scene of their own, shedding numerous different kinds of perspective on a plot element.

For instance, her novel *Second Glance* is about Comtosook, a Vermont town where paranormal events occur when a developer threatens to build on sacred land, and where a long-hidden eugenics program designed to weed out unwanted genes is revealed to have been conducted in the early 1920s. The novel features multiple viewpoints. Each chapter is broken into a series of short scenes told from the points of view of as many as ten different characters that are being affected by the strange events. Note that although there are multiple scenes per chapter, each scene has only one point of view. To show that she's beginning a new scene, Picoult uses a visual cue—a break of four lines (sometimes called a soft hiatus)

---

or a symbol like ï or * * * or ❑—and identifies the point-of-view character within the first couple of lines. These scenes offer different pieces of insight into the plot that is being explored at that particular juncture. Here are three samples of scene launches that all appear within chapter two, in which people are trying to determine whether Angel Quarry is haunted, or whether someone is pulling a prank:

- Ross didn't know whom he blamed more: Ethan, for planting this seed in his mind; or himself, for bothering to listen. Angel Quarry is haunted, his nephew had said, everyone says so. …

- "What do you make of it?" Winks Smiling Fox asked, grunting as he moved the drum a few feet to the left. Where they'd been sitting, the ground beneath their feet was icy. Yet over here, there were dandelions growing. …

- "Ethan?"
  From his vantage point beneath the blackout shades, Ethan froze at the sound of his mother's voice. He whipped his body back so that it wasn't pressed against the warm glass windowpane. …

Each scene may be its own unit, but the three to six scenes within the chapter all play off each other and add up details for the reader. By the end of the chapter, the reader is pretty sure that, yes, Angel Quarry is haunted.

Using multiple scenes within a given chapter is a common and effective way to allow for a mosaic feeling—a feeling of little parts adding up to equal a larger, more comprehensive whole. But it comes with a caveat: When you have multiple scenes within a chapter, you will serve the reader best if each of those scenes has only one viewpoint—and not an omniscient one—since you're already forcing the reader to move around.

Changing POV From Chapter to Chapter

In many narratives, one chapter can be its own long scene. The benefit of this construction is that you don't have to get complex with your POV structure. One scene per chapter is undoubtedly the simplest and clearest structure to work with, and if you are new to writing, I recommend that you use this structure until you've mastered scenes and can move on to more complex structures. When your whole chapter is just one long scene, you can focus on the protagonist's scene intention, decide what kind of scene it's going to be (see chapters twelve through twenty-one), and use your core elements one chapter at a time. This structure requires less work of you, and it also allows the reader to stay in one place and time per chapter. This structure will feel more straightforward to the reader, and perhaps also less textured or layered, but you can guarantee that you will tell a simple, clear story by using this method. One scene per chapter is an ideal structure when:

- You want to keep your characters in a unified time and place

- You're writing a dialogue scene, as dialogue takes up a lot of room

- You're writing a suspense scene, as it requires more time to draw out actions

- Your narrative has a linear chronology—it doesn't flashback in time

- You want to switch to a different type of point of view to achieve a different effect for another protagonist—for instance, protagonist A is narrated in the first person, but protagonist B is better served by third person limited

Consider that when a chapter is one long scene, you have time to devote to a particular protagonist, and you may consider using a limited point of view because, by nature of the length of a chapter, you have more page-time to delve into one protagonist's experience and reveal it to the reader.

DEVOTING EQUAL TIME TO POV CHARACTERS

Now that we've covered the idea of using multiple points of view, it's important to discuss how to let your protagonists share the time on the page. The most definitive way to tell the reader that you have more than one protagonist is to give each protagonist equal time in your narrative. You may devote an equal number of scenes, or give individual chapters to your protagonists, but you do need to be egalitarian if you're going to have multiple narrators.

A lot of authors adopt a simple formula such as this: Each point of view character narrates one chapter or scene, taking turns in order. Character A goes first, then B, then C. Then you repeat that pattern: ABC, ABC, ABC. In other words, you give each character a chance to narrate, then you start all over again. You might give each character a chance to narrate within a given chapter, so you have three scenes for every chapter, or you may devote whole chapters to one character each. You may find the need to do variations on this: AAA, BBB, CCC, for instance, or AA, BB, CC, so long as the time each protagonist gets is as close to equal as you can make it.

23

YOUR PROTAGONIST'S EMOTIONAL THREAD

While all people undergo some change in life, characters in fiction have a dramatic imperative to change in order to give meaning to the narrative they star in. These transformations, however, can't happen all at once, or too easily. The reader tends to be suspicious when a character starts out mean and becomes kind too quickly, for example. So how can you change your characters in ways that lend credibility to each scene and feel authentic in the course of your narrative? Gradually.

Though each narrative has its own variation on shape and structure, it is helpful to think of breaking your novel or story into three parts (or you can use the theatrical term *acts* if you like). Doing so allows you to step back and really watch as your characters grow and change over the course of your narrative, all the while creating a satisfying arc for the reader.

THE FIRST PART: EARLY SCENES

The first third of your narrative is all about establishing the nuts and bolts of characters and their basic conflicts and plot problems, and setting in motion all the seeds for conflict and challenges to come. In these opening scenes, the reader is meeting your characters just as if they were new guests over for dinner. Their words, actions, and reactions to other people will all serve as introductions, and these first impressions will be remembered and will set the stage for their behavior deeper into the book. We'll now look at the ways you can establish information and set up your characters for change in the first third of your narrative.

Establishing Character-Related Plot Threads

At the same time as you establish that your protagonist is a smack-talking hooligan with seductive eyes and a mop of brown curls, or a lonely librarian who reads mystery novels and winds up investigating an actual crime, in this first section of your narrative, you also need to establish:

- **Involvement.** What is your protagonist's relationship to the events of the significant situation? Is the event his fault, centered around him in some way; did he accidentally stumble into it, or is he integral to it?

- **The stakes.** What he stands to lose or gain as a result of the above-mentioned events will create necessary tension and drama.

- **Desires.** What he desires, from material goods to deep and abiding love, will inform the stakes and his intentions.

- **Fears.** What he fears, from bodily harm to not obtaining his desire, will also inform the stakes.

- **Motivation.** What reasons does he have to act upon the events of the significant situation? What is he driven by?

- **Challenges.** How does the significant situation challenge his life, views, status, other people, his status quo, needs, etc.?

We'll walk through these points using excerpts of early scenes from the first part of the novel *House of Sand and Fog* by Andre Dubus III.

Involvement

Co-protagonist Kathy Nicolo (married name Lazaro) is a cleaning woman whose self-absorbed husband divorced her eight months ago. Since then, her life has been a wreck: Financially, she just scrapes by, and her stability as a recovered alcoholic and addict is severely tested. The only material thing of significance to her is the house she inherited from her father, where she lives.

How is she involved in the significant situation? In the first scene she wakes up to find a locksmith and a cop at her door with a notice of eviction for back taxes—an erroneous notice at that. It doesn't matter; until she can prove in court that she has done nothing wrong, they have the right to evict her, and they do. Kathy loses her house and must go live in a motel while she sorts things out. In the time it takes her to get a lawyer, her house goes up for auction and is purchased by co-protagonist Colonel Behrani, a once wealthy man from Iran who is now a struggling immigrant with iron pride.

For simplicity's sake, I'm going to focus on Kathy's storyline for this first section, though Dubus does a thorough job of developing both characters fully and weaving their stories together seamlessly.

It's pretty clear what Kathy's relationship to the significant situation is: She's been evicted from her house. Though Kathy claims it's a mistake, the reader doesn't have enough evidence yet to know if this is true. She seems volatile, and the reader isn't sure if she's trustworthy; she *could* be the kind of woman who might fail to pay taxes:

> "That's all right 'cause I'm not leaving." My throat felt dry and stiff.
>
> The locksmith looked up from his work on my back door.
>
> Deputy Burdon rested one hand on the countertop, and he had an understanding expression on his face, but I hated him anyway. "I'm afraid you have no choice, Mrs. Lazaro. All your things will be auctioned off with the property. Do you want that?"
>
> "*Look*, I *inherited* this house from my father, it's paid for. You can't evict me!" My eyes filled up and the men began to blur. "I never *owed* a fucking business tax. You have no right to do this."

The Stakes

The stakes are pretty clear: Without her house, she's got nowhere to go but to a motel, and on her small income, even that expense is a big one—Kathy could wind up in dire straits pretty quick. This evokes some sympathy for the woman, even though the reader doesn't really know who she is yet. Your stakes must be equally clear; don't make the reader guess. Remember to:

- Show what the protagonist has to gain
- Show what the protagonist stands to lose

Let the reader see in the scenes from the first part exactly what is at stake for your protagonist. Does he stand to be kicked out of his tribe if he speaks his mind; lose his worldly possessions if he loses his job; lose his child visitation rights if he can't pay child support? These questions and their answers must be enacted in scenes in the first part of your narrative.

Desires

Next, through passages of interior monologue, the reader gets a peek into Kathy's desires, which center mostly on her relationships. She remembers the few rare good times before her husband Nick left her; she reflects on the days with her first husband, Donnie, when she was barely an adult, and became addicted to cocaine. The reader feels her palpable loneliness—she's so lonely that even the bad memories are a comfort to her. Because of her desire for love, when Lester Burdon, the deputy who first came to evict her, shows up to check on her, even though he helped facilitate her current unhappy state, her desire makes it plausible that she takes to him:

"I thought I'd check on you, see how you're holding up."

He sounded like he meant it, and he seemed even softer than the day before when he'd led those men in kicking me out of my house. When we got to his car, a Toyota station wagon parked at the edge of the lot near the chain-link fence, I kind of hoped he'd keep talking; Connie Walsh was the first person I'd had a real conversation with in over eight months, and that was more of an interrogation than a talk. I wanted one, even with a sheriff's deputy in the fog.

Kathy's pressing desire to be loved will get her into a lot of trouble later on in the narrative. Her other, more immediate desire, which will drive her actions in much of the rest of the narrative, is more straightforward: to get her house back.

Desires will come in many shapes in your narrative and can be expressed or shown:

- In dialogue between characters

- In the form of thoughts (interior monologue), as in the previous example

- In subtle actions—your protagonists may simply take what they desire, or try to

What matters is that the reader has a feeling for what these desires are, straight away. Desires and motivations fuel a character's intentions in every scene; they help give purpose to their actions, so you'll want to make them as clear as possible.

Fears

Kathy's fears are a bit less direct, but they are there in the subtext of the scenes. The reader knows that she is a recovering addict of both drugs and alcohol, with a penchant for men who liked to be in control of her. This tells the reader that Kathy is not a person with high self-esteem, or someone who feels particularly in control of her own life. The reader sees that she is someone who prefers dependence on others over independence, and that the act of being out of her house throws her whole life into chaos. Kathy is afraid to be alone and afraid to be an adult in the world, to take responsibility for herself. These fears will get her into trouble in the middle of this novel.

Your protagonist should have some kind of fear, whether it is a rational one like the fear of fire, or an irrational one, like a fear of butterflies or of the color yellow, because those innocuous things trigger memories of terrible experiences. No character should be too brave—even heroes have weaknesses. Establish what your character is afraid of early on, because in the middle of the narrative you're going to exploit those fears.

You can establish fear:

- Through speech (for instance, he can admit to a friend that he is "terrified of spiders")

- Through behavior (your protagonist, upon seeing a passenger jet overhead, hits the dirt like he is about to be bombed)

• Through a flashback scene in which the reader sees that the protagonist was traumatized by a specific event

Fear is as much a part of your protagonist's motivations as desire, and it is through fear and desire that you exert change on your characters.

Motivation

Kathy's surface motivation is pretty clear: She's motivated to get her house back because it's all she has, and she sees it as the cornerstone of her ability to live a stable life. This motivation leads her to get legal aid and fight to get her house back. But Kathy is also motivated by older, deeper issues regarding her family and her relationship to her parents. These motivations are the ones that cause her to get involved with Lester Burdon, a married man and a cop; these motivations also cause her to become volatile and enraged at Colonel Behrani, who has her house; and they begin to set the stage for the drama that unfolds in the second part of the narrative.

Your protagonist's motivations will be clear to the reader so long as you:

• Make it clear what the protagonist's desires are

• Make it clear what the protagonist's fears are

• Offer opportunities to thwart the desires and trigger the fears

In chapter eleven, we discussed scene intentions. Motivations—which stem directly from your protagonist's fears and desires—are the foundation of scene intentions. Once you know how your protagonist is motivated, and by what forces, then you can direct him to act in every scene in a way appropriate to the circumstances of your plot.

Challenges

Kathy's challenges are myriad. She lacks money and resources; she has a weakness for using alcohol to drown her feelings; she is attracted to men who are bad for her; and she is literally challenged by Colonel Behrani's takeover of her home.

Challenges are the situations in which you thwart your protagonist's desires and trigger his fears, and they are good and necessary. The more of them you can comfortably create—that is, the more you can create that pertain to your plot and make sense to the character—the better, because they create a sense of urgency and concern in your reader. In the first part of your narrative, your job is to set up which intentions are going to be opposed, leading the way to the middle part, where these intentions will meet with greater opposition and create more conflict.

Assessing Your Character at the End of the First Part

The scenes in the first part are all about potential conflict. You want to ask yourself, have I destabilized my protagonist, given him problems and conflicts that begin to worry both him and the reader? Has my protagonist been directly involved in a significant situation that has brought initial conflict and challenges? Make sure that by the end of the first part, your protagonist is showing signs that he feels tested, forced into action, and driven toward change. Nothing should yet be too conclusive, too fixed in stone, because if it is, the reader has little motivation to keep reading.

MIDDLE SCENES: PROVIDING OPPORTUNITIES

By the time you've made it to the middle section of your narrative, the reader should be a mess, riddled with anxiety and worry for your characters, tense and upset as he wonders what is going to happen next. It sounds mean, but that's exactly where you want him to be. Your protagonist should be in a similar state. After all, you've dangled his desires just out of reach and pushed him toward, or into the midst of, his fears. And you've added a series of challenges along the way so that he can't get out of conflict too easily. The middle part of your narrative is where he'll do the most work. He will be tested and stretched here because you will provide your protagonist with:

- **Opportunities for crisis and conflict.** Now that you've destabilized him and given him problems to contend with, you want to mount the challenges. Complicate his problems. Give him more, new ones. Add other stressors.

- **Opportunities for dramatic and surprising changes.** Under all this change and pressure, your protagonist is going to start to change. He might act out in bursts of rage, or find that he is far more capable than he ever imagined. Either way, the complications you provide here in the middle should cause him to act *differently* than he has before, for better or worse.

- **Opportunities for plot complications.** You may feel that your protagonist's significant situation was bad enough, but if you leave him with no new complications, you also stop the storyline. In this middle section, more will need to happen. Each new scene should provide a new complication or add complexity to the existing problems.

- **Opportunities to test-drive new behaviors.** Even logical people react emotionally to situations—*react* being the key word. Therefore, under all that pressure and stress you've put on him, your protagonist can now legitimately get away with doing something that was previously out of character. That's the nature of conflict—it changes a person. So if you've complicated things enough, then your previously timid protagonist can now pick up the gun and threaten to kill someone, for example.

- **Opportunities for dramatic tension.** As author Steve Almond said, "You have to love your characters enough to put them in danger." This danger, emotional or physical, will create an aura of tension that will drive the reader deep into your narrative.

If all your characters' desires and intentions were met in the middle of your narrative, you'd be done already. Middle scenes are not about resolutions. Middle scenes are the place for characters to experience the classic "dark night of the soul," desperation, uncertainty, and a host of other trials. This element of uncertainty and crisis will bring out a wide range of emotional responses in your characters that will change them, reshape them, cause them to undergo epiphanies and behavior shifts as you move toward the climax of your narrative.

Assessing Your Character at the End of the Middle Part

It's important to be clear that some protagonists change for the worse before they change for the better. When things get challenging, a protagonist often acts out, or behaves badly. In *House of Sand and Fog*, Kathy Nicolo is driven to desperation, and she enlists Lester Burdon to threaten the Colonel—which quickly escalates into physical violence and then tragedy at the climax of the novel. Not the kind of thing a rational, mature person does. You do not need to push your protagonist into some impossibly high ideal of human behavior—if your goal in particular is to redeem a character, you can save that redemption for the final part. In the middle scenes, what is key is that the reader sees your protagonist behaving *differently* than he did at the beginning of the narrative (or historically) as a direct result of the consequences of the significant situation.

THE LAST PART: FINAL SCENES

In the final part of your narrative, it's time to weigh all the changes your characters have or have not undergone and begin to resolve them. Ending scenes are not usually a place for much new character change—this is the place where you let the changes become evident to the reader as you tie up all threads.

Resolve Character Conflicts

In the final scenes of your narrative, the climax has already taken place, and the greatest amount of stress or tension has already been exerted on your protagonist. Now you want to show who he is in the aftermath. You can do this by determining (and demonstrating) the following:

- What are the consequences of having any desires met?
- What are the consequences of having any fears realized?
- Did your protagonist's desires change? How so?
- Did your protagonist's fears change or lessen? How so?
- How does your protagonist feel now about the significant situation?

Demonstrate Character Changes

Depending on the answers to the questions above, you want to show, through some form of behavior, action, or speech that your protagonist

---

really has changed. Perhaps he turns himself in for the crime that his best friend is in jail for. Maybe she finally visits the grave of her dead husband when she was unable to before. Maybe he moves to a new town after being hung up on the past. Or the change might be as simple as a statement: "I'll never go back," a soldier might say, deciding he's ready for peace. In some cases it takes great tragedy to facilitate change, as in *House of Sand and Fog*. I won't give away exactly what the tragedy is, but it changes Kathy Nicolo deeply. Now in jail, up for trial, Kathy no longer is interested in passing blame or getting what she thinks she's entitled to. She's ready to take responsibility not only for what happened to the Colonel, but for her own mess of a life:

> Only two days before, I saw Connie. She's still working on getting my hearing date moved up. I told her I didn't want her to make me look like I wasn't responsible for what Lester had done.

Provide Answers to Plot Questions

You're going to have to tie up all the consequences that came out of the significant situation. Whatever questions you raised must be answered or concluded. Murders get solved. Stolen property gets returned or found. And the thread of action and events that your protagonist has been involved with must taper to a final end.

In literary fiction this will probably come as more of an internal resolution or transformation for your protagonist. In a romance novel your protagonist will finally be ready for the right man and will find him, or consummate the romance that has already begun. In a mystery novel, your protagonist will not only solve the case, or be exonerated from wrong-doing, he will see himself and the world differently. In a science-fiction novel, your protagonist may get in touch with his humanity, or understand the power of the cosmos. There are many ways to tie up plot events in the final part of your narrative—and they all share these elements in common:

- The protagonist has learned something

- The protagonist's behavior or attitude has changed

• The protagonist has embarked on a new direction or path

The key to successful character transformation is to let your character changes unfold dramatically but also realistically. Let the reader see your characters change by how they act and speak, and by the choices they make within the framework of scenes, not through narrative summaries.

24

SECONDARY AND MINOR CHARACTERS

As the creator of all the wily and fascinating characters in your fiction, it can be difficult to assign levels of importance to them at first; after all, they're all wonderful to you, even the evil ones. Yet when it comes to how your characters contribute to each scene, and to the overall journey of your narrative, there is, in fact, a hierarchy that you should work to develop. Even though this is a chapter on the role of minor characters, let's quickly review the role of the protagonists before moving on.

Most important to any narrative is your protagonist—the character around whom your significant situation revolves and who is most challenged and tested in your narrative. In some narratives you might even have more than one protagonist. The protagonists are the headliners of your story, and do the most work and get the most lines; their emotional and spiritual conflicts are of central interest to the reader. In limited point-of-view chapters, each protagonist narrates his own scenes and chapters. It's not as common to show the points of view of secondary or minor characters unless you're writing from an omniscient point of view, and even then, you want to give those lesser characters far less stage time.

SECONDARY CHARACTERS

A secondary character's job is to affect your protagonist in meaningful ways, exerting change and conflict, offering support and sympathy, and enriching your narrative. True secondary characters are neither the stars nor minor players, since these characters have important roles that affect the narrative arc of your protagonist. But if one should die or disappear, the story should be able to go on without him (though his loss will have an impact on the protagonist, of course!).

Here, we'll look at the roles of the two main types of secondary characters: antagonists and allies. Neither type of character should get his own point of view chapters, or, if you've written in omniscient POV, too many paragraphs or pages inside his head. Point-of-view chapters and scenes should generally be reserved for protagonists; the reader will determine who your protagonists are by how much time is spent telling the story from their points of view. Main characters get more time on the page, and the reader sees through the protagonists' cameras more than through the perspectives of any other characters.

Antagonists

The antagonist is the person or the group of people whose objective is to thwart the goals of your protagonist. Antagonists cause conflict and pile on the emotional pressure. (An antagonist can also be a force of nature or other means of thwarting your protagonist, but for this chapter we're specifically going to talk about antagonists as people.)

While the antagonist does not have to appear in every scene, every scene should convey a sense of pressure, menace, or uncertainty as a result of his presence within the story itself. The antagonist needs to be developed well enough that you can understand how he thinks and what motivates him, but he doesn't need to have a full character arc and undergo transformation, like your protagonist does.

With an antagonist you really only need to know the following:

- What is the antagonist's motivation is for trying to thwart your protagonist in the first place
- What the antagonist expects to gain or seeks to obtain by thwarting your protagonist
- What the antagonist stands to lose if he does not attain his goal

Unlike the protagonist, who must undergo some kind of transformation in the narrative, antagonists don't need to be developed too fully. They can start out evil and stay evil. The most character work you'll need to do with an antagonist is to show why and how he came to be the way he is, to uncover his motivations so that the reader understands why he is causing so much trouble for your protagonist. Is it pure evil, greed, lust, or fear? All great villains have a motivation, and the top motivator is usually revenge. He was slighted, injured, thwarted, or insulted, and he is out to set things straight.

What makes the antagonist important to your narrative is not his own individual story, but how he affects your protagonist and acts as a catalyst for change. Here are some ways in which antagonists force protagonists to change or act:

- **By providing a looming threat.** The antagonist has threatened your protagonist with a punishment or consequence if the protagonist does not do something. Think of Lord Voldemort in the Harry Potter books—he is rarely in any scene, but the danger of his return is constant in Harry's mind.

- **By prompting a course of action motivated by fear.** The protagonist behaves or takes a particular action out of fear caused by the antagonist.

- **By prompting a defensive or courageous course of action.** The protagonist takes an action to defend himself or a loved one, or demonstrates an act of sheer courage that is specifically inspired by the antagonist.

Though you are not required to show any change on the antagonist's part (except defeat), you may choose to redeem your antagonist by the end of your narrative so that after his defeat, or at the precipice of it, he decides to help, rather than hinder the protagonist. This is a challenging feat to pull off, and generally works only when the antagonist has already demonstrated the potential for duality early on. For instance, a Nazi soldier may have a sudden fit of conscience and help a Jew escape. You are just as free to have your antagonist meet his demise and never be thought of again.

Allies

The other main type of secondary character is the protagonist's friend, ally, or loved one (we'll lump them all under the category of allies for ease of discussion). Again, these characters don't need to be given their own point of view scenes or chapters, because the story does not require that an ally undergo a dramatic personal transformation. The ally's actions should support the protagonist and make it possible for him to succeed and face his challenges. Your ally may simply be a love interest whose faith in his girlfriend keeps her grounded when everything is going wrong. Or your ally might be a companion on a long journey who keeps your protagonist on his toes and rallies him to keep up his strength to reach his goal.

Though these allies do not need to have a complex character arc, most often they *will* have to rise to some kind of challenge in order to support your protagonist. Allies often must undergo an act of courage or selflessness on behalf of the protagonist—however, the goal is not for the ally to change, but for the protagonist to. Allies will achieve these feats in one of a few different ways:

- **Sacrifice.** It's very common for an ally to sacrifice himself in a narrative so that your protagonist can carry on with his task. All great epic stories have a sacrifice of this kind. My favorite fantasy series, by Robin Hobb, beginning with *Assassin's Apprentice* and continuing on for a total of nine interlinked books, is rich with wonderful allies who sacrifice themselves in many different ways for the protagonists. Hobb is a master of character development, and I recommend her books to anyone who struggles to build characters of any type.

- **Finding surprising strength or courage.** Another wonderful way to use your ally is to have him rally strength or courage nobody knew he was capable of, just when the protagonist needs it most. Think Neville Longbottom—who finds his power in time to support Harry Potter in a big fight. There's nothing more dramatic than a scared ally exhibiting sudden courage, conscience, or strength in the face of danger.

- **Rallying larger support groups.** Sometimes your protagonist must go his journey alone for one reason or another. Secondary characters can rally support on the protagonist's behalf without him knowing they are coming, and show up at the scene of his drama with reinforcements that he did not expect. This might take the form of a group of activists who descend upon their cause at the last minute, or a group of women in a historical novel all showing up to fight for their right to vote.

Allies should be vivid and memorable, but they should also function under this main imperative: to support, bolster, and serve the protagonist. If your secondary character doesn't do one of those three things, you've either got a superfluous character who should be cut or an antagonist in disguise.

MINOR CHARACTERS

Finally we come to the last set of characters that should appear in your fiction: minor characters. Their job is to add spice and realism. These are the store clerks, passersby, beautiful ladies, phone operators, plane stewards, waitresses, strangers on a train, movie ushers, etc., who provide small opportunities for interactions and challenges to your main characters. They can be both disposable and essential, depending on your needs. You will know minor characters by the fact that they do not make frequent appearances in scenes as protagonists or secondary characters—they pretty much appear as needed, which might be once in your whole narrative.

Think of Glenda, the good witch in the movie *The Wizard of Oz*, who turns up only twice to give Dorothy important tips on how to get in—and out of—the Emerald City. Or think even more minor, like the crew on a ship in one of Patrick O'Brian's Aubrey-Maturin novels. Minor characters do not need to be complex. This flat quality works because minor characters exist as foils for your protagonists. In fact, I like to think of them as chemicals that cause reactions in a solution. By that I mean they are there for protagonists to bounce ideas off of, get into brief fights with, and gain tiny pearls of wisdom from in passing scenes. They don't need to be present in as many scenes as your main characters, and they don't need to be vividly drawn.

You most definitely don't have to worry about whether these characters will change. You don't have to give them a love interest or a childhood.

Good uses for minor characters in scenes are to:

- **Offer a piece of plot information.** This should be information that the protagonist needs to know or cannot reveal.

- **Act as a witness to major plot events, helping to tie threads together.** This may be the witness to a murder, the child who speaks up in his parents' vitriolic divorce, the silent neighbor who reveals the husband's betrayal when the protagonist needs to know.

- **Provide a tempering force of behavior.** Your protagonist is fiery and rash, but a friend or acquaintance acts as the calm conscience.

- **Add a touch of realism.** Most of us live near, and interact with, other people on a daily basis in nearly everything we do, so your characters are bound to encounter others, from close friends to clerks at the grocery store. In fact, if your character does not meet people at some point in your narrative, you'd better have a good reason for that—incarceration or a case of agoraphobia, for example.

- **Add comic relief.** A wisecracking joker can be a great addition to balance intense scenes.

- **Act as a trouble-maker.** A minor character can exist merely to add trouble and conflict to your characters' lives: an ex-girlfriend who has a habit of turning up each time your protagonist starts dating a girl he really likes, or a hostile relative who steals from your protagonist's house.

- **Function as a distraction.** A minor character can be a red herring to distract the reader from a plot twist you plan to throw into an end scene. The serial killer might be someone the reader has come to think is a pretty nice guy, so you throw in a minor character who looks pretty bad—a history of drugs and violence, say, and lead the reader away from your true killer long enough to let the truth come as a surprise.

As you might be able to tell from the above list, minor characters almost qualify more as a part of the setting than they do as characters. You don't need to develop them deeply; you simply need to make them useful.

HOW TO KEEP YOUR CHARACTERS IN THEIR PLACES

I'd like to mention that secondary and minor characters can be seductive. You can find them saying a bit too much or showing up in more scenes than is useful. Let's refer back to Harry Potter. Though Harry has many friends and comrades and meets many interesting wizards and creatures who are compelling (without whom he never would have made it through seven books worth of adventures), the reader is not going to waste much time worrying about what happens to Madam Rosmerta, the pub proprietor, or Argus Filch, the Hogwarts school caretaker. It's worth mentioning on this note that Hermione Granger and Ron Weasley, Harry's two best friends, though they are strong and well developed, are still secondary characters. Ultimately it is Harry's journey and story, and he is the character who must undergo the dramatic transformation. As allies, Ron and Hermione exhibit courage and strength, sacrifice and support, but if one of them had been killed off (horror!) the story would have gone on. While your minor characters are important, remember that they will stay minor only as long as they:

- Make infrequent appearances—they should not appear in every scene

- Demonstrate little or no internal reflection

- Are not emotionally complex

- Demonstrate a behavior or personality that challenges or supports your character

- Act as a catalyst to stimulate change or reaction in your protagonist in any scene

If you've got a secondary or minor character present in nearly every scene, the reader will start to think that maybe this character isn't so minor anymore, and then she will begin to expect more out of that character—which means more out of you. Secondary characters can certainly show up in a number of scenes with your protagonist, but again, the focus must be on your protagonist, and these secondary characters must be there to serve, support, or thwart the protagonist in some way.

Make a Scene

Promoting Secondary Characters

From time to time you may discover that someone you intended to be a secondary character is rich and vivid, and fits into your plot so well that you want to bump up his status to co-protagonist—which means that he now would get equal point of view time with any other protagonists currently in your narrative, or even replace your protagonist altogether. Pay attention to how you feel when writing a secondary character. If he fits most of the following criteria, he may be more major than you realized:

- Appears in all or most scenes
- Begins to undergo an emotional transformation separate from that of your existing protagonist
- Becomes so integral to the plot that it falls apart or becomes confusing without him

If he starts to take over the story, or you find that he is more compelling than you first thought, you might consider whether he's been given too low a status in your narrative and needs to be promoted in importance.

Secondary characters thwart or support your main character: They are either allies or antagonists. They are memorable and vivid, but come with no imperative for dramatic transformation. Minor characters are almost a part of the scenery, just simple catalysts to get your protagonist moving on to the next aspect of his plot, and they don't even need to be well-drawn. These characters have no imperative to change whatsoever.

Together, these kinds of characters will create a rich, vivid set of people you can call on in your scenes to provide many challenges and situations under which your protagonist can transform.

25

SCENE TRANSITIONS

So far we have talked about individual scene construction, which is the most important subject of this book, and which will more than prepare you to begin writing a manuscript. Yet a bunch of scenes stacked one after the other doesn't automatically equal a narrative. Now we'll look at ways to link individual scenes to one another to compose a strong, vivid storyline.

It's useful to think of your scenes as the cells that compose a body. Each one is distinct and individual, achieving a different goal, but they all must work together or you won't have a cohesive narrative. The simplest and easiest way to link scenes is through transitions, passages of text at the beginning or ending of a scene, where you condense and shift time, space, point of view, and many other details to create a sense of flow and to bypass mundane or nondramatic moments in your characters' lives.

That last point is very important: fiction is a *simulation* of real life; your goal is to offer only the most meaningful, relevant, and dramatic moments in your characters' lives, and to bypass the other moments that don't contribute to your narrative. Remember this!

Transitions are most noticeable at the beginning of a scene—this is where the reader will make the mental leaps you need: "Oh, I see, he's not on the farm anymore, he's in an airplane! Oh, it's not early morning anymore;

it's nighttime!" So we'll focus first on how to make your transitions clear at the beginning of a new scene, and then we'll talk briefly about how to set up the end of a scene with the next scene in mind.

The reader doesn't like to be jarred every time you begin a new scene, and since a narrative is composed of sometimes hundreds of scenes, you'll need to make sure that each successive scene feels connected to or derived from the scene that preceded it. Chapters are also breaks in your story's action; you may have one or ten scenes within one chapter. Chapter transitions need to be smooth as well.

The end of a scene or chapter is a note to the reader that you are concluding something, taking a break from the preceding events in order to change, refresh, or throw a twist into character or plot details. You might change something basic, such as physical location, or the next scene might take place years down the road. Either way, at the beginning of a scene you are, first and foremost, signaling that changes have taken place since the last scene.

SIGNALING A SCENE CHANGE

When you open a new scene, your first job is to orient the reader as to where the protagonist and other characters are in relationship to the scene (or scenes) before. You start, as the writer, by asking: What has changed? Where and when are my characters now? How can I make this clear to the reader?

Time of Day, or Day of the Week, Month, Year

At the beginning of a scene, it's likely you'll have to somehow make clear to the reader that time—minutes or years—has passed. Condensing time is a handy trick for moving on to only the interesting points of a character's life and story. Here are different examples of leaps in time. The first is from Chris Bohjalian's *Midwives*, and the second is from Caleb Carr's *The Alienist*. Notice how they both rely upon simple expository descriptions, which I've italicized to make them obvious:

> *At some point soon* after my mother started to speak, Corporal Richard Tilley began taking notes. He wrote fast to keep up with my mother, and

the few questions his partner asked usually began, "Could you repeat that please, Mrs. Danforth?"

What has been condensed is the time between Mrs. Danforth's arrest, and the time when she is questioned.

> *I got to Kreizler's house,* at 283 East Seventeenth Street, a few minutes early, white-tied and caped and not at all sure of the conspiracy I'd entered into with Sara—a conspiracy that for better or worse would now play out.

Here, Carr condenses a few hours, and he also condenses the journey from point A to point B. The reader doesn't see the character's entire walk from his office up to East Seventeenth Street, because there is nothing significant to the plot in that journey. Carr simply gets his character to the next place with a few words: "I got to Kreizler's house."

When you want to condense time you can:

- **Use narrative summary.** "Sixteen years later, they stood on the same stoop where they had first met."

- **Use dialogue.** "I can't believe it's been a year since we saw each other."

- **Use setting.** "The young sapling she had planted when she left was now a full-grown tree."

I do want to add a note of caution here. You should only condense time when you need to condense short periods of time, and then only specifically to bypass mundane and irrelevant information. Be aware that large leaps—like many years, or from one plot event to another—undertaken without doing any of the necessary scene work in between to make such a leap plausible, will only get you into trouble with your the reader. If you feel the need to condense large periods of time, or find you jump too freely from one event to another, you may need to renegotiate your plot and figure out how to make events take place in a more plausible timeline.

Location/Setting

Many times the reason for breaking a scene is to move the characters to a new location, whether this is just down the street, or involves putting the character on a steamship to a new country. If you have changed the setting from the last scene, you want to make this clear fairly quickly. Here is an excerpt from Chitra Banerjee Divakaruni's *The Vine of Desire* in which the introduction of a new setting is used to launch the scene:

> Chopra's house is huge and pink, like a giant, lighted cake plopped down on a bald stretch of hillside. There's a uniformed white guard at the gate, to whom Sunil has to show his invitation, then a circular driveway with an illuminated fountain and Grecian-style statuary, mostly nymphs at various stages of undress, or plump, peeing cherubs.

This setting is most definitely not the "tiny apartment" that protagonist Anju and her husband, Sunil, live in, nor is it the university where Anju takes classes. The reader knows right away these characters are not in any of their familiar locales. When making a setting shift:

- Select details carefully so that the setting description is engaging
- Allow your protagonist to interact with the setting when possible
- Allow your protagonist to have opinions about the setting
- Allow the setting to reflect your protagonist's mood, feelings, or inner world in some way

Ambiance and Atmosphere (Mood, Tone, and Weather Changes)

Not all scenes will require a shift in setting, so if your protagonist is in the same location he was in during the previous scene, but you want to demonstrate that something is different—that a new plot twist is coming, or that the character's attitude has changed—you can change the atmosphere or mood. Here's an example from Jean Hegland's novel *Windfalls*, about a struggling single mother, Cerise, who endures a terrible loss. Many of the scenes starring Cerise take place in her small trailer, where she lives with her teenage daughter and young son. The reader is alerted by a literal change in atmosphere that this scene is going to be different from others:

> When the smoke first filtered into her sleep, her dreams recognized it. It was a nasty smoke, the smell of cheap things burning, and for awhile her dreams

engulfed it, offering weird dream-reasons to explain its presence. It was an explosion that finally woke her, a blast that left her unmoored in the darkness, adrenaline prickling her flesh, dread clinging to her bones. A bad dream, she told herself, as she struggled to find a way out of its grip.

The smell of smoke and the loud explosion are not normal occurrences in Cerise's trailer—the reader immediately knows something is wrong (and different from the last scene). These details pique the reader's curiosity and excite anxiety for the welfare of the characters while also suggesting that something has changed from the last time the reader saw Cerise.

Here's another example, from G.K. Chesterton's novel *The Man Who Was Thursday*, a sort of philosophical mystery. One night, the poet Gabriel Syme meets up with a mysterious stranger. Gregory, who initiates a debate about art and anarchy, and gets Syme to agree to come along with him for a "very interesting evening." Syme is unwittingly drawn into a secret society and a mystery that will challenge his view of himself. From the pub—which has a kind of upbeat, jolly energy—where Gregory brought Syme, he is taken by boat on the English Channel to a new location. Notice how the mood immediately begins to turn mysterious and suspenseful with just a few details:

> At first the stone stair seemed to Syme as deserted as a pyramid; but before he reached the top he had realized that there was a man leaning over the parapet of the Embankment and looking out across the river. As a figure he was quite conventional, clad in a silk hat and frock coat of the more formal type of fashion; he had a red flower in his buttonhole. As Syme drew nearer to him, he did not even move a hair. ...

There are many ways to signal shifts in mood or atmosphere:

- **Through weather.** Weather can be used to show that the scene opens in a different season or time of year, but can also reflect and mirror the changed inner world of your characters, or the tone of the new scene. If the scene needs to feel eerie or suspenseful, dark clouds, low light, and other symbols of moodiness can convey this tone to the reader.

- **Through sensory details.** Changes in the way things smell, sound, or feel are giveaways for scene changes. Sounds, for example, can be misconstrued; what sounds like a scream might turn out to be a laugh. A character may step in a puddle of something sticky that wasn't in the house when they were there last, and, in the dark, fear it is blood.

- **Through unusual juxtapositions.** In the Chesterton example, the strange sight of a man dressed in silk and frock coat on a parapet overlooking the embankment signals a new mood. You can use jarring or unusual or just dissimilar images placed side by side to signal that the tone is now ready to shift. The new mood doesn't have to be eerie; you can create comic, romantic, and happy juxtapositions, too.

A Shift in Point of View

Many narratives have co-protagonists who each get their own point-of-view scenes or chapters. In order to show that you've moved into a new character's POV, you may need to use a few simple transitions.

Many authors dedicate an entire chapter to one character at a time, which is a very simple, direct way to communicate whose point of view the scene is in (see chapter twenty-two). To keep the reader oriented, authors use a header below the chapter title that gives the character's name, as in:

Chapter 1	Chapter 2
Mary	Jack

However, if you don't want to use the character's name as a header, you must be sure to drop the character's name or some obvious detail about him into the opening couple of sentences in each scene or chapter devoted to that character, as in these examples from Michael Chabon's Pulitzer Prize–winning novel, *The Amazing Adventures of Kavalier & Clay*:

Josef Kavalier's determination to storm the exclusive Hofzinser Club had reached its height one day back in 1935, over breakfast, when he choked on a mouthful of omelet with apricot preserves.

In a chapter that follows, he shifts to another point of view:

When the alarm clock went off at six-thirty that Friday, Sammy awoke to find that Sky City, a chromium cocktail tray stocked with moderne bottles, shakers, and swizzle sticks, was under massive attack.

In both cases, it's obvious whose point of view the reader is entering, and there's no room for confusion. Don't make the reader wait for a page to figure out whose eyes he is looking through!

SIGNALING PLOT AND CHARACTER TRANSITIONS

Consider your character and his plot as you start each new scene. You do not need to drop the scene's new piece of plot information into the very opening of that scene. Your protagonist or another character could also use words (dialogue or written text) to express that a transition has taken place. "You're not so powerful now," the villain might say to the superhero. Or a character might find a letter in place of his wife that reads, "I've left you."

Sometimes the shift in location or mood is enough to signal that, later in the scene, something is coming. But you do want to be sure that the opening sets up the scene for whatever you have in mind. So consider the following:

- **If your plot is event based, and an important event happened in the prior scene.** Maybe a building exploded—where is your protagonist in relationship to that event now? On the phone with the cops, for instance, or hunting down the arsonist?

- **Is your character picking up from a cliffhanger?** Perhaps your character is beginning an action after an epiphany ending? Don't forget to conclude that action.

- **Does your character need to express feelings (interior monologue) related to the plot in the scene after an event?** Is he afraid for his life, or refreshed after a long vacation? You might launch the next scene with a line of interior monologue that tells the reader how your protagonist's feelings are different from, or related to, the previous scene.

Transitions are the way you speed past the dull and the mundane, and condense time and space so that your characters can get right to the important work of the plot. What has taken place in the scenes before is your clue to effectively linking the next scene.

26

SCENE ASSESSMENT AND REVISION

So there you are, with a finished draft or even just a finished scene still smoking from the sheer effort of your labor. First, put it aside. In a couple of weeks (or more), when your work is cool to the touch and you've had enough of a break that you're ready to tackle revising, there are many ways you can approach the process. A scene-by-scene revision approach is a good place to start—it's a bit like unpacking the boxes full of interesting, but not necessarily organized, stuff in your garage and putting everything in order.

IDENTIFYING VIGNETTES

Anyone can learn to dance by following the footwork, but not everyone who learns to tango can actually perform for an audience with any grace or dramatic effect. This is true of scene writing. You can learn how to write a basic scene, and still write scenes that just don't do anything for your plot. This assessment chapter hopefully will prevent you from becoming a very competent vignette writer—that is to say, someone who is very good at writing scenes that don't add up to much.

It's important for you to be able to recognize when a scene is just a free-floating vignette that doesn't serve your narrative. There are multiple definitions for a vignette. My favorite is "a small, graceful literary sketch." To this let us add, "which does not necessarily relate to the plot, and is therefore extraneous." Vignettes may be some of the most beautiful passages in your entire narrative, but are vignettes—and not scenes—because they are conspicuously out of plot context, or missing an important scene element. In order to determine whether your scene is really a vignette, you must run it through another set of questions:

- Does the scene introduce new plot information?

- Does the scene relate to the significant situation?

- Does the scene build upon the last scene?

- Does the scene involve, inform, or affect the protagonist?

- Does the scene make the reader feel smarter or more clued in?

- Does the scene move forward in time (even if only by seconds)?

If the scene in question is relevant to your plot, the answer to every one of the above questions will be a resounding yes. If you answer no to *any* of those questions, you have a vignette, which needs to be fleshed out into a proper scene, or cut.

A vignette can be a half-formed scene, which is missing one of the core elements or lacks one of the necessary parts of its structure—a launch, middle, or end. But vignettes often get written because the author is taken with language or finds a character's inner life compelling. Among my editing clients, vignettes often show up as tangents; the writer stumbled onto an inspiring idea or a description, and ran with it. Unfortunately, vignettes usually please the writer far more than the reader.

Every scene is part of a larger matrix of scenes that add up to the outcome of your narrative. A vignette usually leaves the reader scratching his head, wondering why the scene was necessary. Ultimately, the most important question you can ask of a scene to determine whether it is a vignette, and thus whether it can be cut or transformed, is: Will my narrative still make sense and flow if I cut this scene out? If the answer is yes, you've got a vignette on your hands, and it doesn't belong.

TRANSFORMING OR CUTTING VIGNETTES

If you've determined that your scene is *not* relevant to your plot or character development, and thus is a vignette, then you have two options: Cut it, or make it relevant. If you decide to make it relevant, your next step is to determine what's missing so you can add it in. Here are some common missing elements when a scene feels too much like a vignette:

- **Character motivation.** You have forgotten your character's motivations and relationship to the significant situation of your plot, and you have had him behave in an unrealistic or unrelated way. **Fix:** Go back to your character sketch (or do a new one) and see what more you can learn about your character that will fill in the blanks.

- **Pertinent dialogue.** You've written a scene full of dialogue that goes nowhere, is too mundane, or does not pertain to plot. **Fix:** Edit or cut dialogue and look to the other methods described in this book for demonstrating character and revealing information.

- **Setting.** You put your characters in a setting that does not make sense to your plot, or your setting is so vague that the reader doesn't understand how it relates. **Fix:** Ask yourself how important your setting is to your story. Determine if you have too much setting or not enough.

- **Information.** Nothing new is revealed, so the momentum peters out. **Fix:** Think about what happens next and how can you reveal it.

- **Action.** Your scene lacks enough action, and the reader finds it boring or gets distracted. **Fix:** Remember to think in forward motion. Ask what action could get your plot or characters moving in the most interesting way.

- **Conflict.** There's not enough push-and-pull energy in the conflict, and the scene feels too easy to the reader, and, as a result, loses his attention. **Fix:** Consider the consequences. Refer back to your significant situation and make a list of all the consequences that have developed so far. Consider whether you have enough, and think about what additional ones you can drum up that will make sense to your plot.

When it comes time to cut a vignette, you're likely to suffer a moment of doubt, even panic. Always save your last draft of something before you revise, or save the excised pieces, so that you can reclaim them if you make a mistake and cut too soon. Generally, however, true vignettes will not be missed. In fact, you may feel a sense of clarity once they're gone, because all they did was obscure the plot.

If you feel empty or your plot stops making sense after you cut a scene, then most likely that was a valuable scene, and you should put it back in and try to fix what rings false about it.

PARING DOWN NARRATIVE SUMMARY

If you find that you have trouble assessing how much narrative summary to snip out, ask yourself these questions:

- If I cut the narrated section in question, will the plot or characters suffer? If no, then it can go.
- Can the narrative summary—family history, backstory, explanations—be revealed through dialogue, flashback, or action? If no, it can go.
- Have I repeated this information in another scene? If so, it can go.

The following are checklists for you to run through when it comes time to assess individual scenes that don't feel quite right to you.

ASSESSING SCENE ARCHITECTURE

One of the most important questions to ask when you're revising is whether your scenes are cohesive in structure, and if each one is not only a working individual unit, but also sets up the next scene. Does each scene:

- Have a beginning, a middle, and an end?
- Launch vividly and engage the reader?
- Have a rich subtext, with texture, themes, and imagery?
- Include complications that up the ante on the characters?
- Leave the reader hungry for more upon its ending?
- End in a logical way that leaves room for the next scene to launch?

ASSESSING CORE ELEMENTS

Because there are so many core elements in a scene, you'll really want to take a solid look at each scene to see if it fulfills the goals of setting and the senses, if characters are well-developed, and if it contains enough tension to keep the reader's interest.

Visual and Sensual Details

Does each scene:

- Have an effective setting that is vivid but not overbearing?
- Reveal the time, place, and culture of your setting?
- Use objects to reveal details about plot and character?
- Engage the senses to create a sense of realism and authenticity? (Don't forget those seemingly mundane senses, like taste and hearing.)

Characters

Does each scene:

- Include a distinctive protagonist within the first two paragraphs?
- Feature useful minor characters as catalysts and antagonists?
- Use voice, dialogue, and behavior, rather than narrative summary, to reveal character?
- Keep consistent points of view?
- Offer your protagonist a chance to act or react?
- Force your protagonist to reevaluate or change?
- Engage your protagonist in the plot?

Plot

Does each scene:

- Introduce at least one new piece of information (who, what, where, when, how, or why)?
- Build upon the information revealed in the last scenes?

- Relate only information that ties directly to the significant situation and its consequences?
- Dole out plot information slowly, creating a sense of mystery?
- Use flashback scenes in place of backstory where needed?

Dramatic Tension

Does each scene:

- Employ subtlety over melodrama?
- Create an emotional response in the reader, not just the characters?
- Create the feeling of potential conflict?
- Thwart your protagonist's goals, delaying satisfaction?
- Throw in unexpected changes without immediate explanation?
- Shift power back and forth?
- Pull the rug out—throw in a piece of plot information that changes or alters your protagonist in some way?
- Create a tense atmosphere through setting and senses?

ASSESSING SCENE TYPES

At the end of each scene type chapter you will find a bulleted list of muse points. Refer to these when assessing a specific scene type.

◎ ◎ ◎

All in all, any "no" answers to the questions on these lists gives you an instant indication of where your scene needs to be strengthened.

When you assess individual scenes, you create a cohesive sense of integrity in your overall narrative, because you assess each scene not only on its own merits, but on its contribution to the adjacent scenes and to the storyline as a whole.

INDEX

Index　　　　　　　　　　　　　　　　　　**275**